C000060176

STRAWS IN THE WIND

The betrayal of Poland and one family's incredible journey

EUGENE KRAJEWSKI

First published in 2001 by Cromwell Publishers, London

Second Edition Published in 2003 by WritersPrintshop

E-mail - print@writersservices.com
Website – www.writersservices.com

ISBN 1-904623-01-8

Book website – www.strawsinthewind.com

Contents

Images

Introduction

My name is Eugeniusz Krajewski. Though I was born in Poland I have spent most of my life and all of my professional life as an engineer in England. Throughout these years, and even more so recently, I have found the English to be curious about my name, my background and my childhood experiences, which are so different to their own. I have made one concession in adapting my Christian name to the English equivalent of Eugene but I have always refused to tamper with my surname, of which I have always been proud.

I am often asked by new acquaintances to tell them how I finished up in this country. After I have told them one of my shortened versions of my life history, during which story they are usually very quiet and fascinated, I normally get a response like, "You should write a book".

They are often completely ignorant of the crimes perpetrated upon the Polish Nation by Stalin's regime at the start of the Second World War - it is a fact still often met with reactions of amazement by many that Stalin was responsible for far more deaths than Hitler.

The fate of my father had always preyed on my mind and after the death of my mother in 1992, a "journey home" seemed like an opportunity to discover the truth about what really happened. I made the trip but my investigations were not crowned with success – only a few signs and bits of gossip, *"straws in the wind"*, which strongly suggested that the actual events surrounding my father's disappearance were very different to those our family had been led to believe. As the Russian Authorities had removed all physical trace of our family's life in that area, I was determined to ensure that the Communists' attempts to rub out my father and the rest of the Krajewski clan from history would not succeed. So I find myself writing this book, with the hope that in telling our story, the fate of our family and families like us will not be forgotten.

Lately I seem to meet a lot of young people with Polish or mid-European sounding names who in most cases cannot speak their native tongue and have no knowledge of their parents' history. I hope that some of these young people will read my book and that it will stir them into investigating their own heritage on the Polish, Ukrainian or Belarusian side as the case may be, and I hope that they will learn to be proud of their mid-European roots.

To all the other readers, regardless of their ethnic or cultural background, I say that, if you find my book enjoyable and entertaining, then I consider my efforts to be worthwhile.

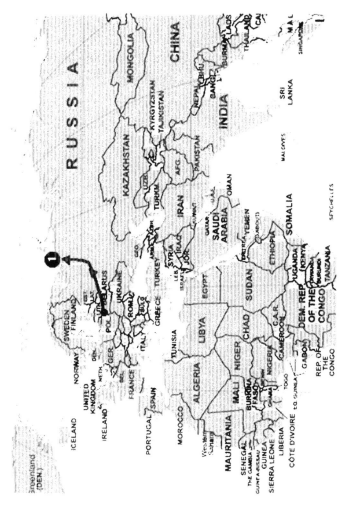

Map i Taken from our home in Poland, we were transported
to a labour camp in the frozen north

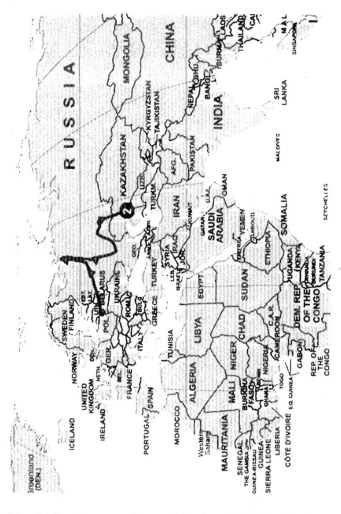

Map ii After the amnesty, we drifted south to Kazakhstan

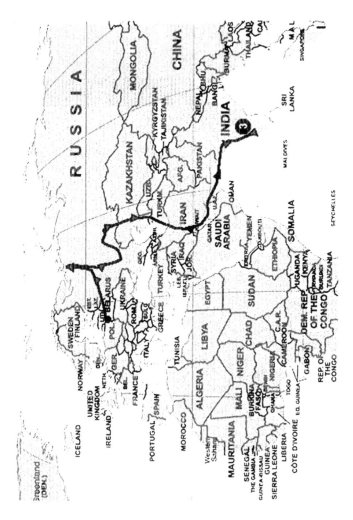

Map iii Having escaped the Soviet Union we travelled
over land and sea to the camp of Valivade in India

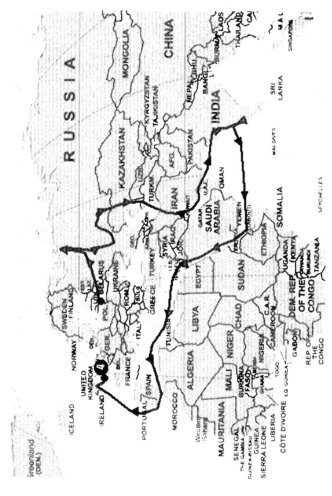

Map iv The final leg of our journey took us to Bombay,
then all the way to England

Dedication

This book I dedicate to my father, and to all the other victims of what President Ronald Reagan once called "that Evil Empire."

I wish to acknowledge and thank my wife Halina for her encouragement and patience, and also my daughter Suzan for her moral support.

I also wish to thank my daughter Julia and to express my gratitude for the ways in which she has helped me with the text.

Chapter 1

It was a scorching hot day. Flat open fields stretched out all around us as we motored along the dry, dusty road. On the right hand side, far in the distance, I could see the outline of a forest. Ahead, growing rapidly, was the outline of a town.

Before long we were in the outskirts. The sun continued to beat down, baking us inside the car as we travelled along, all the windows open. We carried on to the centre and eventually reached the Market Square. My cousin finally pulled up and we all alighted.

At long last we had arrived. This was Piaski - a small provincial centre in Belarus. This little town hadn't always been part of a state named Belarus. Sixty years ago, when I had last seen it, Piaski was part of an independent Poland. This was the place of my earliest childhood memories.

Sixty years since my enforced departure, and this was my first sight of the place. And here it was. Still standing. Much changed, but still standing. And now, here we stood. In the baking hot sunshine. Despite the heat, my mind was suddenly launched backward in an instant to the cold of winter. To the cold and the panic. Back to our last desperate moments here and the even more desperate times that would follow. I was four years old when they came for us. It was the 9th of February, 1940.

Outside the thick snow glistened. That winter was severe, even for Poland. But inside our house all was quiet. I was warm in my bed and fast asleep. My mother, brother and two sisters, like me, were sleeping soundly. When the insistent hammering begun on the door, it was so loud we all jumped up in our beds, terrified. After some hesitation, Mother called out asking who was making this racket at such an unearthly hour. The reply she got was,

"Let us in, in the name of The Soviet Union – immediately!"

Upon opening the front door, Mother was confronted by an NKVD officer, his handgun drawn, two Red Army soldiers and two local communist Belarusians.

They all pushed past and entered. The officer looked around and barked an order in mother's direction.

"Get all your children up," he shouted. Then after inspecting the premises further, he demanded, "Where is your husband?"

The order to get us up wasn't necessary. By that time we were all out of our beds, watching the proceedings, holding our breath, terrified. In response to the second enquiry mother said that, due to some misunderstanding her husband was currently detained by the local police. The Russian simply grunted in acknowledgement, and left it at that.

After a hurried conference with the Belarusian escort, the officer addressed my mother:

"Your family together with other undesirables are to be resettled elsewhere. Get your belongings together and start loading onto the sleighs waiting outside."

Mother could hardly believe what was being said.

"Surely you can give us a few days to prepare? My baby (meaning me) has a bad toe and can't walk. In any case, I'm sure my husband will be home soon and will help us pack for the journey."

The Russian was implacable. "You must pack all your belongings and get yourself and your children onto the sleigh now. We will inform the local authorities about your destination and they will make sure your husband joins you in due course. You have two hours and no more."

After having said this, I remember sensing something in him soften just a little. "The weather is bad," he said. "I suggest you take all the warm clothes you can. Take your husband's things as well. It may be that he will join you without coming back here. Take some food as well. It'll be a long journey."

It was typical of my mother that in moments of disaster, instead of giving in to despair and consequent inaction, she would suddenly stop complaining and start behaving in a calm, purposeful and even businesslike manner. So it was on this occasion. To our astonishment, without a further word, mother launched herself into the sudden task of packing. She took out our large wooden bathtub and placed it in the middle of the room. Then, systematically, she sorted out everybody's winter clothes, bundled them up and loaded them into the tub. She then went into the kitchen and brought out what little we had of bread along with all the cold meats and preserves she could lay her hands on.

Lastly, and by that time she was being hurried by the Russian, she grabbed what she thought were the most important family documents and stuffed them into her handbag.

Before we could make sense of what was happening, holding onto what belongings we could take with us, and too frightened to make a sound, we were all sitting on the sleighs. The early morning of 10th February was incredibly frosty, the temperature dropping to minus 40 degrees Celsius. In getting us prepared for the journey, Mother faced a difficult problem. My left big toe was too sore to accept a shoe. If my foot was not adequately protected however, in this weather I was sure to loose my foot altogether. She hit upon an idea. She took one of my down pillows, split it open, stuffed my foot into it and bandaged it over.

And here I stood sixty years on in the very same place, in the glorious sunshine on two healthy feet.

I remember as we sat there, cold and bewildered, the horses suddenly started forward and we found ourselves moving away from our house and with it, all the security we had ever known. As we departed, we saw that our house had been completely surrounded by a dozen Russian soldiers, with their bayoneted rifles pointing in the direction of our home. It was just as well none of us had any thoughts of running away. Clearly, the consequences would have been fatal.

Our journey to Hell had begun.

The first leg of the journey didn't take long. To our surprise, only fifteen minutes after setting off, the sleigh pulled up outside the Parish Council Offices of Piaski and we were ordered to get off and take our belongings with us.

As we entered the building, the loud chorus of howling children assailed our ears. It appeared that around twenty other families of Polish army settlers and foresters had arrived there ahead of us. Looking around we soon discovered our disadvantage. Almost without exception, the other children were accompanied by both their parents, and in some cases, by one or more grandparents. The four of us only had our mother to care for us and shield us from disaster. Immediately filled with fear and foreboding, we all found ourselves infected by the unearthly howling and joined in the chorus.

We sat there, crying, all night. The air carried the bone-chilling sound far along and into the houses of the remaining townsfolk lucky enough to have been left alone by the New Authorities. Not many people slept that night in the town of Piaski.

In the morning small groups started to collect outside our makeshift prison. Some brought food to pass on to their detained friends or relatives, while others came out of sheer curiosity. After a while mother spotted her friend Mietek Puciolowski in the crowd and waved to him. Mietek moved cautiously towards the open window and handed mother a large freshly baked loaf of bread. It was a gift none of us was ever to forget.

At mid-day a long string of large horse-driven sleighs collected outside the Council Building. Our 'guardians' ordered each family in turn to board the nearest vehicle. When all were loaded, the whole train moved off down the road. As we moved along the Main Street, we could not help but note an eerie silence all around us. It appeared that our captors, afraid of possible rescue attempts by the remaining Citizens of Piaski, had ordered all inhabitants to stay inside.

"Anybody found on the street when transport starts will be shot without warning," the NKVD Commandant announced through a loud hailer.

Quietly, the transport moved forward.

Chapter 2

The fact that only Polish Army Settlers and their families were taken away from my little town that night was no coincidence.

What we didn't know at the time was that Stalin had worked out this detailed and highly secret plan and had it put in place one whole year previously. In fact we were not the only group deported, as we later discovered. That same night, all along the whole stretch of Poland's eastern borderland, many Ex-army Settlers and their families were also taken from their beds.

The Russian Dictator was settling an old score.

It was these Polish soldiers after all, that delivered to the proud Red Army, a humiliating defeat in 1920, when the Soviets decided to re-invade our Fatherland.

After this war, partly to show gratitude and partly to secure the eastern border, Marshal Pilsudski, granted the Ex-combatants parcels of land in the eastern regions, and all along the Russian border.

This not only helped to protect the Nation from it's unfriendly neighbour, but also had the effect of reversing the process of Russification that the Tsar had enforced before the First World War. The Settlers became a great re-vitalising Force in the Region, and being fiercely patriotic - a very effective bulwark against the communist Fifth Column.

The fact that my father was one such settler, more than explained our predicament. In his case though, there was more to it. Most recipients of land, hailed from various parts of Poland. For most, these were new parts. An opportunity to have a farm of their own. Something they probably wouldn't be able to achieve where they grew up. Our farm was part of a settlement called Marszalkowa Wola and was established next to the large existing village of Rogoznica. Unlike his neighbours and Ex-Army pals however, Father was a born and bred 'local'. There was also another and, to a Pole, obvious difference and that concerned his surname. Father's last name of Krajewski had an ending of "ski," whereas the surnames of our neighbours were Loj, Kowalik etc. Traditionally, Polish surnames ending with "ski" or "wicz," (like for example Juszkiewicz), indicated noble ancestry, while others suggested a peasant background.

The notion of 'knighthoods' in the Middle Ages in Poland was no different to the similar traditions practised throughout most of Europe. However, where Polish tradition differed from the others was in the numbers of those it 'ennobled', and the subsequent growth of those entitled to the various honours, rights and privileges this implied.

Here, I must fall back on a brief outline of Polish History.

Our first king, Mieszko I, pulled together a series of Slavonic tribes during the decade of 950 – 960 A.D. to form Poland; a powerful and unified State in Central Europe. This was particularly noteworthy, as most European Regions were at that time organised into city-states, Principalities and the like. Soon after, in the year of 966 A.D., our country accepted Christianity and so joined the European Mainstream.

Located in the centre of Europe, Poland throughout its history tended to get involved in frequent wars and battles on various fronts. These were usually conducted in the defence of it's own sovereignty, but even on occasion to protect Christian Europe itself from the 'Eastern Hordes'.

Such actions required a constant supply of fighting men. Again, going back to the traditional social structures of the Middle Ages, wars were conducted by Landed Gentry, Nobility and Knights. In the case of the "well to do," this included their retinues. Peasants, together with the villages they lived in, belonged to particular Squires and were simply regarded as chattels. They had no surnames, no training in combat, no sense of allegiance other than that to their Master and certainly no sense of National Identity. Therefore, to ensure future supplies of fighting men, Monarchs got into the habit of knighting commoners who had distinguished themselves in battle. This wasn't the only way however, a person might have been ennobled.

One particular true story may serve as an example.

One day, King August 'the Strong' went out hunting in the forests of Eastern Poland. As he rode through the relative wilderness along the bank of the river Niemen, he suddenly came across a substantial patch of cleared land. The soil had been ploughed and was obviously under cultivation. Intrigued, he started looking for signs of habitation. Before long, his courtiers discovered an insignificant but sturdy looking hut located nearby. On entering, the King was greeted by a surprised yet delighted young couple. The hosts humbly introduced

11

themselves as Jan and Cecilia. They said that, back West where they hailed from, there were no opportunities for them to own land and have a farm of their own, so they had decided to move out into this Eastern wilderness and carve one out for themselves.

The King was so impressed by their pioneering spirit, that he called their action no less than heroic. In fact there and then, he made the grant of the cultivated land official and gave the couple the name of *Bohatyrowicze* or in English, '*Heroes*'. Today the settlement of Bohatyrowicze still stands on the bank of the river Niemen.

The actions of various Kings over the ages tended to multiply the number of noblemen in Poland. However, there was yet another factor that caused their numbers to increase still further.

In England, landed gentry always took care that their Estates were preserved to keep intact over generations, and if possible, to grow. To ensure this, Rules of Inheritance were introduced. These stated that only the eldest son was entitled to inherit the Land and Property, the Family Crest and all that went with it. The result was that the English Gentry stayed wealthy if small in numbers. And with every male member of the family who was not the first born, the crest was added to so that an altered version of the original was carried down their families, without encroaching on the rights of the principal successors. Poland followed a different set of rules. The Polish sense of fairness demanded that all offspring be treated equally. This meant that each son was equally entitled to the use of the family Coat of Arms and the name of a nobleman as well as a portion of the Estate. In such a way, the Polish nobility quickly became both numerous and impoverished.

As, unlike the English, each male member of a Noble family was entitled to the use of the Family Coat of Arms, there was no need to make changes or add embellishments. It can be seen therefore that, by comparison, Polish Crests remained less complicated in appearance than the English ones.

The Krajewski Coat of Arms is one such example. Although simple in design, it tells its own story. The design itself indicates that it must have been granted in the thirteenth or fourteenth century. The content suggests that the distinction was a reward for valour in battle, and probably as a result of some particular action involving the defence of the King's own person.

To justify their illustrious ancestry, and repair their finances, many young men of noble birth joined expeditions directed towards the eastern borders to fight the invading hordes of Tartars or Turks. Land was plentiful there and largely uninhabited. Many stayed on after the fighting ended, and settled down in the Eastern Borderlands. Some indeed made tidy fortunes, while others finished up either in service to some Magnate or other, or made their living as small farmers. In this, they differed little from peasants who by then, were also free men and tilled their own soil. Despite appearances however (as their pride didn't allow them to admit the obvious), they held onto their titles proudly and refused to mix with common peasantry. Their settlements were called *Zascianki* and not *Wioski* to ensure that they weren't mistaken for ordinary village dwellers.

It was from just such an ancestry that my grandfather came - Jozef Krajewski. My grandparents lived in a modest lodge by a forest on the outskirts of a town called Wolkowysk in, what used to be called "Greater Lithuania," and which for many centuries past, formed part of the Polish-Lithuanian United Kingdom.

He made his living as a forester, taking care of a part of the great Radziwill Estate. On occasion, he supplemented his income by fixing coaches and repairing farm implements at the 'Big House', as he appeared to have a talent where machinery was concerned. It was in that Lodge that my father Leon was born in 1898. His parents doted on their only son and spent what little income they had on his education. Unusually for that time and region, my father not only received Primary tuition, but also went on to complete a course in the local Secondary School. Of course the lessons were all in Russian. By the time my father was born, Poland had been under occupation for over a hundred years. Our powerful neighbours had shared out our lands between themselves. One part went to Austria, another to Prussia and the last, but by no means least, to Russia. It was therefore under the yoke of Tsarist Russia that my father was born and raised. Alongside his formal Russian schooling, Father attended clandestine gatherings where he not only developed an excellent command of his native Polish tongue, but also learned about Polish Literature, Polish history and something of his noble ancestry. It gave him great pride and satisfaction to discover that his Clan boasted many famous and heroic

13

figures, which had made significant contributions to the welfare and sovereignty of Poland. One of his particular heroes was called Rafal Krajewski.

As I said earlier, Poland had been under occupation for over a century. During that time, many attempts were made to free my country from invaders, but all to no avail. One such revolt, known as 'The January Uprising' took place in 1863. Unfortunately, just like previous attempts, the Russian Army quelled the rebellion. Its leader Romuald Traugutt together with all the members of his Emergency Government were captured, brought to Warsaw and eventually executed in the town's Citadel. In the secret gatherings, Father heard many first hand accounts of this most recent attempt at regaining the freedom of the Polish Nation. Amongst others, he learned that Traugutt's Second in Command was named Rafal Krajewski, his namesake.

As he grew and his interest in his family history increased, he begun to develop a deep pride in his lineage and a determination to live up to his ancestors' glorious past. And before he knew it, his opportunity had soon presented itself. In 1914, while he was still a very young man, the First World War broke out.

Chapter 3

For some time before the start of the Great War, Josef Pilsudski who hailed from my father's part of the world, was engaged in actively organising and training Polish youth with the intention of leading yet another uprising in Poland to free his Fatherland from the Invaders. After the breakout of the 1914/18 war, taking advantage of our enemies' falling out, Pilsudski formed a Polish Liberation Army popularly known as the Polish Legions, and proceeded to harass the invaders – and the Russians in particular. My father, by then a young man, hungrily absorbed all the news of the Polish Legions and the exploits and his hero, Joseph Pilsudski. Before reaching the age of 16, full of patriotic fervour, he could no longer curb his impatience and joined up (lying about his age).

His trials and tribulations during that period were many. It was his zest for life however, as well as his sense of humour and his commitment to the Cause that helped him survive. One story, often repeated in our family, may serve as an example.

At one time during the campaign, the Russian Army captured Father's unit. My father, ever the practical joker, told the Russian Guard that he was wasting his time because he was in any case going to escape. The Guard took the threat very seriously and showed more zeal than ever in trying to herd the soldiers together with his bayoneted rifle. They were at the railway station, and the Russian soldiers began to push their prisoners onto the waiting train. The Guard in question was so concerned with pushing his charges onto the train that he swung his rifle and elbows in all directions. In the scuffle, he swung his elbow against my father and pushed him out and away and into the neighbouring crowd of ordinary citizens waiting on the platform. Suddenly my father discovered that his fellow prisoners and their Guards had boarded the train and were gone, leaving him behind. Palms sweating, he rushed to the nearest toilet on the platform in order to conceal his whereabouts, and tried to stay there as long as possible. Whenever somebody came along, knocking on the door, he would call out using different voices each time, responding first of all in a deep voice, calling out "engaged!"- then if another person came, trying to gain entry, he would call out in a high-pitched female voice, saying "go away, can't you see the toilet is occupied?" He continued this charade for as long as he dared and eventually surfaced to discover that the platform was almost empty and no one appeared to be looking for him. Quietly, he sneaked out of the station, and (after overcoming many further trials and obstacles), managed to re-join the Polish Army. He later met his comrades from the prison train, and had a good laugh with them about the episode. They in turn told him how upset the Guard was to discover Father's disappearance, and that he just kept repeating, "The son-of-a-bitch said he would escape and he did!"

Eventually the war ended.

Marshal Josef Pilsudski, established as the leader during and after the War, took full advantage of the disintegration of the neighbouring Empires and re-established an Independent Polish Republic.

My father now in his early twenties, returned home to find that his own father had died while he was away, and only his mother and young sister Jania were left.

It was time to gather up the pieces and start building a "New Poland".

Father set about bringing the small farm, inherited from my grandfather back into some shape and re-establishing his social contacts. It was as the result of the latter that my parents got to know each other.

A few months later, a wedding took place in the neighbourhood. The bride invited her best friend Konstancja Juszkiewicz to be her Head Bridesmaid. At this point I must explain that Polish customs differ somewhat from the English ones when it comes to wedding etiquette. In England, the groom goes to the altar with only his best friend for company and nervously awaits the arrival of his bride on her father's arm, followed by a number of her bridesmaids. In contrast, Polish custom requires the couple to approach the altar hand in hand with their respective male and female friends behind them, also formed in couples. It was also a local custom in my part of the country for each bridesmaid to receive a present from her partner, once the ceremonies were over.

As I mentioned earlier, my mother led the line of bridesmaids. Her partner was a local farmer's son and a close friend of the groom. My father Leon, also a friend of the groom, accompanied another young lady in the second row of the wedding train.

Mother often told us the story of how it was that she met my father on that day. It went a little like this:

The marriage ceremony went off without a hitch, to be followed by the wedding festivities. My mother took a seat at one of the tables generously laid out for the occasion, thinking she would have a brief rest before the start of the dancing and other activities. She suddenly saw the rather handsome young man from the second row approach. He came over and said rather formally, "As we have not been introduced, I hope you don't mind if I now rectify the matter. My name is Leon Krajewski, I come from Mostek near Wolkowysk and I am a distant cousin of the groom."

With that, he sat down, and proceeded to engage my mother in conversation. After a while, he produced an impressive box of chocolates and offered them to my mother. Mother became highly impressed by the young man's manners and was enjoying his witty conversation, as they together consumed the chocolates.

Suddenly it occurred to her that protocol required for her to be squired by her partner from the marriage ceremony, and started looking around to see where he might have gone. Just then she caught sight of him at the far end of the hall, frantically searching for something under the benches. When she heard him accuse his friends of stealing his chocolates, she looked at the last of the chocolates in her hand, realised what had happened and burst into uncontrollable laughter.

This sort of audacious stunt was typical of my father. He saw where the young man had secreted his gift, pinched it and used it in order to impress my mother.

It was just as well that my mother saw the funny side. Whenever she told this story, I never heard any further mention of the butt of the joke - my mother's escort. I always wondered what he thought about it and whether he also considered it at all amusing.

The couple soon discovered that they got on well, and started courting.

Having in due course decided to get married, on Mother's insistence and to satisfy the requirements of social etiquette, Father had to send an official matchmaker to see my maternal grandfather in order to formally request her hand in marriage.

My father, being a rather modern individual, wouldn't have normally bothered with all these old fashioned customs. Modern or not however, and although he certainly married for love, it was clearly no coincidence that his bride, a Juszkiewicz, was of local nobility and thus his 'social equal'.

Having gone through all the proprieties, my parents were married a year later, and proceeded to arrange their new life together.

As a veteran from the War of Liberation, and a volunteer, Father was entitled to the Government Grant of a parcel of land and a low interest loan to get a farm started. This was Pilsudski's doing. Unlike other leaders in history, the Marshal didn't forget the boys that had made it all possible.

The farm they selected was part of a settlement peopled by couples just like themselves and was located on the edge of an existing village called Rogoznica. It was also conveniently within walking distance of my mother's old home in the settlement, (or zascianek,) of Lawry. The new settlement was eventually named Marszalkowa Wola to honour the Nation's hero Marshal Pilsudski.

Whereas my mother's ambitions were focussed on making the farm a success, Father's interests lay elsewhere. He (and also my mother) would have had a higher level of education than most of their neighbours. In addition, Father had outstanding talents in many directions and had developed many interests over and above farming matters. As the Chairman of the local Ex-combatant Association, he tended to get involved in local politics. He also put his influence to good use by helping local farmers and advising them on how best to approach Government Officials etc. But his inventive mind didn't allow him to limit his activities there. When it came to farming, he devised and put to use a threshing machine to separate wheat from chaff. And once he got involved in the building of the new Church in Rogoznica, he invented and manufactured concrete hollow building blocks to be used in its construction. He even wrote poetry.

Life on the farm went on, and with it came children. Both my parents were delighted when their first child, a daughter arrived. It was

18

therefore a massive shock to them both when not long after, the little girl (christened Leonarda) contracted scarlet fever and died. My father was inconsolable. Having been instrumental in erecting a Church in the neighbouring village, he now had the unenviable distinction of being the very first to make use of the adjoining cemetery. Another girl-child arrived a couple of years later. She was named Stanislawa, after my maternal uncle and is still my eldest sister. Things were beginning to look good. Not long after, another child had arrived. Another girl. Unfortunately, disaster struck yet again. Regina, his third daughter, contracted pneumonia when she was only a few months old and also expired. Father was completely shattered by this second terrible blow. Regina was buried in the same grave as her sister. Later my father, by then highly skilled in the art of crafting objects out of concrete, cast a monument. Upon it he carved an inscription with a poem to his "angels," and placed it on their grave.

In due course other additions to the family followed. The next was a boy. Father insisted that he be called Romuald, to honour the hero of the last Polish uprising. Next came another girl. Her name was to be Zuzanna. The last of the children was one more little boy - ME. On arrival, after a decent pause, I was taken to the parish church in Rogoznica and christened Eugeniusz.

Life on our farm proceeded without any further major disasters. But the loss of his infant daughters hit my father very hard. As time went on, he would spend a great deal of his time in the cemetery, making improvements to his work.

When I said that there were no further disasters at that time, I should have possibly said, "no further fatalities". In fact a major setback did occur. Father, having made a trip to the forest one winter to gather wood for fuel, caught a chill which due to the long journey home, had turned into pneumonia. He spent a considerable time in hospital recovering and was left with serious side effects. It seemed that he had developed fierce allergies to pollen and other elements to be found in the air in the country. The attacks were so severe that they would often result in haemorrhages. These attacks were to prevent Father from doing any work in the fields.

Something had to be done.

After discussions, my parents decided to move to town and make their living in some other way.

On enquiring around, Father discovered that veterans of the last war like himself could apply for licences to trade in alcoholic beverages. This was Pilsudski's way of, again helping his "boys" who delivered Poland in its War of Liberation, and also of ensuring that this very sensitive trade was placed in responsible hands.

Having agreed that route with Mother, Father made the necessary application and was immediately awarded the licence in question. So the venue then, for the next stage of my family's life and the place of all my childhood memories of Poland, was to be the nearby small market town by the name of Piaski. I was only eighteen months old at that time, and so the farm in Marszalkowa Wola left no imprint in my memory.

Chapter 4

My parents initially rented a house in Piaski next door to my mother's friends, the Puciolowskis. Father soon decided however that, although the business took off, he needed to be located more centrally if he was to establish and maintain a turnover, sufficient to provide an adequate income for his family.

One possible location, Father thought, was a hardware shop in the market square, run by an old man called Szmaja.

He approached the man with an offer to rent the shop as well as the dwelling higher up on the hill. Szmaja's health was ailing and he was already thinking of retiring in any case. If he was to acquire such a "money spinner" as the licence to sell liqueur, he might have still been tempted to stay in business. The sale of alcohol was in those days, controlled very strictly. Given the appetite therefore for the liquid amongst Poles, anyone holding a permit to sell the stuff was bound to make a mint. He did try to persuade my father to part with the document, but when he realised that Father wasn't going to sell, agreed terms and rented the property to my parents.

The shop was big enough to house a snack bar, as well as a number of separate dining rooms. In the rear there was sufficient space for a big kitchen and sleeping accommodation. Mother put her culinary talents to work in the kitchen. To take care of the children while they both worked, my parents brought over from Mostek my ageing grandmother. While the whole family got itself established in the house on top of the hill, my parents tended to sleep in the back of the shop in order to protect the stock.

At the back of the house there was a large shed sufficient to house our horse and cart. I addition, my parents brought with them our best cow "Malwa" from the farm and also found a place for her in the outbuilding. This last move was intended to ensure an adequate supply of milk for the children.

Father rented the farm out to a local tailor by the name of Kuprianczyk. Initially, when approached with a proposition, Father hesitated. He knew that the man was suspected of belonging to the communist underground movement. Still, on the principle that

21

"business is business" he struck a deal, a decision he would have reason to regret later.

Business started developing satisfactorily. Mother was in her element. The quality of her cooking was generally acclaimed and its fame soon spread around the town. Eventually, a private "dining club" was established. This comprised a small number of select members of the town's "society" like policemen, schoolteachers etc. The group gathered in our private dining room on a daily basis for reason of social intercourse and, of course, in order to enjoy my mother's wholesome cooking.

My parents soon made themselves known to the local Parson. The Roman Catholic Church was located just along the main road and off the market square, literally a couple of minutes' walk from our establishment. The church was only a few years old. The fact that it was reminiscent of the structure in the neighbouring Rogoznica was no accident. After the church in Rogoznica was erected, Roman Catholic parishioners in Piaski decided to follow the example of that village and put up a new and better place of worship for themselves, than the one they'd been using up to that time. After all, like elsewhere, the numbers of the faithful wishing to attend Mass on Sundays grew rapidly in the post war years.

Slowly, my parents started being absorbed by the social life of this small provincial town. They found themselves mixing socially with the so called "important and influential members of community," their elder children Stasia and Romek found themselves receiving preferential treatment from teachers in school etc.

My father being by talent and inclination a poet and a man of letters, started contributing to the local weekly paper by writing short articles and publishing some of his poems. That activity immensely elevated his standing in the community but his outspokenness eventually bought him into open conflict with another one of its greatly respected members - the local Priest.

My father intensely hated social injustice and exploitation of one human being by another. In order to expose some of the (in his view) unsavoury activities he could see all around him, he resorted to writing short satirical stories, usually in verse.

22

Some of his poems dealt with the tendency of town's folk to look down on peasants and unfairly regard them as ignorant and stupid. On other occasions he would highlight the fact that Belarusian peasants, traditionally of Russian Orthodox religion, were being enticed away from their heritage by "religious carpetbaggers" from America and being lured to join various peculiar American sects and forsake the faith of their fathers. (How strange to see history repeating itself! Now, with Eastern and Central Europe finally free of the communist yoke, the process observed by my father in the nineteen thirties is again in full flood.)

There were equally times when my father would turn his critical eye on the activities of his own Roman Catholic Church. Although he always was a firm believer in the Church's teachings, he found some practices, like for example the notion of selling "a piece of heaven" by a priest in exchange for a donation to the church, distasteful. With his typical forthrightness, he could not avoid expressing his views in private conversations and, occasionally, in print.

A couple of my father's poems dealing with such matters were published in the Journal, provoking discussions on the subject in some social circles in the town. This was too much for the Priest who met my father and demanded that he desist from expressing such controversial views in print in the future.

Father considered the priest's demands an infringement on his liberty, a big word in a newly independent Poland, and refused point blank.

So it was so that a feud between the Priest and my father started. The priest started making sideswipes at my father during his weekly Sunday homilies, (all carefully veiled, of course). My father, undeterred, continued to deliver his contributions to the Editor. My mother, mortified at the notion of even questioning a priest's pronouncements, tried to persuade my father to do as the man demanded and retract his previous statements, but to no avail. The fact that father's articles appeared to contain more and more bite and seemed increasingly venomous, was no coincidence.

The battle continued for quite some time. It was only, just before the outbreak of the Second World War that the situation (with the intervention of the Bishop) was finally resolved.

23

They struck a deal. My father was to stop writing the more provocative articles, and in return the Parson agreed to cease lambasting my father from the pulpit. The feud, thank Heavens, was over. No one was more pleased or relieved at this outcome, of course than my mother.

In spite the friction between my father and the local representative of the Roman Catholic Church, things were progressing well. The business was going from strength to strength, and my father's health had also visibly improved. There were occasions, when his physical strength as well as his resourcefulness was badly needed. On market days, some peasants, having generated cash by the sale of farm produce, would come in to the snack bar to relax over one or two vodkas. Unfortunately with some, it tended not to end with "one or two". There were occasions when sudden drunken brawls would explode in the bar. Such fights could easily become very serious. Some of the more aggressive individuals had a habit of carrying knives and some would even have axes on them. Normally, at the first sign of trouble, Father would send for the police. However there was one occasion when trouble flared up suddenly and without warning. Half a dozen men were tangled up in a fight in the middle of the room. Father, realising that it wasn't possible to summon help in time, started pushing and shoving the whole bunch, until he managed to manoeuvre them all out through the front door and onto the street, where, by now, the police were waiting. His friends expressed their surprise and admiration that a man of not very great stature like my father (he was five foot five inches tall), could single handedly manage to control such a frenzied bunch of drunks. It spoke volumes for father's strength as well as his bravery and ingenuity.

By this time, my father's sister Jania was well into "marriageable age". Up to that time, she seemed to be too choosy to make any lasting relationships, so my father, as always, concerned for his sister's welfare and her future, unburdened himself to his wife one night. Mother suggested they do a little "matchmaking" between Jania and Mother's own, still unmarried brother Stas. Mother proceeded to arrange a series of "coincidences" when the two found themselves alone together. Eventually my aunt took my father on one side and told him that; nice as my mother's brother was, she didn't think they were

24

suited to each other, and suggested my mother doesn't waste any more of her time and energy in pushing them into each other's arms. Father relayed the message and the "matchmaking" attempts were dropped.

It was some time later that Jania sought out my father to ask his advice. For some time, she had been frequently seen in the company of one Joseph Wysocki. One day she turned to her brother. She told him Josef asked for her hand in marriage. Aunt Jania and my father were very close and she always valued his views. On this occasion, she wanted his opinion of the man, before making up her own mind.

Father pondered over the matter and eventually responded. After some thought, he said what he thought of the man, his position and the proposal. In his view, the fact that Wysocki was somewhat older than my aunt was of no import. He clearly adored Jania; his financial situation was sound, (with a substantial farm in the nearby Zienciki), and on top of all that, he was of noble birth and so "her social equal". To sum it up, my father's advice was to accept the proposal.

My aunt Jania took this advice and before long, married Joseph and moved away to Zienciki. It must be said with hindsight, that my father's advice proved right. His sister and Joseph Wysocki were to enjoy a long and a harmonious marriage.

The "Juszkiewicz Clan" on the other hand proved to be a continued source of trouble and discord. My mother, being the eldest, was accustomed to resolving family disputes among her siblings and advising on appropriate action when life's important decisions had to be made. In that, she always and inevitably involved my father. She became concerned when she discovered that her sister Elzunia (Elizabeth) had developed a "serious liaison" with an older man called Joseph Juszkiewicz. The coincidence of the surname did not signify any close blood relationship. Joseph's blood ties with Elzunia were probably very distant if any. The problem lay elsewhere. Joseph had, in his time made unsuccessful advances to my mother (while she was still free, of course); to be followed by equally doomed approaches to my aunt Jadzia. My mother felt, and my father agreed, that the man was too old for Elzunia and his approaches were probably opportunistic. They had a family "conference" and decided that Elzunia must give him up.

My young aunt Elzunia met Joseph, her intended, and told him about the family verdict. His response was that of anger and unwillingness to accept their authority. To his comments that she should ignore the opinion of her siblings, she responded with her view that, without such a "blessing," she would be unable to bring any dowry to their union.

Undeterred, Josef advised her to secretly pack what she thought she was entitled to, and sneak out to him.

One morning uncle Stas got up at dawn as usual to start work in the fields. He was surprised to see that the oven was still cold. He called for Elzunia, his sister, to get up and get the fire started. There was no response to his call. After a while, he saw his youngest sister Gabrunia (Gabriela) creeping out, trying to find out what all the commotion was about. Her brother Stas was, by then running around the whole house, looking for his other sister. Aunt Elzunia was gone. What was worse, she took with her most of the treasures carefully and painstakingly collected by them all, to be shared out equally to each on their respective wedding days.

This was too much. Uncle Stas, furious, rushed to Piaski to my parents for support. It must be said that my uncle was an excellent farmer. When it came to horseflesh he was an acclaimed expert. When it came to intellect however, he was no giant. More often than not, he needed someone to tell him "what to do next".

My parents agreed with my uncle that aunt Elzunia's behaviour was disgraceful. Father offered to go to Joseph's house to face his sister-in-law and get things straightened out. Uncle Stas agreed but insisted on going along as wall. Reluctantly, father agreed to take him along.

They found my aunt and Joseph Juszkiewicz getting ready to set off to church to organise their wedding. When tackled, aunt Elzunia denied vehemently having taken away anything that didn't belong to her, and became angry with her brother for even suggesting it. She also added that, in her view she was entitled to a third share of the farm at Lawry, and she was going to make sure she wasn't to get cheated out of her inheritance.

This was too much for my uncle. He rushed at his sister, fists flying. It took a great deal of effort on the part of Joseph Juszkiewicz and my father to separate the two. Father for once, returned home empty handed. He realised that, taking my uncle along with him was a great mistake. Still, what was done could not now be undone.

Joseph Juszkiewicz and aunt Elzunia married in due course. Needless to say, nobody from the family attended. She was branded the 'black sheep' of the Juszkiewicz family. The arguments over land eventually finished up in Court. My father argued that whatever happened, Elzunia's claim of one third of the farm was erroneous. The total number of children left by old Joseph Juszkiewicz was five and not three. The fact that my mother and my aunt Jadzia didn't claim their rights did not mean they were null and void. He thought that, breaking up a viable farm was a big mistake and constantly tried to persuade Elzunia to accept a notion of "common ownership," with Stas running the farm and paying out one fifth of annual profits to his sister. The argument dragged on right up to the outbreak of the Second World War and was never properly resolved. One result however, was that a mortal feud started within the family, which survived through time and all adversities. At the time of writing, my aunt Elzunia is the last remaining member of that family still living. Her brother lies buried in the cemetery in the parish church of Rogoznica, where my aunt, still highly religious, used to go to Mass. In spite of her religious upbringing however, she couldn't bring herself to visit her brother's grave even once.

The youngest of the clan, aunt Gabrunia, also eventually married. Not wanting to follow in the footsteps of her sister, she made sure she took my father's advice and married a man father thought was "a good match".

It was the year of 1938 before my uncle Stas married at long last. Uncle met a girl and instantly fell in love. It's remarkable that, although his wife came from a village and was clearly not of "noble stock," no objections were raised to the alliance. It would appear that my father had by that time had enough, trying to keep the Juszkiewicz lineage pure. One must add that uncle Stas in his state of infatuation wouldn't have suffered the slightest criticism of his intended. It must also be said that my new aunt Hela looked pretty, knew how to dress in the latest fashion, and most importantly, had such a winning personality that she soon managed to get everybody on her side. So it was that without fuss, the spell was broken and the "noble" family of Juszkiewicz accepted into its fold, a peasant girl in a marriage "for love" and not just in order to make a suitable match.

Time was passing and I continued to be the youngest child in my family. This was no coincidence. Soon after I was born in Rogoznica, Mother persuaded my father that it was crucial for her to help him in turning around their fortunes. She clearly couldn't be relied upon to do that if she was to become pregnant as soon as the last infant ceased to suckle. The only solution was "the most reliable form of birth control known to man" - i.e. abstention. Father, handicapped by his ailing health, had to accept the logic of my mother's argument. Sleeping arrangements were modified accordingly.

Whenever the matter came up (usually after father had a couple of drinks), Mother would remind him that their circumstances were still precarious and that they still couldn't afford to lose her input into the business. Father could see that in truth, mother's argument couldn't be denied and reluctantly he accepted the situation, however unpalatable. To my mother this was no sacrifice. She always found demonstration of emotion (particularly sexual contact) difficult and alien to her nature. That, in her mind, didn't contradict her largely unspoken emotional ties to my father and high regard for him. Although she was determined for the arrangement to continue, she was aware that my father was "made of different clay". Whenever she saw father being attentive to an attractive woman, or worse still, when such a woman indicated that she found *him* attractive and started flirting, Mother would begin to feel insecure and become highly annoyed.

There were many occasions when conflicts arose as a result of this concealed tension. The following example is but one of many, as told by my mother herself, still clearly unaware of the real significance of her actions that day.

One evening, father came home and after a while casually remarked to mother that a week next Sunday the Town Traders' Association was holding their Annual Dance in the Hall. He had struck a deal to provide a snack and drinks buffet. This, he thought, should bring them a tidy profit.

They discussed detailed arrangements for a while and agreed that father would set out the stall at the dance and serve the clients as best he could on his own to start with. Meantime, so as not to lose regular business, mother would keep the restaurant-bar open until eight o'clock as usual.

The arrangements went smoothly. Father dutifully stayed at his post alone waiting for mother to arrive. He was always fond of dancing and the music was so inviting that he couldn't wait to have a go. As soon as mother arrived he said, "Great. Hold the fort for a while. I'm going to grab a dance." With that he rushed off and, with a big bow, invited the very attractive wife of the local schoolteacher to join him on the floor. Within moments, mother saw them floating along to a waltz, the woman loudly laughing in response to some joke of my father's. This was too much for Mother. Sudden anger welled up inside her. She dropped the sandwiches she was preparing onto the table and marched onto the dance-floor towards the couple. "How dare you treat me like this!" she shouted at her husband. "You think that as soon as I appear you can dump all the work on my plate and go off gallivanting. What do you think I was doing when you were running the bar? You know damned well. I also had to work. I run the restaurant single-handed. If you think I'll put up with this sort of treatment from you, you're sorely mistaken." Having delivered her tirade, and seeing that it had had the desired effect, she stormed out of the dance hall and went home. Father stood there in the middle of the floor stunned. The band stopped playing and other revellers stopped and watched the unexpected show. Father was of course extremely embarrassed. After a moment, he apologised profusely to his partner and retired behind the bar for the rest of the evening. In spite of everything, business had to be conducted. Apart from the question of immediate profit, there was the matter of fulfilling his commitment to the Committee. A failure on his part to maintain the service would have had serious long-term repercussions on his future trade. Needless to say, throughout the evening, father would have much preferred to be somewhere else. *Anywhere else.* Mother had always described the episode as her way of punishing father for his lack of consideration. She never saw the physical distance between them as a factor. And she would never admit, even to herself, the real truth - that she was simply jealous.

For me, these precious few years in Piaski represented an idyllic childhood. It was also the time of my first real childhood memories. Life was settled and secure. A child's needs were easily satisfied. Food was always plentiful. All I needed to do whenever I felt like a snack was to run up to the counter in the snack bar. There would always be some Polish sausage or some other cold meat on the worktop. I would help myself and be off again in pursuit of some other pleasure. Of my many memories from those days is a clear picture of my grandmother sitting on a stool and plucking goose fathers. The feathers seemed as pure and white as the hair on her head. My playground was our backyard as well as the street and the square at the front of the establishment. One must remember that in those days, children were not in constant danger from traffic and public spaces didn't represent an undue hazard. In spite of that, with my usual sense of curiosity, I managed to get myself into trouble. One day I walked out onto the street to find the square ahead of me deserted. There was nobody to be seen and there was no sign of any activity anywhere. There was however one object in the middle of the square I hadn't seen before. A single-decker bus stood in the middle of the square seemingly abandoned and forlorn. On top of the vehicle was a luggage rack with a few suitcases and sundry bags. At the back, there was a metal ladder stretching from the luggage rack almost all the way down to the ground. I was fascinated. The temptation to investigate more closely was irresistible. I approached the vehicle and gingerly climbed a couple of rungs of the ladder. To my horror, just at that moment the bus started moving forward. It was my good fortune that my father had been observing my activities and, petrified at what was developing, ran out of the shop and grabbed me before the vehicle had a chance to build up any speed. In spite Father's anger I felt enormous gratitude towards him for saving me from what I perceived to be certain disaster.

On yet another occasion, one Sunday morning I suddenly woke up from a nap only to find myself alone in the house. I remembered that a little earlier, everybody was getting ready to go to Mass. "Where have they all suddenly disappeared to?" I thought. Little did I know that the whole bunch quietly slipped out, leaving me in the care of my ageing grandmother. They must have gone and forgotten all about me!

Without a second thought I marched out onto the street and down towards where I knew the church would be. After a fair stretch, I reached the church and entered. In front of me I saw rows of people standing very quietly. To the left at the far end stood a man higher than the rest. He was dressed all in white and appeared to be shouting at the people in a very loud and angry voice. (It should be noted that 'fire and brimstone' sermons were the order of the day in Poland at that time, and particularly from that priest.) Terrified, I scuttled to where from past experience I expected to find my family. To my relief I soon reached the protection and security of my parents.

Some other adventures I experienced could not be ascribed to me or to my sense of curiosity. One example was an incident on the riverbank. I often played with my siblings on the bank of the river Zelwianka that flowed through the bottom of our back yard. One warm and sunny day my eldest sister Stasia (Stella) decided that the river had become so shallow that she could cross it with me on he shoulders. Unfortunately she miscalculated. Halfway across, the ground suddenly fell away and Stasia, with me still attached, found herself under water. Luckily she managed to scramble out and drag me out with her. (I wonder if this has anything to do with the fact that deep water has filled me with dread all my life ever since!)

Another of my early childhood memories was a time when the circus came to town. I still have a vivid picture of a beautiful lady twirling in the air, holding onto her partner only by means of a leather strap and her teeth.

The above examples of my earliest childhood memories may give the wrong impression. In my opinion, a child's mind registers most strongly, moments of greatest personal emotional experience. What it usually allows to go by un-noted, is the sense of security in one's surroundings and the caring of all the people around. In general I can only describe these few years of my life as a time of a normal and a happy childhood.

My father, always on the lookout for new ideas, came across an article one day in a Journal describing the invention of the radio. The writer then went on to describe how, with simple and primitive materials anyone could construct a "crystal wireless set". Father became fascinated. He immediately decided he must construct one for his own use. The description in the Journal wasn't particularly detailed, and it took a lot of "trial and error" on my father's part before finally and to his delight, he succeeded in making an instrument which, with the aid of ear-phones allowed him to hear a transmission from Warsaw. Having perfected his receiver, Father got into a habit of listening to the nine o'clock daily bulletin from Radio Warsaw. Soon he became known as the best-informed person in the town on current affairs.

It was on one such evening in the autumn in the year of nineteen thirty nine that Father, ashen faced, came over to Mother after his regular stint with the radio and said;

"Dear Koscia, I have just heard on the radio that Germany has declared war on Poland. There have already been reports of aerial attacks. All reservists are ordered to report to their points of assembly without delay. My place for reporting is the garrison in Sokolka. I'll have to go tomorrow morning first thing."

My father's words signalled the end of an era for my whole family and the end of my carefree childhood. The catastrophe that was to befall us was never to be righted.

Chapter 5

Things changed rapidly. Within days of my father leaving to join the army, rumours started circulating that Communist Russia was readying to take advantage of Poland's problems on its Western frontiers and re-invade our country from the East.

News from the Front was not good. It seemed that the Polish Army was no match for the might of the German Military Machine. From the East, it was said that the Red Army was on the march and some said that they had already crossed the Polish border. It seemed that the cause was lost. That is certainly how various Local Authority officials read the situation. Almost without exception, they abandoned their posts and set about organising the means of escape for themselves and their families. Members of the Communist Party, a secret and illegal organisation until that time, suddenly started taking charge.

Suddenly, everybody seemed to be either a communist or a communist sympathiser. Our landlord Szmaja was no exception. One day he knocked on the door and was invited in by my mother. She had no reason to be suspicious. My parents' relations with old Szmaja had always been cordial throughout the time of their tenancy and even before that. Szmaja in turn always made it be known that he valued them as reliable and profitable tenants. The old man sat down and, for a while, said nothing at all. The expression on his face betrayed feelings of discomfort and embarrassment. Clearly, what he had to say did not come easily. In the end he looked up at my mother and said,

"You must understand the situation Mrs Krajewska. With your husband gone to war and him being as prominent as he was, your presence on my premises is likely to cause me problems. Don't take it personally, but I have no option but to ask you to vacate the place as soon as possible."

Mother was shocked at this unexpected turn of events. As if she didn't have enough on her plate trying to take care of her family with my father gone "only God knew where". She couldn't even be sure father was still alive. In a few moments she recovered her composure and said,

"Mr. Szmaja; I'm disappointed in you. You well know that you have no basis for your attempts to evict my children and me. The rent

33

is fully paid up and we have done nothing to breach the terms of our lease. If you think I'm some sort of criminal I suggest you report my crime to the police. If your accusations have any basis, I'll be arrested and that'll be that."

Seeing his obvious discomfort she continued,

"No; this is our home and this is where my husband expects to find me on his return. The word is, that fighting with the Germans is over. I'm sure Leon will soon be returning home and we'll be picking up where we've left off. I think you would be wise to put any notions of evicting us out of your mind. We are staying put."

Szmaja's face slowly distorted with growing anger.

"It's all very well," he responded. "You know perfectly well we are now living under the Communists. Your husband's anti-Communist activities are well known throughout the town. The people now running the show quite obviously have no love for him or his family or for that matter for anyone associating with your lot. I can't afford to have you around. If you don't want any unpleasantness I suggest you get out of my house and preferably out of Pieski (he had already started using the Russian name for the town) without delay."

Having delivered his ultimatum, Szmaja got up and left without a further word.

To add to her troubles, mother suddenly discovered that many prominent members of the community were shunning her. Many of the people that now treated her like a stranger, only recently professed to be close friends of the family. Her "circle of diners" started to melt away, and with it went her income. The behaviour of some of her previous customers and now only debtors was infuriating and worrying.

There was one past-time client in particular whose attitude my mother found particularly annoying. Mr Sawicki was a teacher in the Town Primary School. He was a young man, recently appointed to join the Staff and even more recently accepted as a member of my mother's "circle of diners". His bill for the last month was still unpaid when he suddenly discovered that he would be 'better off' dining with a certain young widow a little further down the street. Mother approached him on a number of occasions asking him to settle his account but was met with poor excuses and thinly veiled derision. She was furious. Yes, the lack of money was a serious problem, but what hurt her more was to be bettered by this young upstart. She kept observing him on his regular visits and brooding. Finally she came up with an idea.

One lunchtime Mother spotted the young teacher cycle over to his new haunt, rest the bike against the wall as usual and enter. She gave him time to settle in, and approached the house. Through the window she could see the woman's guests, including our young teacher, deeply absorbed in some discussion. No one was interested in what might be happening outside.

Mother very carefully, grasped the handlebars and started slowly walking away with the bike. Nobody spotted her. "So far so good," she said to herself. She continued to walk along the street towards her own house. On the way she had to pass the Police Station. Her calm and deliberate walk belied her inner terror. "What if somebody runs out at this moment and accuses me of stealing the bike. I'd be under arrest and branded as a thief before you know it," she agonised silently. Fortunately, nobody noticed her action and she wheeled the bike into her hall, closed the door and waited. Eventually our diner said his good-byes and reached for his bike. It wasn't there. He couldn't believe his eyes. Who would have had the nerve to steal his precious machine right from under the window! He came out and started wandering up and down the street with a vain hope of spotting his cycle somewhere along. At that point mother came out and feigning concern, approached the dejected individual.

"What's the matter, Mr. Sawicki?" she said. "You look as if you lost something."

"Yes," he innocently replied. "Would you believe it? Somebody stole my new bicycle!"

"Don't worry, Mr Sawicki," responded mother with a sweet smile. "Your bike is safely under lock and key in my house. You can have it back just as soon as you give me the money you owe me."

The young man's face briefly showed a sequence of emotions passing through his mind. First was the feeling of relief that his precious bike was safe. This was immediately followed by irritation at being outwitted by a woman. Next, the reminder that he needed to retrieve his machine without delay.

"That was very clever of you Mrs Krajewska," he said. "I can assure you there was no need for all these dramatics. I fully intended to settle my account with you as soon as I could. In fact I have twenty Zlotys on me, which I intended to deliver to you this afternoon as part payment. You can have it now. If I can collect the bike, I'll bring you the rest of the money tomorrow. How would that be?" he ended hopefully.

Mother was beginning to enjoy this. "Not so fast my dear Mr Sawicki," she said. "The bike stays with me until you come up with all the money you owe me." The young man, crestfallen, walked off promising to return the following day with the money.

So it was that the young teacher, having been taught a lesson, turned up next morning with the full sum and having settled his debt, disappeared grumbling, riding his bike.

The incident gave Mother a lot of satisfaction and a much-needed boost to her morale. The situation however, continued to deteriorate. The "dining circle" was now a thing of the past. Even if she could retain some of her customers, Mother could no longer get the necessary produce to cook a half way reasonable meal. The Snack Bar tended to be deserted and she even started having problems with her deliveries of vodka. To add to her troubles, Szmaja's behaviour was getting more and more aggressive. What was she to do? Where was Leon? Fighting had apparently now ceased and she'd heard that some men had made their way home while others made off south in an attempt to get out of the country all together, join our Allies and give our enemies battle once again. Of Leon there was no word. Had he lost his life in the defence of his country, or was he languishing in some German or Russian prison? One thing she never doubted - that my father would never have deserted us and chosen to save himself by leaving the country.

There was nothing for it. She had to act.

Her first problem was what to do about Leon's old mother. The notion of dragging this old and infirm woman around seemed unreasonable. Having given the matter some thought, she came up with a solution. Why, Jania, Leon's sister could take care of her own mother. After all, by all accounts, the farm at Zienciki was well to do and the large house well able to accommodate another occupant.

She sat down and wrote a note to Jania Wysocka, explaining her situation and asking her to come and take her mother away. She didn't have to wait long. Just a few days after posting the letter she saw a cart arriving in her yard. On the driver's bench sat Jania and her husband. Mother greeted the couple warmly. She went out of her way to explain that the old woman was no burden and that they got on very well. It's simply, that as things stood, she saw no other way but to leave the restaurant and get out of Piaski. What was going to happen to her and her children she was not certain. One thing she was sure of however, and that was that, it wouldn't be fair to drag the old woman with her into this uncertain future. The couple readily accepted her explanations and assured her that they would only be too glad to take Jania's mother away with them. Jania expressed her concern for Leon's welfare and said she hoped he would re-emerge soon. "After all," she said. "You can't put a good man like Leon down very easily. You know yourself how resourceful he can be. Don't worry. He'll be home soon."

The farewells were charged with emotion. In the end the couple left, taking my grandmother with them, and we were left alone.

Mother knew she had to get out of this place but "where to go?" she thought. These were strange times. All pre-war deals and agreements seemed to be off. After all, she only had to look at the way Szmaja was behaving. The fact that she had a fully paid-up and valid lease seemed to make no difference. Surely this meant that she could simply ask Kuprianczyk to vacate her own house in the Rogoznica Settlement, and move back in with her brood...didn't it?

The following day, on Thursday, her brother arrived to the market as usual to sell his farm produce. Mother dragged him over to the house and told him her troubles.

"Why don't you go back to your farm in Rogoznica?" he said.

"That's just what I was thinking," Mother replied. "If I turn up there with my whole family and demand my rights, Kuprianczyk will have no option."

After some further discussion they both agreed to 'strike while the iron was hot'. Mother packed some clothes, bedding and some personal belongings and waited for her brother to finish his day's work at the market. When he returned, she loaded all her belongings onto the cart, planted all us kids inside and went over to see Szmaja.

"I wanted to let you know that I've decided to close the restaurant down for the time being and go with my children to stay in Rogoznica for a while. I'm leaving most of my belongings behind. Soon, when my husband returns, I'll come back and we'll open the business up again."

She delivered her speech with the defiance and determination she did not feel, turned around and walked out before the old man had a chance to respond.

It was evening when we all finally arrived at our homestead in Rogoznica. Mother asked her brother to pull up outside the barn and discharge his burden from the cart.

"Thanks for your help, Stas," she said. You might as well carry on home. I'll take care of things from here on."

Uncle Stas, glad to be relieved of further involvement, promptly complied. Once he'd gone, mother walked up to the house and knocked.

After a moment the tailor appeared at the door.

"What can I do for you?" he enquired.

"Mr. Kuprianczyk, I must apologise for coming like this unannounced. The fact is that we've been forced out of our accommodation in Piaski and I have no option but to reclaim our property and move back into our house. I know this is out of the blue and so I have no intention of being unreasonable. We'll crowd into the spare room in the back for now. Tomorrow you can start looking for alternative accommodation. Until you are ready to move we'll muck in together as best we can."

The man looked at mother in silence for a while and then burst out in sardonic laughter.

"These are new times, my lady," he finally said. "*We* are in charge now. (Meaning that the Communist Party, of which Kuprianczyk had been an enthusiastic member for many years past, was now ruling this country.) This is my house now and I intend keeping it. You'd best collect your belongings and go. You're trespassing. If you are still here in the morning, I'll get my dog to see you off my property."

With that he gave her a cold stare, stepped back and shut the door.

Mother was taken aback. She didn't know what to do next. It was pitch dark by then. We children sitting in the barn quickly sensed her distress. The smaller ones (including yours truly) were beginning to whimper. Suddenly she felt completely abandoned. She didn't seem to have anywhere to go to gain shelter even for that one night. Eventually in her desperation she thought, "I must go to Kowalikowa next door. She was always a good friend and neighbour. I'm sure she'll help us in our hour of need."

Having made her decision, she told us all to sit tight in the barn and wait for her return, and then disappeared into the night. Without Mother, time seemed to drag forever. Outside the barn as well as inside it, all was pitch black. Deep inside the barn we could hear some rustling noises. It appeared that we were sharing the barn with some rats nesting amongst the heaps of potatoes. The notion that they might come anywhere near us was terrifying. Far in the distance we could see a light. It was the kitchen window of our own house. It was even more depressing for us to realise that we were barred from access to the familiar warmth of the place. What was to become of us?

After what seemed like an eternity, we heard faint sounds in the distance. A light appeared, swaying in the air. Within moments, voices started getting stronger and the storm lamp getting nearer and nearer. Before long we saw a horse and cart pulling up alongside the barn next to where we here huddled. To our relief, we saw, alighting from the driver's bench, our next-door neighbour Franciszek Kowalik followed by his wife Jadwiga and our mother.

Soon we were taken to our neighbour's house, given a nourishing hot meal and settled down for a warm night's sleep, trying to put the recent tribulations out of our minds.

Early next morning, Mother set off again; this time once again to see her brother in Lawry. She returned later that day with Uncle Stas in tow. Mother thanked our hosts profusely for their help and hospitality, and again we departed.

On arrival to uncle's farm in Lawry we were greeted by his by then very pregnant wife. After things settled down a bit, the adults sat down to a "council of war".

"I'm sorry to burden you with my troubles," Mother started, "but as things stand I and my children have nowhere else to go."

"Don't distress yourself. That's what families are for." responded the aunt.

Uncle Stas quickly chipped in, "Of course. I'm only sorry I didn't stay with you long enough yesterday. Maybe if Kuprianczyk saw a man beside you his response might have been very different. This is your home. Stay with us as long as you need."

Mother, heartened by the couple's words thanked them both for their generosity but then added;

"I know you won't say it, but we'll be a severe burden on you. Things can't be easy for you either in these days of turmoil. I bet you didn't have much luck with your trading at the market the other day."

After some thought she continued, "I can see that Hela is too far gone to be able to do too much around the farmyard. That's something I can take on. The two small ones can't be of any help. I'll keep them with me out of harm's way as best I can. I thought Stasia and Romek might go and stay with Gabrunia. They're big enough to help around their farm and earn their keep."

Stas and Hela raised no objections, and so the following day Mother set off to my aunt Gabrunia's, with Stasia and Romek alongside.

She related her tale of woe to her sister and finished by asking if she would help by taking her two eldest off her hands for the time being.

Aunt Gabrunia was known in the family for her grumbling and her sour disposition, however Mother soon discovered that in adversity her heart was in the right place. She didn't hesitate.

"My dear Koscia," she said warmly, "You can't imagine how sorry I am to see you in such distress. Of course we'll help in any way we can. The children can stay with us and are very welcome. If it makes you feel better, Stasia could help me with some needlework and Romek can take care of the cows out on pasture."

Slowly we all started settling into our new life. Weeks were passing by. It appeared that the War for our country was over. Germans halted their advance, forming a new border approximately half way across Poland, and occupying the Western part. The Russian Red Army moved across from the East and took over what remained. Of Father there was no sign.

I found our stay on uncle's farm at Lawry fascinating. For a child of my age a farm represented a treasure house. There were so many things and places to be investigated and explored. I often trotted behind my uncle, fascinated by his everyday farm activities. My uncle was a devoted horseman. One day he thought he'd impart his fascination for the animals to me, his young nephew. His favourite mare had a growing foal. Uncle, without any great enthusiasm on my part, sat me on the young horse to give me my first taste of horse riding. The young colt's back was sharp and bony, and I was pleased to have the exercise out of the way as soon as possible. Another occasion that left an imprint on my young mind was a time when uncle decided to "break" an untrained mount.

One day an army platoon arrived at the farm and demanded to inspect the farm stock. They soon spotted the mare and told uncle that the animal was to be requisitioned by the Army. All the pleading on his part proved to be fruitless. His beloved Kaska was being led away in spite of his protests. In response to his argument that he couldn't run the farm without a beast of burden, they presented him with a young and completely untrained stallion before they left.

Unconsoled, uncle was left with the task of turning the creature into a useful farm animal. One day, as we all sat by the window looking onto the farmyard, Uncle Stas appeared out of the stable doors, mounted on the new beast. As soon as they were out in the open the horse started rearing, bucking and jumping around in all sorts of unpredictable ways. We were all terrified. "Surely the stallion will throw his rider to the ground any minute and then trample him to death." I thought. As a few more moments passed however, Uncle Stas was still in the saddle. Eventually the horse, exhausted, started slowing down. In the end, all his energy spent, the stallion accepted defeat and calmed down completely. This was the first time I'd seen a "wild" horse ridden into submission. No such scenes in the future on cowboy films would impress me as much as that moment.

Of course, I shouldn't have worried. My uncle, after all, was known to be an outstanding horseman.

While I tended to shadow my uncle, my sister Zuzia decided to make herself agreeable to our aunt. This was, at least in part attributable to her curiosity at the aunt's condition. She had no experience of our mother carrying a child and found the situation fascinating. (She was too young to remember my arrival, and much too young to remember the one before.)

Away at the homestead of aunt Gabrunia, Stasia and Romek coped with their exile as best they could. Stasia seemed to show little talent for needlework, in spite of patient coaching by our aunt. Romek, a little more cunning, appeared to take to the idea of cow herding. However, every time the cows were left with him in the fields, they would run home to the shed as though demented. Nobody could understand what was happening and it was eventually decided that it would be better for Romek and better still for the cows if he were to give up 'taking care' of the animals. It was many years later that my brother let us in on his secret. Hornets in England are unpleasant and dangerous insects. They cannot however, be compared to their cousins in Poland. Those monsters would attack, without provocation, any creature within their area of activity. The sting was literally unbearable. Cattle on pasture were particularly prone to such attacks with the result that cows became extremely wary of the distinctive sound of approaching hornets, and tended to run for cover to escape imminent attacks. My brother observed such events and one day, thought he'd try out an experiment. When the cows were nicely settled on the field he came up behind them and made the best attempt he could of reproducing the sound of an approaching hornet. It worked. The cows first went rigid with fear, then with the sound getting nearer, raised their tails right up into the air and galloped away. They didn't even slow down until they were safely inside their shed where to their relief, the sound of the hornet could no longer be heard.

Eventually, and inevitably, my aunt went into labour. Uncle started pacing up and down in the traditional manner of all expectant fathers, utterly beside himself with anxiety. Although he was looking forward to the arrival of a possible son and heir, his prime concern was for the welfare of his beloved Hela. While uncle Stas stayed outside trying to cope with his emotions, my mother stayed with her sister-in-law and acted as mid-wife. Eventually the child arrived and uncle was allowed to view it. Moments later he run out of the house holding a child in his arms and shouting;

"It's a girl, it's a girl."

He was clearly overjoyed with the new arrival. The fact that only a short while ago he said he was hoping for a boy was completely forgotten.

Time came to choose a name. After a brief discussion, aunt Hela said to my mother,

"I'd like to call my little one Zuzia. It seems only fitting. I know how close you and my Stas have always been. You've even called your eldest after him. I think this idea of naming children after another member of the family binds people together, and I certainly wish and hope that our families will continue to be as one in the future. Yes. Our first born will be called Zuzia after your little girl to whom, incidentally, I've taken quite a shine."

Nobody contested the decision. My mother said she felt honoured and agreed wholeheartedly. Soon after, we all made our way to the church in Rogoznica where my new cousin was duly christened.

It was late autumn in the year of 1939 when rumours started circulating that some Polish prisoners taken by the Red Army were being freed. The Communist Russian Authorities, not wishing to appear to the Outside World as Imperialist aggressors, decided to hold a plebiscite in the part of Poland they occupied. It was their intention to demonstrate to the naive West that their action really was intended only to "liberate the Polish Proletariat" from the oppression of their home-grown Capitalists, and that the expansion of the Communist Russian Empire was the last thing on their mind. To encourage "the right result" they decided to release a percentage of Polish prisoners of war, who were expected to vote for the New Order.

One-day mother came home from town, and finding it difficult to contain her excitement said to her brother,

"I've just come back from Piaski. I saw a man there who said he'd just arrived from Wolkowysk and that he was sure he saw Leon in town, trying to make his way home."

After that, the strain of waiting for Father's return was unbearable for all of us. Eventually, one afternoon, mother ran into the house and called to us,

"Come, children! Your father is coming home!"

We followed mother outside as quickly as we could. She stopped at the edge of the field and scanned the far horizon. In a while, as we watched, a small dark figure appeared in the distance, set against the overcast sky. As we stood there, transfixed, the figure grew larger and larger. In the end we could all see him clearly. There was no longer any doubt. It was Father.

For a moment we stood there, shocked at his appearance. Father was bedraggled, his face pale and covered by a fortnight's growth of a greying beard. We all started to walk across the field to meet him. Soon the walking turned into a run. The reunion when we finally reached him was very emotional and tearful.

Father was home at last.

It took a few days for father to recover, at least partially, from the effects of his recent privations. It was then that he told us his story.

"You'll remember that as per "standing orders" I reported at the Garrison Headquarters in Sokolka..." he started.

"...when I arrived I discovered the whole place in a state of chaos. There was a constant stream of new arrivals entering the camp without any organised reception and induction facility. Eventually, by trial and error I managed to get myself registered and fitted out after a fashion. The uniform was a poor fit and the rifle of the Great War vintage. Still, in the end I found myself attached to a regiment and put in charge of a platoon."

"Early next morning our regiment was ordered to move out. We marched west for the next few days, apparently with the intention to reinforce our units giving battle to the German armies. Suddenly, after we passed Warsaw, our Commander received new orders. Apparently our lines of defence had been breached and our Army was in a full-scale retreat. The intention now was to fall back and form a new line of defence, using the unbloodied units from the East. We were to fall back and await further instructions. In response to further orders we kept on retreating. The journey was exhausting. We were getting worn out, even before we faced the Enemy. You must remember that our division comprised foot soldiers only, and that we had no mechanised transport facilities whatever. This meant that, not only did we have to march with the complete kit on our backs, but in addition, had to carry all the heavy equipment and supplies."

"My platoon was chosen to transport the Field Altar. This comprised all the equipment and paraphernalia required for the Regimental Chaplain to celebrate Mass in the field and various materials he would need in order to discharge his pastoral duties towards the soldiers. This was quite an onerous duty as the materials, although precious and sacred, were bulky and heavy and so difficult to transport."

He paused for a moment, the strain of telling the story visible on his face. After a moment's rest and a sip of tea, Father continued.

"Suddenly, in the middle of the day, with the whole regiment in full marching order, a call came from the front to halt. As soon as the soldiers settled down, unit leaders were gathered to receive instructions. The news passed on to us by our Commander was hard to accept. Apparently, Germans, having driven our Armies East half way across our land, stopped their advance. This seemed like good news until we heard what followed. The reason for the German Army's halt was the fact that we were now to be invaded by Stalin's Red Army from the East, who were to take over what remained of our land."

"Once that news reached the Army Headquarters, the situation was deemed hopeless. Instructions were issued to all units to disband and for all soldiers to seek their own individual means of salvation."

"Our Commander delivered the final order with a sombre expression to a stunned and silent gathering. He finished by saying that he wished all the best of Fortune and asked all assembled to return to their units and disband them as ordered. He then turned to me and said,

'Krajewski; I must ask you to undertake one last duty before you and your soldiers look to your own security. As you know we now stand in lands that will soon be occupied by the Godless Russian Communist Army. We cannot allow the sacred artefacts your team was transporting, to fall into their hands. Before you disband, I must ask you to bury the Field Altar in some secret place so that the invading Hordes will not have a chance to defile it.'

With that final statement, he wished us all good luck once again and disappeared behind the screen of his tent."

Father, fatigued, paused for a moment and then continued. "I took my lads to a copse on the nearby hill, and there we dug out a big pit next to a large oak tree. Before we deposited our sacred cargo, I invited each to take for himself whatever item they wanted to take away with them. I took a few sacred pictures and a hand-full of medallions of Our Lady of the Immaculate Conception. We buried all the remaining items and made sure the location was well concealed before leaving the Wood."

"As we started down the hill we suddenly found ourselves completely surrounded by Russian soldiers. There was nothing to be done. We gave ourselves up and were promptly marched off to a nearby Prisoner of War Camp. There, to our dismay, we found, incarcerated, most of my regiment. Of the Commandant there was no sign. I think his escape arrangements were prepared more carefully than the rest of us."

"Soon we were marched off to the nearest Railhead and transported by cattle-truck to a large POW camp outside Minsk. Conditions in the camp defied description. We were squashed like sardines in meagre and rickety huts. Hygiene was non-existent. In order to attend to one's bodily functions it was necessary to use a large open ditch on the edge of the camp. What passed for food was a daily bowl of dishwater with a hint of potato peelings and a small piece of black bread. There was no doubt about it. We were not intended to survive for long. To add to our despair, guards kicked and abused us at every opportunity. I managed to befriend one of the Russian soldiers and in secret offered him one of the pictures of The Sacred Heart of Jesus. The man looked at the picture and started weeping. Through his tears he thanked me profusely for the gift and secreted the picture on his person. I'm sure a lot of them behaved the way they did because it was expected of them. They all knew that to show mercy for Poles or even worse, to indicate any religious beliefs, could mean that they too would find themselves behind bars."

"Several weeks had passed. On top of all my troubles the old chest sickness came back. I was loosing my strength fast and was getting too feeble to cope. The end was not too far away."

"Suddenly, one day I and some others were called up before the Camp Commandant."

"Listen carefully, you Polish scum," he said.

46

"Our Loving Father, Marshal Stalin, having first rescued you from the chains of Capitalism, now decided to give you Poles an opportunity to join Us and share in the benefits of being a part of The Soviet Union. You have been pardoned. Get your belongings together and go home. When you get back you and your families will be required to vote in the Plebiscite asking to be allowed to join The Soviet Union. Make sure that you, your families and your friends vote the right way. The names of all the subversives voting against will be noted."

"We couldn't believe our ears. Without argument, each one of the selected group collected his meagre possessions and, before we realised what had happened, found ourselves outside the Camp gates, and on the road leading to the railway station."

"At the station the group broke up. Each of us started looking for a means of transport that was likely to bring him closer to his family. I found a goods train departing in the direction of Grodno and sneaked into one of the wagons. On arrival I begged a lift from a peasant travelling with his horse and cart towards Wolkowysk. After that point my luck run out and I found myself having to make the rest of the journey on foot. When I got to Piaski, I found our restaurant deserted. Szmaja wasn't very helpful. In the end I made my way to the Puciolowskis and there I was told that you were here. They gave me something to eat and I set off across country to join you."

Father, his story finally told, looked at us and smiled.

"And so here I am at long last. My war, thank heavens, is over. Do you know that throughout all that, I haven't fired a single shot?"

He then put his hand into his coat pocket and produced a handful of medals of the Virgin Mary. Father then called each of us in turn and presented one of the medals to each. Having finished dispensing the amulets he gathered us together and said. "You must take great care of these gifts. Always wear them around your necks. These medals have the power to protect you from evil, just as they saved your father from the Hell of the Russian prison."

You see, in spite of his quarrels with his parish priest, my father really was a deeply religious person. His problem was not with the Roman Catholic Faith but rather with the way it was sometimes proclaimed to the faithful.

Eventually he turned to mother,

"Tell me your story my dear," he said. "What happened after I left? How did you finish up here at your brother's, and where are the other kids? I haven't seen any sign of Stasia or Romek."

It was mother's turn to tell father of her experiences. She told him about the business collapsing, the landlord old Szmaja forcing her out of the house in Piaski and finally about her unsuccessful attempt to reclaim the farm in Rogoznica.

Father listened to it all intently. When mother finished he said,

"Here I was feeling sorry for myself. I see you and the children went through quite an ordeal of your own."

He sat there for a while, deep in thought then finally sighed and said,

"We've all lived through some terrifying experiences. Still, thank Heavens; we are all alive and well. It's time to start re-building our lives."

He then became quite excited and started pacing up and down the room.

"Tomorrow morning we shall go to visit you sister Gabrunia and see how our children are doing," he said. "In the evening I'll go over and see if I can persuade Kuprianczyk to hand over our property. This would give us a chance to settle back down and start a new life. This nightmare will surely pass soon. In the meantime the thing to do is to survive somehow and keep our heads down."

Early next morning they halted their horse and cart outside aunt Gabrunia's front door. Gabrunia and her husband greeted the couple warmly and said how pleased they were to see father return from the War safe and sound. Father's reunion with Stasia and Romek was highly emotional. Tears were flowing freely not only down the children's faces but also all over Father's cheeks while they all hugged and squeezed each other.

Later, when children disappeared to be return to their usual activities, Father said to his hosts, "I must tell you again how grateful I am for your help. I must ask you however to bear with us a little longer. I'm going to try to get our farm back so that we can all move in and start our life as a family again. Meantime, will you please allow

Romek and Stasia to stay on with you? It won't take more than a few days."

Aunt and Uncle readily agreed and my parents set off for home. On the way back they saw something moving under a blanket in the back of the cart. It was their young Stasia. While my mother and father were talking with my aunt and uncle, Stasia had hidden behind the stove and eavesdropped. She didn't like what she heard. No way was she staying behind with the aunt she disliked so much, with her "precious daddy" back home again. When nobody was looking, she sneaked out and hid on the cart.

Having discovered her, my parents didn't have the heart to take her back, and so Stasia joined us all at Uncle's now overcrowded house.

Next, father set off for our homestead in the Rogoznica Settlement. He returned very late that night and related his encounter with Kuprianczyk to Mother.

"As you would expect, I arrived in Rogoznica fully expecting to have a flaming row with the man. In the beginning, after I put my case to him, I received a very hostile and even abusive response. After a while, however an evil smile appeared on his face, as though he had just thought of some amusing secret and he suddenly changed his tack. "I'm not using the whole house these days. Maybe I've been a little hasty in turning you down. I can see no reason why you and your family couldn't move in and occupy half of it." He seemed to be trying to conceal some secret joke as he continued, "Move in as soon as you like. Do it tomorrow if you like." I thanked him for his generosity and said I'd discuss his suggestion with you before making a decision and left." After a pause for reflection he added, "On the face of it, I should have grabbed the offer and told him we'd be moving in straight away. The reason I played for time was that there was something about the expression on his face I didn't like. I don't know what this snake is up to but he's definitely up to no good. I don't think we'll be safe living under one roof with him. If you agree, I suggest we give it a miss and look for another solution to our problems."

Over the next few days father made some trips to Piaski. He called on many friends and old business acquaintances and enquired about prospects for renting suitable accommodation as well as opportunities for making a living.

One evening he returned home, clearly having sampled someone's hospitality. "Our problem is solved!" he announced. In response to mother's enquiries he explained, "I ran into a chap with whom I used to do some business in the good old days and we started chatting. It appears that he is doing very well bartering. He needs someone to help and asked me to join him. On top of that, he has a large house, a good part of which he's not using. I've seen the place and reckon there's plenty of room for all of us. As a partner, I wouldn't be required to pay much rent." He then looked at mother inquiringly and added, "What do you think. It kills two birds with one stone. We get somewhere of our own to live and I get to earn a living. Shall we go over tomorrow and have a talk with the man, if you like what you hear, we can have a look at the rooms."

As usual mother found her husband's deal to be sound and readily agreed to go along with it.

A few days later we all set of again for Piaski. By that time Romek joined us and the family was complete.

We first arrived at our old house by two carts and father went over to talk to Szmaja. He came out soon after and called for mother and the elder kids to help in loading all our furniture and other belongings mother left behind, onto the carts. While the work was progressing, Szmaja, no doubt anxious to see us off his premises, kept nagging and harassing us. Father, who was known for his mercurial temperament, kept his temper on this occasion under iron control and did not allow himself to be provoked. Onto the carts went beds, tables, chairs and the large ornate bureau father brought with him from Mostek.

At last we settled in as a family yet again. The part of house we occupied comprised two large rooms and a small but well equipped kitchen. Mother took time arranging the furniture and seemed very pleased with the end result. The house was situated well off the beaten track and, my parents thought, would be unlikely to be spotted by Communist activists who knew us and might be inclined to exact their vengeance on a Polish patriot like my father. Slowly, we all started to relax and enjoy our new situation.

One morning in the late January of the year 1940 my father, as usual, went out on the town to organise some deal or other. On his travels between town and country he would observe objects in town that the owners would part with in exchange for fresh food. When he established that some farmer needed an object father could locate, he knew he had a potential deal.

That day, he seemed to be much later returning home than usual. Mother wasn't too concerned. He might have met someone and stopped off for a drink. These kinds of encounters were often very good for business.

Late that afternoon we heard a knock on the front door. Moments later Mother ushered in two men into the front room. The first was older, possibly around 40 years of age. The man's build was slight and height below average. His hair, combed straight to the back, showed significant streaks of grey. His face had a severe expression. It seemed unlikely that it ever lit up with joyful laughter.

The other man was much younger. Probably not more than in his mid twenties. His unruly blonde hair and animated fresh face gave the impression of a friendly and innocent character. Both men wore what we quickly recognised as the light green uniform of the self-styled Communist Militia. None of us had ever seen either man before.

On entering, the older man, clearly in charge, announced rather formally to mother, "Your husband Leon Krajewski has been detained for questioning at the Police station. He is suspected of Anti-State activities. We are here to conduct a search of your premises to help us establish his guilt or innocence."

Having made his announcement, the leader of the team looked around and went over to the roll-top bureau my father brought with him, and which he treasured as his only heirloom. As he started to rummage through father's papers, the younger Militiaman, at a loose end, asked mother for a glass of water to quench his thirst. He seemed a little ill at ease and his dry throat was probably the result of nervous tension.

As though sensing that the younger man represented the softer option, I approached him as he raised the glass to his lips and asked out loud, "What have you done with my father?"

An awkward silence followed. After a while, ignoring my enquiry the man re-started his activity with the glass and everybody returned to normal behaviour, as though I hadn't even uttered a word. 'After all I was only a baby, and what do babies know?'

The officials conducted a very thorough search of the whole premises, inspecting all and any documents and other sundry paperwork particularly closely. They couldn't have found anything incriminating, because after hours of searching they left, taking nothing away with them. As they left, Mother, heartened by the fact that they apparently found no incriminating documents, asked when Father would be allowed to come home. The reply she got was that they couldn't say. "If he isn't back by tomorrow morning, call at the station. You may be told something more definite then."

The night came and went and there was no sign of my father. Early next morning my mother, mortified, took father's winter jacket and went over to the Police Station. Her request to see her husband was refused. Not being able to make any headway or get any information about father's circumstances, she asked if, at least they would pass on to him his warm coat. She remembered that he had left our home scantily clad, and the nights were getting very cold. The Militiaman accepted the coat and suggested that, if Father was not released soon, Mother should come and enquire in a few days' time again.

A few more days passed and there was still seemed no prospect of father coming home. Mother went to the Police Station yet again. This time she was told that my father was moved to a prison in the borough town of Wolkowysk and mother must make enquiries with the authorities in that town in due course. "For now, no more information is available," said the duty sergeant.

Only a few days later, in the middle of the night of 9th of February in the year of 1940, after we had all turned in, we were suddenly awakened by that terrible knock on the door.

At a stroke, our life in the place where I was born, as were my siblings, my parents and their parents before them, was torn away from us. We were on our way, being transported away from everything we knew, to some completely strange and unknown destination.

Life was never to be the same again.

Chapter 6

After having spent the first night in the Parish Council Offices in Piaski with twenty or so other families crying all night, the next day at mid-day a long string of large horse-driven sleighs collected outside the Council Building. Each family in turn was ordered to board the nearest vehicle. When all were loaded, the whole train moved off down the road in silence. Not one of the inhabitants of Piaski who had been lucky enough to remain dared venture out for fear of being shot on sight.

As the sun was setting we arrived at the railway station in Wolkowysk. In front of us stood a battered goods train. The large sliding door was opened in the front wagon and the deportees started transferring their wares from the sleighs into it. Eventually it was our turn. As we entered, we discovered that these were no ordinary goods wagons. Our Russian hosts, no doubt anticipating this moment, converted the vehicles for "passenger" use. As I said, the middle part of the vehicle wall was taken up by the original and unmodified sliding doors. Directly in front as one entered, was located a cast iron stove with a sheet metal flue running straight up and through the roof. On either side were added two intermediate floors, thus making it possible to pack the unfortunate travellers on three levels. There were no windows.

The sleighs soon departed and we were left wondering what was to happen next. Clearly, keeping the Detainees informed was not a top priority item for our Guards. The train remained in the siding for the next three days during which time a continuous stream of transports of Polish families kept pouring in, each being promptly loaded into the next vacant wagon on arrival. To keep us alive during this period of waiting, a Guard would come down once a day with a bucket full of slops which he laughably called cabbage soup, followed by another, carrying dark brown bread cut up into small pieces. Each passenger's daily sustenance was a bowlful of the so-called soup and a small piece of bread. A starvation diet.

All the doors were sealed and the train set off on its journey. None of the travellers had any idea where they were going, how long their journey would be or even, how long it was to be before the next stop.

In fact this last item soon proved to be the source of serious problems. The train kept pounding on hour after hour. After some time 'calls of nature' started making their needs known to the occupants. With their arrival dawned the knowledge that the vehicle had no provisions for dealing with them. Initially, parents used whatever pots they brought with them to allow their children to relieve themselves. Soon, however it became apparent that this short-term solution was insufficient. In the end, somebody came up with the clever idea of cutting a hole in the wagon floor to allow desperate passengers to relieve themselves and dispose of any refuse. (The main sliding doors were locked from the outside.) A hole was promptly cut behind the stove. (There was no shortage of wood - saws and axes on board.) The facility was very inconvenient and offered no privacy and so it's use was limited to extreme emergencies. After many hours of travelling the train finally stopped and the prisoners were allowed to come out. The train didn't halt for the convenience of the travellers. The only reason it halted was for the locomotive to replenish its water supply. While the engine was taking on water from the tank, the whole of the train emptied as each occupant rushed out to attend to his call of nature. A pattern was quickly established. All the men crouched on one side of the train, while the women used the other side.

Eventually we arrived at the main railway junction in the town of Baranowicze and the train was yet again parked into a siding. The wagons were unlocked and, uncharacteristically, our captors chose to impart some information to us regarding our current circumstances. Apparently the train was to remain in the sidings for some days, and was in any case not going to move again until our Guards received further orders. The feeding regime from our previous period of waiting in Wolkowysk was resumed. The contents of the slops they called soup varied a little. Sometimes we could even find odd pieces of potato peelings in it. Our Guards became slack and people started to make long excursions away from their wagons. A couple of young men from our wagon decided to take advantage of the situation and run away. One day they both disappeared and we never saw them again. Many years later I discovered that their escape was successful. The story was that they both made their way across the Russian/German border and finished up in Warsaw. In fact they both later died defending the Capital from the Germans during the Warsaw uprising.

Some of the people came back with some incredible tales. Apparently the whole of this International Junction was being filled with prison trains like our own. Hundreds of trains were already amassed and new ones were arriving all the time. We stayed there for over a week, while other trains kept coming in. During our stay we continued to be fed the standard diet. The food was, of course not sufficient and we supplemented it by dipping into the supplies we brought along with us from home. This we did very sparingly for we still had no idea what was ahead of us.

Suddenly, early one morning Guards started shouting as they walked down the length of the train:

"All that belong on this train; get on board and settle in. We are setting off straight away."

As they went the enormous sliding doors were closed and sealed from outside.

We all sat anxiously in the dark waiting. After what seemed like an eternity, the train suddenly jerked violently and we were off.

Again the train run on at a break-neck speed into the unknown. The occupants of our compartment started to get more and more uneasy.

"Where are they taking us?" people stared asking no one in particular, "Are we really being resettled? Are they going to take us out into some desolate place and kill us? What is this all about anyway?"

As time went by, some people on the top deck, having discovered gaps in the wall panelling, sat at their observation posts and occasionally shouted out their comments;

"We are travelling East into Russia," one would say.

"We have just passed Minsk," would call another.

Later a despondent voice would whisper, "We have entered Russia. I've just seen the sign of the Smolensk railway station."

After we passed Moscow, the train changed direction and continued northwards. The towns we passed were less familiar to Poles. However as the names were called out, "Jaroslaw...Wologda..." it became obvious that our destination was to be the region of Archangel in Siberia. The train left the main track after the town of Wologda and proceeded northwards on a side-track. We travelled on through desolate snow-covered countryside for a long time. In the end the train run out of track and we came to a halt. The whole journey took three weeks.

As the wagons were unlocked, the travellers started to emerge and survey their surroundings. It soon became apparent that the rail terminated in the midst of a small village or a hamlet. All around were endless forests.

Our guards dispersed into the settlement. After a couple of hours we were told to alight from the train. As we came off, the guards took individual families and ushered them into one of the houses. We were thus foisted onto the poor villagers and told that we were to spend the night there. The next morning we were to continue our journey.

It must be said that in spite of the fact that our host's huts were suddenly filled to the brim with uninvited guests, their attitude towards us was friendly and hospitable. They raided their own meagre supplies to give us all warm and nourishing meals. Truly, this behaviour was in the age old and ancient tradition of Slavonic hospitality. The evening in our hut went by very pleasantly with our hosts quizzing the arrivals about life in "the outside world" and then, after sharing some home-made vodka with the new comers making music and singing. In our misery it didn't occur to us that these apparently free people had experienced isolation equivalent to long-term prison confinement. They listened with wonder, and sometimes with disbelief, at the description of the life in Poland we left behind.

In the end all agreed that it was time to get some sleep. After all, we still had no idea what privations we were to face the next day.

After only a few hours' sleep we were woken by our Russian guards and ordered to get up, get our belongings together and come out. We were all confused. "Surely, the sun hasn't even come up yet!" somebody said. The NKVD officer in charge responded, "We have a long journey ahead of us. There is no time to waste on idle chatter if we are to reach our destination by nightfall. Hurry up."

Outside, we found a row of sleighs with the local Siberian ponies harnessed in at their heads. The equipment and the animals obviously belonged to the inhabitants of the village, and were now being arbitrarily commandeered by the Red Army soldiers for their own purposes. It seemed to us that the "free Russians" were no freer than us.

We settled in on the vehicles and the next phase of our journey began. The group travelled further north throughout most of that day, stopping only to rest and feed the horses and, of course to dish out our meagre daily ration.

On the horizon we saw a large lake, and soon discovered that we were in fact heading towards it. Arriving at its bank we saw a row of long barracks. The buildings were constructed of rough timber logs and appeared to have been there for some time. We could see no sign of life in or around the buildings. The horses came to a halt alongside the nearest building and the leader of the convoy shouted out:

"This is it. This from now on will be your home. Come up to the front one family at a time and you'll be allocated your accommodation. Remember. This is not a holiday camp. You are here to work for the greater glory of the Soviet Union and the Revolution. You will earn your food by working."

"Remember; He who does not work , does not eat."

After this speech was over, one by one, the bewildered groups started alighting. Eventually it was our turn. The Guard directed Mother to the top of the next building and we all followed, dragging our belongings with us. The room we entered was split into two by a makeshift screen. Our part, for we soon discovered that only one third of the room was allocated to house our whole family, was neglected and dirty. In the far corner stood a crudely constructed wooden bunk bed with nothing but wooden planks and thin straw-filled mattresses to lie on. In the middle we saw a stained table and alongside it a crude bench. A tiny window provided sparse daylight. We were surprised to note that the opening housed a glass pane. A small brick-built stove, now cold and unlit, stood against the corridor, midway between our accommodation and that of our neighbours behind the low screen. It's chimney extended through the sloping roof.

"So this is to be our home." Mother said, despair in her voice.

While we all unloaded our belongings, our captors prepared our evening meal. The usual thin hot soup and a small piece of brown bread of course.

Hungry, we all ate the offered food rapidly and then, exhausted by the long journey, fell upon the bunks as we stood and fell fast asleep.

The next day at dawn, we were woken by one of the guards hammering on the door. On entering he loudly announced:

"All adults and youngsters over fifteen are to get dressed and gather outside in ten minutes. Today you're starting your work in the forest. Children will stay behind."

Our first day in exile started with Mother gone and the four of us left alone, cold, frightened and hungry. One would have expected my eldest sister Stasia, who was then almost in her fifteenth year, to take charge. In fact it was my brother Romek who more quickly rose to the occasion. Saying nothing, (Romek was never much one with words), he got dressed, put on his shoes and overcoat and went out. After a while he returned carrying a big bunch of twigs. From his pocket he produced a handful of dry moss, he must have found outside, and placed it in the oven. He then built a small stack of twigs and lit the lot with a match he must have cadged from someone outside. As the flame developed, he added more wood until, before long a cheerful fire was established and the room started getting warmer. Later that day, another officer arrived at the camp accompanied by two Russian women and all the children were told to gather around them outside.

Firstly, the officer told us that one of the women has something to say to us. As an incentive, and to ensure our attention, he added that hot food would be brought for us all immediately after the speech.

The head teacher stepped forward and delivered her well-rehearsed speech. Most of the words went straight over our heads. For a start the delivery was all in Russian, a language most of us had no need to acquire up to now. After discarding the unintelligible propaganda and communist slogans, what it all boiled down to was that, we were all to attend school every day starting the following day. Next, followed instructions how to get there.

"If you take a path along the lake to the left of the camp you will eventually reach the Administration Compound. There you will find the School Building, a shop and the Camp Commandant's Office," she said.

"Truancy won't be tolerated," she continued.

"Your parents, who will be responsible for your attendance, will be severely punished for all your transgressions."

Her final incentive was to say that no food would be distributed in the camp in future, except on Sundays. Adults would be given their rations at their place of work during the week and children would be fed when they attended school.

After the assembly was disbanded we were left alone to our own devices and proceeded to settle in and investigate our surroundings.

As I said earlier, the camp was sitting on the bank of a large lake. At this time of the year, with the daytime temperature hovering around minus thirty degrees Celsius, its surface was frozen solid. The settlement comprised thirteen identical barracks, all in a row alongside the lake, like an army platoon. The unlucky number was not lost on my sister Stasia who saw gloom and doom everywhere. Each building contained six rooms, which were in turn divided in two by screens. In that way twelve individual chambers were formed. If you then plant three families into each area you get a barrack housing thirty-six families.

All around the camp was a deep, seemingly impenetrable, dark, virgin forest. It appeared to be mainly made up of tall and ancient spruces and fern trees, but it also contained a variety of bushes and some isolated groups of leafy trees like maple and birch.

We tried to make friends with the group of children behind our screen but to our surprise, the response seemed to be indifferent or hostile. Not accustomed to such behaviour, we did our best to keep our distance from that time on.

That evening Mother returned, visibly exhausted. She told us that she was put to work cutting down trees and chopping branches off felled logs alongside men. When she complained to the guard in charge of the unit, she was reminded of the slogan she heard on our arrival to the camp,

"If you don't work, you don't eat," he said. "If you want to get a full ration, and something to take home to your children, you must do the work of a man. Lighter tasks mean smaller rewards."

Hearing this, Mother realised that she had no option. Families with men and grown-up children would have it comparatively easy. If she was to keep her children alive, she had to compete with men felling trees.

Next morning, bright and early, we all marched off to school. Stasia and Romek were assigned their places in classes relative to their age. Zuzia and I, being below school age, were guided into a Kindergarten.

After lunch we were all allowed to return home where, with our parents still away at work in the forest, we were left to our own devices.

It's surprising how in spite of all the adversities, the force of life, curiosity and sense of adventure overwhelms children and young people generally.

Before long some kids decided that the lake was perfect for skating. Obviously nobody brought such luxuries as skates with them. It was time to innovate. Some young man came up with an idea. From a piece of wood he whittled out a skate, which he fastened to his boot with screws. To give his gadget "glidability," he attached a thick wire along the underside. The skate worked perfectly, and he soon found himself the envy of all boys and a few girls. Soon others set about copying the invention. Others found yet other ways to entertain themselves. In spite of the depravation and hunger we were beginning to have fun.

At the end of the week Mother discovered how the system worked. She was awarded an income based on her output. It fell far short of the "norm" set by the Commandant and her income was reduced accordingly. From that money the administrators deducted the cost of food dished out to her as well as all of us children. After the whole thing was reckoned up she found that her earnings didn't cover the cost of basic food and she started the following week in debt to the authorities. There was nothing she could do about it. She couldn't allow for her children to starve to death. Mother had to accept that her indebtedness would continue to grow. She also realised that even this inadequate income relied entirely on her continued effort. She certainly couldn't afford the 'luxury' of falling ill.

Stasia gained little from her attendance in school. Torn away from her beloved father and familiar surroundings, her thoughts and emotions were in turmoil. She didn't concentrate at all and allowed all the lessons as well as the propaganda to go over her head. Romek's response to this time of trial was very different. He quickly picked up the Cyrillic alphabet and rapidly developed his ability to read and write Russian. As his comprehension grew he discovered that a lot of the propaganda they were fed was fiercely anti-Polish. He found some songs so insulting that (at a risk of severe punishment) he refused to join in singing. Luckily the teacher pretended not to notice and my brother's demonstration brought no wrath upon him. Zuzia and I, as toddlers, were spared the more intensive attempts at indoctrination. No doubt this was reserved for us when we grew older and more able to absorb and believe the lies and double-talk of the communist system. We spent our time playing and learning "patriotic" songs. I can remember some of them even now.

One of the first items the older children were taught was our new postal address. This was:

Szamp Oziero (nearest English translation would be Lakeside Camp)

Region Onega

District Archangel

USSR

The location was a far northern region of European Russia and strictly speaking not Siberia, which is the name of the Asian expanse to the east of our location. This minor detail was ignored by all at that time, as well as in all future references I know of. The name of Siberia was for ages synonymous with exile and slave labour and any other description of our location would seem inappropriate.

Our parents were then informed that, if they wished to contact their relatives. They could write letters and were assured that these would reach their destinations. Should people back home wish to send letters or provisions to us, this would also be permitted. On hearing this, Mother proceeded to write a letter to each of her sisters, her brother and Jania, her sister-in-law, telling them something of what things were like, (of course, one had to be circumspect as all letters were censored) and asking for help with food. While she was at it she decided to write to the Soviet Authorities enquiring about the whereabouts of her husband.

It may seem strange that, although we were, in some ways, treated like convicts, according to the Communist Propagandist double-talk we were free citizens of the Soviet Union resettled to live in a more appropriate location. As such we were allowed to communicate with other citizens as freely as anyone else.

Hence the, to us surprising, permission to write and receive letters and parcels.

The first to respond was my uncle Stas. Just before Easter we received a parcel. To our hungry eyes, the contents were delicious beyond belief. There was a large leg of cured ham, a big chunk of speck and a couple of rings of Polish sausage. Our Easter celebrations that year were a feast never to be forgotten.

Some time later, Mother received an official communication from the Authorities. It was brief. In response to my mother's enquiries about her husband Leon Krajewski the letter simply stated, "The person described is not known to us."

The reply seemed strange to us, but there was no more that could be done about it.

My big toe had healed up long ago. Slowly I explored my new surroundings and became acquainted with other kids of various age levels. There was one little girl in particular I befriended. She was a year younger than me, but seemed quite bright. She wasn't tall. In fact she was definitely shorter than I was, and I wasn't very tall myself. Her head was covered with a mass of curly blonde hair. In general she gave the appearance of being frail and delicate. The two of us spent a lot of time playing together.

Some adults made skis for themselves. With their aid, some of them ventured far away across the snows to outlying villages, where they would trade some of their belongings in for food. The local Russian inhabitants weren't much better off than we were, however they readily traded their modest supplies for Polish clothes. They certainly had no prospect of buying items of such design and quality through normal channels, even if they had the money to pay for them. The only clothes available to them were the drab and utilitarian products of the Soviet State factories.

Amongst my other adventures, I remember being fitted out with someone's skis and making my first, terrified attempt at making use of them on frozen snow. I never did master the art.

After some time I didn't notice my hunger. The thing, however, that I found disturbing was an abnormal development in my mouth. Stage by stage, I found my teeth were becoming looser and looser. Then I found that something even more disturbing was happening to my gums. Flesh around my teeth started to come off in slabs. Next, unsupported, my teeth started dropping out one by one. Soon I finished up with no more than three or four teeth left. What I didn't know was that I was suffering from Scurvy - a disease borne out of malnutrition and vitamin deficiency.

Children can be cruel. Instead of showing concern for my condition, my siblings made fun of me, calling me a " toothless old man". This annoyed me intensely, but I was too small and weak to do anything about it. My visible anger only served to encourage them to taunt me even more.

Although she couldn't really afford it, Mother visited the camp shop and took on credit some essential implements. I remember being particularly fascinated by the painted wooden spoons she brought home with her. I've never seen anything like it. To me they looked beautiful and pleasant to handle. Not at all like the normal metal utensil we all knew.

At the beginning of May, winter started to show signs of abating. The temperature rose to only a few degrees below freezing, and ice on the lake started breaking up causing loud reports, like cannon fire.

The vast majority of Poles practised the Roman Catholic faith. In Poland traditionally, the month of May was dedicated to the Virgin Mary. Back home during that month, most women and quite a lot of men would gather in church every evening to pray to Our Lady and sing hymns in adoration of the Mother of God. It wasn't surprising that at the beginning of that month, almost out of habit, a group of women in our barrack got together and started saying (to them familiar) prayers. They had to be very quiet, for they knew well that such activities were forbidden by the Soviet Authorities, and that transgressors were normally very severely punished. Unfortunately for them, one of the families living in the same building was that belonging to my little blonde friend. The family by the name of Wasek comprised my friend's father, mother, two adult brothers, a grown-up sister, two brothers in their early teens and a girl a few years older than my friend as well as my little playmate. With so many people of working age the work output of the family was a lot higher than most of the others. The parents hoped that the Camp Commandant might recognise this and that he might commend them to the Authorities as "Heroes of the Soviet Union". Success in such an endeavour would confer upon them great wealth and many privileges. "If only the Commandant could be persuaded..." thought the girl's mother.

One evening as she walked down the corridor, she heard strange group mutterings emanating from one of the cubicles. She came closer and put her ear to the door. Through the wall she could hear a group chant of;

"Hail Mary, full of Grace, the Lord is with Thee..."

"I've got them!" she must have thought. "I'm sure the Commandant would be pleased to hear about this blatant breach of regulations. I wonder how he would show his gratitude to the person who would help him in exposing the culprits! He might even put such a person's name forward to the Committee for decoration."

Having made her decision she kept a close eye on the goings-on in her barrack for a number of days. She discovered that most of the women from her barrack and some from the one next door attended every night. The group gathered in a different cubicle each evening at eight and conducted their devotions for about an hour. With this information she made her way to the Commandant, also secretly and under the cover of darkness. The last thing she wanted was for it to be known where the Russian had got his information.

The following evening the Commandant entered our building and told all the women to gather in one of the rooms. Pointedly, he did not invite his informant Anna Wasek.

He cut straight to the reason for his visit.

"You all know very well that religious gathering is strictly forbidden in the Soviet Union and breaches of this regulation is punishable by imprisonment, and maybe worse. Your neighbour Anna Wasek told me that you make it a habit to gather together and perform various religious ceremonies. You are all grown women with children to look after. I can't believe you could be so stupid as to risk your lives and the welfare of your children with such foolish activities. I must admit that I haven't personally observed any of it and assume that the story amounts to no more than a malicious lie. I warn you, however. It'll be the worse for you if you should prove me wrong." Having delivered his speech the Major turned round and quickly departed.

The women were dumbstruck. When they recovered their wits silence turned into a loud babble. Over the general noise could be heard occasional exclamations, "How could she!"..."What sort of monster is this?"..."May she burn in hell!" In the end some women decided to confront Anna. They walked down the corridor, knocked and entered. The woman leading the delegation stepped forward and faced Anna Wasek.

"We've just had a visit from the Commandant," she said. "He told us that you informed on us, and said that we gather for prayers. How could you have done such a thing? Have you no conscience whatsoever?" she continued, "Are you not afraid of God's vengeance?"

Anna stood there in front of them. She went as white as a sheet. Her hands started to tremble. In her eyes appeared large teardrops.

A long and heavy silence followed. In the end Anna spoke: "The man lies," she said. "I don't know why. I know that he was eyeing my eldest daughter, and she told him where to get off. I can only assume that it's his way of taking revenge on us."

Seeing that the gathering remained unconvinced she added, "I swear to God on the lives of my children. May they all die if I'm not telling the truth."

At such a profound oath the gathered women had no reply. "We'll take your word that what the Commandant said is a lie. We hope for your sake that your vow isn't false. Remember. God sees all and hears all. We don't wish your children any harm." After that, the women, rather subdued, quietly dispersed.

Until that time the whole family boasted remarkably good health. The fact that they always had more (and better) food than most of us might have had something to do with it.

A couple of weeks later however, Anna's youngest and best-loved child, her little blonde Angel, was suddenly taken ill. The child had

65

suddenly developed a high temperature. Her mother put her to bed and used every remedy she could think of to break the fever. In spite her every effort the child's temperature kept rising. Only a few days after she fell ill, the girl, under the influence of very high temperature, started hallucinating and calling out the names of her dead grandparents. Before dawn the next day, my little friend lay dead; her final sufferings were at last over.

Needless to say, her mother, together with the rest of her family, was beside herself with grief. As was our custom, a couple of days later the child was laid out in her coffin. Everyone in the camp came to see the little girl lying there in her best dress and to say their final respects and farewells. Nobody mentioned the recent incident or the terrible oath uttered by the dead child's mother. I remember being paraded alongside the coffin myself. At my age the gravity of the moment didn't seem impressive. I wasn't even particularly shaken by my little friend's death. After all, death was something I saw around me all the time in this place. No. What stuck in my mind was my impression of the girl as she lay there in front of me. Suddenly, she looked a lot taller in that posture than she was only days ago when we played together outside our hut. I could have sworn she seemed taller than me. "How could that be?" I thought.

Soon the incident passed and was forgotten. Other, more urgent matters attracted our attention.

We discovered the secret of the camp we now occupied. Apparently, Ukrainian peasants had built the settlement some years ago.

In the early thirties, Stalin decided to "collectivise" all agriculture in his Empire. This wasn't too difficult to accomplish in the central regions of Russia, as traditionally, most of the peasants in those areas earned their living before the Revolution by working on the vast estates of the Russian Aristocracy and Nobility. Most of them owned little or no land of their own. It was a simple matter to convert the country estates into collective farms and employ the local peasants as farm workers.

Unfortunately, for our "Uncle Stalin," the Ukraine, known as "the bread basket of Russia" used to be organised differently. For centuries, Russian Tsars granted parcels of land in the fertile steppes to their soldiers, released from service after some particular campaign was over. The plan had many advantages. It ensured that the area, previously peopled, not by Muscovites, but a different Slavonic ethnic group called Ukrainians remained loyal to the Tsar. In addition, the supplanted Russians were obliged to present units of cavalry during time of war or civil unrest. These fierce horsemen were known as the Cossacks.

Cossacks, by then well mixed with the indigenous Ukrainians, proved to be highly independent in spirit and refused to be "collectivised". When the Ukrainian peasants found their land confiscated under Stalin's orders, they simply refused to work on State farms.

Stalin's plan wasn't working. The collectives in the most fertile, and traditionally, most productive part of the Soviet Union were failing to deliver their wheat harvest. Something had to be done. Determined to crush the people's resistance, Stalin ordered more prominent families to be deported and resettled in Siberian regions. Of those that remained, only the ones that worked on the collective farms were to be fed. The result was the infamous Genocide of the Ukrainian people. Over five million died of starvation in a land famous for it's production of food. Hundreds of thousands were deported to far away northern regions. There, they had to build their own dwellings and eke out a miserable existence by working in the forests, felling trees.

Stalin had succeeded, but the Ukrainian people had paid dearly for their resistance. His cruelty wasn't forgotten. When the Second World War broke out, Ukrainian divisions allied themselves with the Germans, against Stalin. "We will even join the Devil himself to fight this Monster" they used to say.

The rate of mortality amongst the displaced Ukrainians was also high. After a few years not many survived. When the time came to deport us Poles, there was plenty of spare room left in the camps built by the Ukrainians. The Soviet secret police NKVD simply re-located the remaining, still living Ukrainians into a few camps, leaving the vast majority of the original settlements vacant and ready to receive the wave of Polish transports.

We later discovered that the previous inhabitants of our barracks didn't take all their belongings with them. Behind them they left us their legacy - BUGS.

As winter started coming to a close, all the horrible creatures started surfacing. We soon discovered that our bunk beds, mattresses and the very fabric of our accommodation were completely infiltrated by bed bugs. Unaccustomed to this lack of hygiene, we all found this invasion impossible to cope with. The creatures would attack us in our beds at night and suck the blood out of our anaemic and under nourished bodies. In the morning they could be seen trying to scurry away. Enormous, bright red and so pumped up with our blood, that they could hardly move. You could easily squash and kill a few, but you knew well that a whole regiment was waiting to replace them. We tried every trick we could think of to rid ourselves of the pestilence, but to no avail. When the temperature outside improved sufficiently, we would drag our bunk bed outside and pour boiling hot water over the creatures to kill them. Next morning we would find ourselves bitten all over again. The pests still remaining in the crevices of the cabin walls would climb onto the ceiling and dive down onto our sleeping bodies. As if this torment wasn't sufficient, we soon found our clothes and our scalps alive with lice. Again, all attempts of trying to kill them off, with our limited resources were doomed to failure. We simply had to accept that being infested and at the mercy of those creatures was simply part of our existence in this living Hell.

The month of May was the harbinger of spring in Archangel. By the latter part of that month Nature, abruptly awakened from its long slumber, immediately commenced its frantic activity. It was as though all the plants, trees, animals and insects knew that there was no time to waste. Abruptly the temperature rose causing all remaining snow and ice to melt. The result was mud everywhere making walking along the old paths just as difficult as it was before when they were covered with slippery ice. With the rising temperature, and to accelerate the thaw, came torrential rains. Even before the thaw was over, the grasses and forest clearings became suddenly covered with spring flowers. This was followed by the springing up of grass as well as leaves on the forest shrubs and bushes to add to the few existing leafy trees. Instead of the (until now) predominant colours of white and grey, the whole area became bright green, with patches of riotous reds, blues, and yellows.

On the heels of plant life followed insects. Soon the riverbanks, forests and meadows became alive with every kind of crawling flying and biting creature. As was the case with flora, the Arctic bugs seemed to have a genetically in-built imperative to feed, develop and reproduce as quickly as possible. Time was short. Unfortunately for us and to our cost, most of them found human flesh to be the easiest and most rewarding source of sustenance. The most vicious were mosquitoes. They normally concentrated along the banks of the lake and inside the forest. Northern mosquitoes should not be compared to the midges of moderate climate. They are much larger, bolder and more persistent. The prospective victim would find himself or herself attacked by several insects simultaneously. On landing the mosquito would proceed to extract the person's blood at an amazingly high rate. What remains after is a maddening itch that lasts for days, or until the next attack, after which things get even worse.

Seeing our discomfort, the Russian guards would only laugh and say;

"Don't worry. You'll get used to them."

Surprisingly, in the end, as our hosts predicted, we got used to being drained of our meagre blood supply at night by the bed bugs as well as being bitten by mosquitoes during the daytime.

Rapidly, spring turned to summer. The days became surprisingly warm, considering the Northern Latitude. Days started getting longer and longer until, in the middle of summer the sun never quite set and we experienced life in perpetual daylight. It was very strange and difficult to get used to. The sun would dip low on to the horizon and hover there for some hours, only to start climbing again eventually. We had to establish an artificial "night time" for ourselves, and go to bed pretending it was pitch black outside.

In spite of our miserable existence, the summer warmth lifted our spirits. Some young people, (not children like me, of course), took to swimming in our lake. One morning, a young man came running up to the camp with terrible news. A young woman was caught out by cramp some distance from the bank and, before others could come to her assistance; she had drowned.

69

When the name of the victim became known, a feeling of foreboding spread like wildfire throughout the settlement. The young woman was in fact the eldest daughter of Anna Wasek.

"A second Wasek child is dead," women were whispering. Could it be the result of Anna's foreswearing?

Imperceptibly, summer changed into autumn. Ripening berries now covered the forest shrubs, instead of the recent flowers. Many were known to us as edible fruit. Some of the others, we soon discovered by trial and error, could also be eaten. All children and youngsters below working age started making excursions into the nearby forest. In the first instance, the fruit supplemented our inadequate diet and became a vital source of vitamins. Having gorged ourselves, we would start filling our baskets to bring something home for our parents, still hard at work in the depths of the forest. Our mother, thinking ahead, instructed the elder of her children, Stasia and Romek, to go a little further away from the buildings and other people and bring home as much of the summer fruits as possible. It was in her mind to make as many fruit preserves as possible and store them for use in the wintertime when food supply was bound to be meagre.

One evening, Mother came back and as usual intended to prepare and stow away that day's fruit harvest. She saw Romek's basket full of berries. Of Stasia's container there was no sign.

"Where are your berries?" she asked, turning to her daughter.

Stasia replied, "I didn't bring any to day."

"Where is your basket then," Mother said.

At that Stasia, never very good at concealing the truth, went beetroot red and blurted out the whole story.

"I went alone deep into the forest," she began, "because most of the bushes nearby were all picked out. I was doing very well. My basket was almost full of blueberries, when suddenly I heard a sound of movement behind me. I was frightened. I thought it might have been a bear. I remembered people saying that a big brown bear was seen recently not far from the camp. As I watched, the bushes were pushed aside and a man appeared, I think it might have been one of the soldiers from the Commandant's barracks. He was going straight for me. As soon as I saw him coming, I panicked and started running. I didn't stop until I got home."

Mother listened to the story without interruption. When her daughter finished she simply asked,

"And what happened to the basket and the berries?"

Stasia stopped short, embarrassed again and admitted, "When I started running I must have dropped the basket. I didn't even realise it was missing until some time after I got back. I'm sorry."

Mother looked at her daughter for a long time, an expression of tiredness and exasperation on her face.

"Listen," she finally started. "You know how hard things are. If we don't make some provisions for the winter we will all die. You are my eldest child. You're almost fifteen. If I can't rely on you for help, I don't know what to do. Surely you knew how important it was to bring the fruit home?"

Feeling helpless and alone in her struggle she started weeping. After only a moment, however she regained her composure. Moments of weakness like that were very rare for my mother.

"Right," she said. "Tomorrow you will go back berry picking. Don't come back until your basket is brim full."

Stasia wasn't known for responding positively to Mother's orders. On this occasion however, she took Mother's strictures to heart. She immediately applied herself to building up the stocks of berries, making sure that each one of us also contributed. As a result, by the time first frosts arrived, Mother had stored up one sizeable wooden barrel of blueberries and another of other mixed berries - a substantial supply with which to face the oncoming winter.

Mushrooms were another traditional forest crop. We all did what we could to pick them. This northern forest however, wasn't ideal for them. We found few traditional types inside the forest itself. Typically a clearing would have been a better bet. There we sometimes found a profusion of white mushrooms, a type not known back home, but established to be edible. These would be dried or marinated (if you could get your hands on some vinegar), and stored away for the harder times to come.

People better placed than my mother, cleared parcels of land on the edge of the forest and having saved some potato peelings planted them with the hope of a crop of potatoes before winter came. Their success very much depended on the seed material used. Most failed completely, however some people succeeded to recover an impressive amount of potatoes in the dying days of the short Siberian autumn. Unfortunately, as I said, this exercise required a substantial input of labour. All of Mother's effort was directed towards achieving her allotted norm in her forest employment. She had no time or energy left to work on the clearing of fields or planting of crops. Needless to say, we were all to young to carry out such tasks in her place, and so we had to do without advantages available to others.

Before we knew it one day in early September, steely heavy clouds gathered above us and it started snowing. Once it started, snow continued to fall for several days and nights without respite. When we eventually surfaced we discovered the whole countryside covered by a thick blanket of snow. The nearby trees were also affected, with their branches bent to near breaking point under the weight of snow and ice.

Another winter had arrived.

The rhythm of life changed yet again, this time to a familiar cycle. After all, it was winter when we first got there almost a year ago.

Grown-ups continued to work in the forest felling trees and lopping off branches, while children carried on with their schooling. We no longer made excursions into the forest. There were no pickings left, except for dried boughs and twigs for the furnace. The children, ever resourceful, soon rediscovered skis, toboggans and skates that had been put away for safe keeping at the end of last winter.

Although I, by then fully recovered from scurvy, thanks to vitamin-full forest fruits, my general state of health continued to be fragile. In spite of the respite from starvation occasioned by fruits of the land, a lot of people's resistance started waning. Some would collapse in the middle of their work in the forest only to be carried back home by others; others succumbed to frostbite and found themselves developing gangrene. That winter we lost many people from our camp. Many more than in the previous year.

It was just a few days before Christmas when Anna's eldest son was caught by a falling tree. The poor soul didn't make it alive back to camp. Yet another funeral for the Wasek family.

Just before Christmas we, on the other hand, had a pleasant surprise. Another food parcel had arrived. This time from my Aunt Jania Wysocka, my father's sister. Needless to say, the contents helped us all cope with the daily starvation diet. It also helped us celebrate Christ's Coming with a spirit of renewed hope.

Before we knew it, spring of the year 1941 was upon us.

This time Mother was given a new job. Together with other women and older men she was assigned the task of mowing wild meadows and gathering hay. As suitable lands were located some distance away, Mother, together with the rest of the contingent set off, initially by boats across our lake, then continued on foot until they reached the banks of the Great Onega river. There, often waist deep in water, they hoed the tall and wild riverside grasslands. As could be expected, and as was in fact anticipated, the area was full of particularly nasty and aggressive mosquitoes. Without protective clothing, the work would have been impossible. Mother like the others, was issued with tall, waterproof boots, and an overall and jacket to suit. For her head she was given a hat with a large brim, to which a long screen of netting was attached all around. The group stayed on site throughout the week and slept in a makeshift camp. No money was paid to reward them. Instead they received something they regarded to be even better. It was good food. In addition to regular hot meals, they received better quality bread and dried goods.

Every Saturday night we would anxiously await our mother's arrival. To tend to her children she was allowed to knock off earlier each Saturday and set off back to our camp. She would be given a ride part of the way and walk the remaining few miles until she reached the bank of our lake. There alone she would board a small boat and row it right across to the landing at the foot of our camp. With her she would bring the supplies she was issued and share them out amongst us. In my memory all the food she brought was welcome and tasty. The one item that still stands out in my mind is a yellowy dried fish the Russians called "treska". To my hungry pallet this was a delicacy beyond description. I could never have enough of it. On occasion Mother didn't have the time to change into ordinary clothes and arrived in her working apparel. The gear was certainly impressive. With her tall boots and hat surrounded by long netting she looked like something out of this world. Sunday lunchtime Mother would board her little boat and set off on her long journey back to her work camp, only to repeat the exercise in a week's time. She was half starved herself during the whole period, but she kept us all alive.

Younger and more able-bodied men stayed behind. Their task was to transport all the logs cut down and trimmed in the previous months to the side of the lake, float them on the water and tie the logs into enormous rafts. When the work was completed a couple of tugs arrived to tow the timber to the other side. From there, by canal and river, the produce and result of Polish slave labour would be transported all the way to the port of Archangel and abroad. I wonder how much of it finished up in English furniture factories.

To man the rafts, only the fittest and most agile men were selected. Anna Wasek's husband, together with his eldest remaining son, was amongst the chosen few. It was some three weeks before the team returned, having discharged their cargo. Young Wasek was not amongst them. It seems that in the middle of the lake some logs got loose. The young man tried to repair the damage, fell between the masses of floating logs, disappeared under the raft and drowned. The others watched horrified. There was nothing they could do to help him.

The spring tasks over, the work teams were returned to the forest felling trees all over again.

During the latter part of that summer, strange rumours started circulating. Some said that The Soviet Union had fallen out with its ally The German Reich and that the Germans had already crossed Russian occupied Poland and were attacking Russia itself. Later there was even talk of Polish armies being formed again on the Russian soil. It all sounded to us like fairy tales and wishful thinking. Mother, however with her ever-practical approach to life, decided that we must rapidly gather what supplies we can in case we were to be released.

What actually happened on the European Continent, far away from our Siberian exile was that the Germans really did attack the Russians. Hitler, having failed to subdue Great Britain, found his armies more and more heavily engaged in Southern Europe and North Africa. With the British exercising effective control of the seas, he found himself relying more and more heavily on the oil the Russians doled out to him.

Before long, he snapped. "Why should we have to beg to get meagre supplies from these Slavonic savages, when their stores of oil

74

in the refineries of the South are overflowing?" he must have thought to himself. "Why, let's simply go out there and get it. While we're about it we can clear out the large expanses of fertile land for our farmers to occupy. They'll soon see what kind of output can be got out of that land with our German efficiency."

Without any warning, Hitler broke his pact with Stalin on the 22nd of June 1941 and attacked along the whole of the new Russian-German border. Russians, unprepared for this act of treachery, pulled back rapidly.

Stalin, under severe pressure quickly switched allegiances and joined Great Britain to form a United Front against the common German foe. By then Poles had firmly established themselves as part of the British Fighting Force. With Polish Forces clearly overwhelmed by the invading German Armies in 1939, Polish pilots grabbed old biplanes and anything else they could get their hands on and flew across to England to continue their fight against Hitler. Their contribution in the Battle of Britain is generally acknowledged. With the Polish armies crushed one by one, the Government moved down south and later moved to Rumania. As Army units were being broken up, some soldiers and many officers made their way South in their effort to evade the twin enemy of Germany and Russia. They crossed over to Hungary and Rumania and then, with varying success, tried to make their way across to France.

At the time the Second World War broke out, a major Polish statesman, General Wladyslaw Sikorski found himself in France. Due to political differences of opinion between himself and those in charge in Poland before the outbreak of the War, the General chose to leave his Homeland and settle in France. This proved to be a very fortunate turn of events for the battered Polish Nation. As the dispirited members of the Government and others started filtering through to the free world, Sikorski took charge. Soon foreseeing the collapse of France he moved "The Polish Government in Exile" to London. With him came the few Poles he had managed to gather around him on the other side of the Channel.

It was when Hitler's invasion of Russia commenced that General Sikorski, by then acclaimed as the new head of the Polish Government, saw his chance. Stalin, as a price of his joining of The Alliance, demanded military and material assistance to help him resist the onslaught. This was when Sikorski made his masterly move.

As a member of a British delegation he arranged a private meeting with Joseph Stalin. After brief formalities the Pole said:

"Marshal; I hear that you are making urgent demands for the British to come to your aid. You must understand that their human resources are limited and you may find yourself disappointed." Seeing that Stalin was showing signs of impatience he quickly continued,

"I think I have a solution to your problem the Allies might go along with." Having at last captured the Georgian's attention he asked,

"Who do you think hates the Germans the most?"

Seeing the puzzled expression on the other man's face he offered the answer, "Why, the Poles of course. Now, how many good Polish fighting men do you have languishing in your prison camps? I think you'll agree that these people, if properly trained and equipped, could make a much bigger contribution towards defeating the German foe than digging salt in the mines of Ural Mountains or felling trees in Siberia."

"Now this is your master stroke;" he continued, "You demand that the Allies take those people across the border to Persia or Iraq. There they are to feed them, clothe them and generally prepare them for war. Once the units are ready to fight you can demand that they be brought back to face your enemy. Now, this whole business won't cost you a penny and the Allies will be glad to get you off their backs. Remember; they are short of fighting men, not food or equipment."

Having set the trap he waited with bated breath. Stalin was a wily old dog, not easily fooled. He sat there for a while and turned the proposal over in his mind. "I can't see anything wrong in it," he thought. "Those Polish dogs would certainly fight the Germans more fiercely than anyone I know. As he says, I'll gain a crack Army, eager to fight my enemy, and it'll cost me nothing. If I don't do this, who knows when the English will come up with any effective help."

His cunning countenance lit up with a smile and he roared, "Sergeant, bring a bottle of good Polish vodka immediately. My friend General Sikorski and I have an agreement to seal." The general heaved a mental sigh of relief. All he had to endure now was a binge of vodka drinking with this monster. Not to worry. He had a strong head for alcohol. The charade of friendly drinking with Stalin wasn't something he looked forward to. Still, the sacrifice was worth making.

So it was that on 12th of August 1941, the Soviet authorities issued a decree announcing an amnesty for all Poles currently on Soviet soil. The official news didn't reach our camp until the end of that month. On the last day of August the camp Commandant gathered all the adult population and read the Decree out loud. All assembled listened to the announcement in stunned silence. "So its all true" they thought. "God works in mysterious ways…"

After he finished reading, the Commandant looked up and waited for a response from the gathering. When after some time none came, he started,

"As of to-day you are all free people. Papers to that effect will be issued to each family in the next few days. This means that you'll be able to go wherever and whenever you please, without asking anyone's permission. If any official tackles you, all you need to do is to show him the document and he'll leave you alone." Having regained the people's interest he went on, "As I said; you are free to go, but where will you go. There is no point in trying to make your way back to Poland. As you well know, the Germans now occupy your Country. On top of it all, we have no facilities to transport you away from here."

He let it all sink in and then continued, "Think about it. I've treated you fairly and as well as I could. Why not stay here and earn your living as free men. In future your pay will be doubled, the camp store will be supplied with good cigarettes and other quality goods. You could build yourselves houses to your liking in the clearings around and your children would continue to benefit from our school. If you still insist on leaving, let me know of your destination so that I can make arrangements for your journey. You must remember, however what I said earlier. Transport is not easy to organise. You may have to wait for some time before arrangements can be made."

He let the notion hang in the air and finally added, "Think about it. Meantime, as from now on, new conditions will apply. Thank you."

The gathering dispersed quietly. It was all too much to absorb. The notion of staying on in this hellhole was out of the question. Little groups started forming to discuss the situation. "Where to go?" they would say. "The Commandant is right that return home is out of the

77

question, but where else can we go?" Various suggestions were floated. One woman said, "Yugoslavia is an attractive place. I once knew a girl from Sarajevo. I think I'll ask to be sent there." A man, clearly with a background in classical education, followed, "For me it's got to be Greece. The climate is beautifully warm, and what about the culture! If I can't go home, that's the place I'd like to end my life in."

After some days of animated discussion, groups would go over to the Commandant's office and register their chosen destination.

Time went by. Things went back to normal. True, the food improved, the pay was better and the store had large supplies of good cigarettes and other useful items for sale. As the weeks passed, the occupants of the camp started to get impatient. The Commandant's staffs were fobbing off all enquiries about travel arrangements. We were beginning to despair. "Was this newly won freedom to be only a mirage? How are we to get out of this pit of death?"

The name of "Pit of Death" was no exaggeration. Ever since the last winter, the lethal effects of malnutrition, cold, exhaustion and poor hygiene were becoming more and more apparent. At first it started with chills, followed by persistent coughs. Later more and more people seemed to develop diarrhoea. With time the awful realisation started to dawn on the camp occupants that they were witnessing major illnesses within the settlement such as Tuberculosis, Dysentery, Night Blindness and others. With no medicines or let up in the regime, the infections continued to spread. Before the arrival of summer, the first death occurred from T.B. This was soon to be followed by other fatalities from infections of the lungs as well as Dysentery and other illnesses. By the time the Amnesty was announced, a third of our number had perished.

People were getting very nervous. In spite of the improved conditions, the death toll was accelerating. The small patch of open ground at the back of the camp initially used to bury the first few casualties had quickly grown to a large expanse filled with wooden crosses. If something were not done soon, none of us would survive.

As everyone knows, 'necessity is the mother of invention'. Out of desperation a scheme emerged. A small group of men, on some pretext or other, made a journey to the town of Wologda. There they discovered a Consulate of the newly formed Polish Government in Exile, set up to process and take care of Polish ex-prisoners. They told the Consul their story and asked for his advice.

The elderly gentleman, a Polish Officer from the First World War, thought for a while and told them';

"I think official representations will get you nowhere. Your problem is how to get from your camp to Wologda. Once you're here they can't touch you. What I'll suggest may surprise you, but remember that I've had a lot of experience in dealing with our freshly baked allies. Get as many good quality cigarettes as you can and make a deal with the Station Master. I suggest four hundred should do it. Give him half to start and the other half when he gets you here. Be sure not to part with the final payment until you arrive in Wologda. Remember. Those people can't be trusted."

The delegation saw the man in question and after some protracted haggling struck a deal. They promised to send one of their number back with two hundred and fifty cigarettes within a week of their return home. The Station Master would then make the necessary arrangements to divert an empty train down our siding.

The emissary went off as arranged and on return told his group;

"The Station Master promised me to send the train over in the next few days. He couldn't be specific. It'll all depend on the circumstances. I think we should tell all who want to leave to get their belongings together, get themselves over to the rail terminal and wait."

A couple of days later the trek to the railhead began. Amongst the travellers was Anna Wasek. It didn't escape other women's notice that just before departure her only remaining daughter had died of tuberculosis. She still remained the subject of much gossip.

The whole camp, without exception, gathered at the Rail Terminal. There was no sign of any trains. By then, in the month of October 1941, the Siberian winter began to establish itself in its full splendour and severity. To protect ourselves from frost, numerous bonfires were set up all round. As their warmth represented a matter of life or death by freezing, the campers organised regulars forays into the forest to keep adequate supplies of wood and ensure that none of the fires were ever allowed to go out.

Days were passing and still there was no sign of transportation. One day the Camp Commandant came to visit the bivouackers. "What are you doing?" he said to groups huddled round campfires. "I told you before. There are no trains to be had. Come back to your warm barracks where hot soup is waiting for you. Mark my words. If you don't return soon you'll all perish here." Seeing that his words were having no effect, he turned around and made his way back to his quarters.

On the fifth day of waiting, when some were beginning to voice their suspicions of betrayal, a train appeared on the horizon. The Station Master of Wologda had kept his promise. The train comprised one locomotive and six converted goods wagons. By now, we realised that our mode of transport from Poland wasn't particularly noteworthy; all passenger transportation in the Soviet Union was by then arranged in that fashion.

. Quickly, we clambered in, closed the huge sliding doors against the frost, and waited. The train started moving. At long last we were leaving this God forsaken place. Almost unanimously, a song left the breast of each of the travellers. It was the ancient hymn known to all Poles, that speaks of deliverance and offers heartfelt thanks to the merciful God.

Yet another journey had begun.

Chapter 7

The train started and we were on our way. It continued to accelerate, and having gathered full speed, kept racing on as though chased by some terrifying Furies. It continued on at this break-neck pace without a single stop until we reached the station of Wologda.

In fact, the notion of being pursued wasn't so far fetched. On reaching the station we were told that the train was indeed being pursued. It seems that our Commandant had over-played his hand. He saw no prospect of a train arriving at our Rail Terminal in the foreseeable future. He had gambled on the notion that, when enough time had passed, the conditions on the Terminal would start to get worse, perhaps through lack of food, lack of fuel or even through the spread of disease. In the end the spirit of the travellers would be broken. However reluctantly, they'd decide that the prospect of freedom was just an illusion. Eventually they'd conclude that life in the camp Szamp Oziero was all life had to offer. The risk was worth it. If things went his way, the Commandant would finish up with a resigned and compliant workforce. The last thing he expected however was to be outwitted.

When news reached the Commandant that a train had indeed arrived at the terminal, and all his Polish captives were already on board, he panicked. Where would he be if all his workers disappeared? The Head Office would soon establish that camp Szamp Oziero showed considerable expenses and no income. The conclusion would be obvious. The camp would be closed down and the Guards, including himself, be re-assigned to more useful duties, like the Front Line against the Germans in the West, for instance.

Having decided, he quickly shouted out his orders. "Get half a dozen sleighs ready immediately and harness up the fastest horses without delay," he said. "We're going after them!"

The pursuit started in earnest. Unfortunately for our Commandant, his movements could be observed over many miles in this flat country. The train driver, having gone out on a limb already, didn't fancy getting caught and having to explain himself to the local dignitary. His reaction was immediate. The moment he spotted the contingent in full flight, he started stoking up the engine fires and didn't let up until the train was blasting at full speed, and the pursuers left behind.

On arrival in the town we made our way to the Polish Consulate. There, we were told that we needn't be afraid of our Camp Commandant's pursuit. We were safe. The Polish officials, assisted by Soviet Authorities, issued us all with the necessary travel permits, fed us and organised rail transport. We were told to make our way South towards Kazakhstan. "The new Polish army is being formed down there," the Consul told us. "Aim for the town of Taszkent. The men will be able to join up. The families will also be taken care of. Later, with God's help, you will all leave the Soviet Union and will then be in the care of the Allies."

Yet again we set off on a train journey.

Strangely enough, our journey as free men and women was far more arduous even than the trip in prison trains out to Siberia. We all brought with us what food supplies we could manage to save up. Nothing could prepare us, however for what was ahead and the length of time it was to take for us to reach our destination. In addition, we were all lousy, dirty, under-nourished and many of us, disease-ridden.

The train, just like all the previous ones and, it seemed, all the trains in the Soviet Union at that time, comprised twenty converted goods wagons. Each coach was fitted out in the standard way, with three levels of sleeping accommodation, a stove in the middle and a large sliding door.

At the start at least, we had enough fuel in our wagon to keep the stove going red-hot. I well remember one of our fellow passengers performing a strange ritual every morning. On waking he would walk over to the stove, take off his shirt and shake it over the stove. This resulted in the appearance of a cloud of sparks all around the stove. It took me some time to realise that the sparks represented individual lice being burned. It was in fact his feeble attempt at delousing. Needless to say, his shirt was amply replenished during the course of the next day, with the resulting pyrotechnics the following morning, no less impressive than the previous ones.

As I said earlier, a lot of people died of numerous diseases in our camp. Many also managed to board the train bringing their infections with them. Many died during the subsequent journey from various illnesses, the cold, starvation and pure exhaustion.

My family was lucky. Apart from my earlier complaint of scurvy, we all escaped the various deadly infections raging all around. On boarding the train we were all in good health. I seemed to have caught a chill and was running a slight temperature, but that was nothing compared to the condition of some of the others. At first everybody was good humoured and full of hope. We were all enjoying the journey and the promises it was leading us to.

Time went by. Our rate of progress seemed incredibly slow. At times the train would race on for days without stop. On other occasions the driver would stop in the middle of nowhere and stand for a period impossible to predict. Sometimes this amounted to five or ten minutes, other times it could be hours or even days. Many times, under instructions to which we weren't privy, he would backtrack for hundreds of miles, and then take a new route.

The meagre food reserves were fast running out and we were all getting frightened and desperate. The small piece of bread rationed out to each of us at irregular intervals was certainly not enough to keep body and soul together. We took all means possible to gain some more food. It was literally a matter of life or death. When the train stopped at stations or elsewhere where groups of people or signs of habitation were spotted, all the passengers made their various pitches to win sustenance. Some would bring out some of their belongings to trade, others would produce money they still had on them and yet others, not having anything to barter away, would beg or even steal.

While all this activity was taking place, out of necessity, parents would leave their compartments and wander off and away from the train. As I said earlier however, whenever our train driver decided to continue his journey, he never considered it necessary to warn his passengers of imminent departure. The result was that many people got left behind, with the rest of the family on board, not knowing when and if they'd ever see their loved ones again. Sometimes the mother or father would re-appear on board some days later on other occasions the family member in question would not be seen again for a very long time and often, never again.

What happened to the helpless children, while their parents, in search of food, went missing is another matter. As I said earlier, everyone was on the point of literal starvation. In those circumstances, unfortunately, all morality is abandoned. The only imperative is for the individuals, and their offspring to survive. In general it meant that abandoned children were doomed. Not only would they not receive any help from their fellow passengers, but what little supplies they might still have about them would be stolen or simply torn out of their feeble hands. I, together with my siblings, had seen sufficient examples of this to be fully aware what awaited us all, should Mother no longer be there to take care of us. It was on one of those typical stops that Mother, our stocks of food almost completely depleted, decided to take a chance. The train stopped alongside a small settlement. A modest amount of trading in farm produce was in evidence in the little market. Mother took Father's winter jacket, one of the very few of Fathers items still remaining and stepped off the train. We could all clearly see her approaching the market, carrying the jacket on her arm. After a short while, mother's endeavour was obviously crowned with success. There she was departing, with a substantial sack of produce on her back.

"Look," my elder sister called out. "Mother bought some food for us. We'll be all right now."

Excited, we all gathered near the massive sliding door, waiting to greet her as she boarded the wagon. As we watched, to our horror, our train started moving gently forward. Slowly, very slowly it started to pick up speed. Mother, not far by then from her destination, saw what was happening and started to run. The picture that I saw then, and that has stayed with me forever, imprinted on my mind was that of Mother running for all her might, the train going faster and faster, and finally, Mother's silhouette disappearing past the horizon limited by the size of the opened wagon door.

"Mother didn't make it! We are lost!" cried out Stasia, always there with helpful information when you needed it. At that, gripped with despair and terror, we all started wailing inconsolably. Unfortunately, it was only too easy for us to believe that she was indeed right and that we were all now doomed.

As though to spite us, the driver decided to make up for lost time. The train blasted on at break neck speed for the next three days and nights without a single stop. Our travelling neighbours slowly moved away from us as though we all suffered with leprosy or some other vile and contagious disease. We were indeed doomed.

In the end the train came to a stop. And, miracle of miracles; as the door opened, we saw our mother standing in front of us, the bag still hanging over her shoulder. Once we satisfied ourselves that the figure in front of us was real and not an apparition, we all rushed forward to hug her. When the excitement finally died down, Mother told us her version of events.

"As you know, I went out, determined to get us something to eat," she said. "The little bit of berries left wasn't going to last us for long. Before long I found a man who was selling potatoes. He couldn't conceal his interest in the jacket I brought along to barter with. Before long we struck a deal. He kept the jacket and I walked away with a whole sack-full of potatoes. It was a good deal. I was delighted. As I started on my way back to the wagon however, I saw the train start to move. Terrified, I started to run. The train was going faster and faster. I wasn't going to make it. As I ran on I thought, "I've got to do all I can to get onto that train, however no way am I dropping those potatoes. If I reach my kids without any food to give them, they and I will all die of starvation anyway. It would be better for them if I were to be left behind. Maybe some merciful soul would take pity on my children and help them to survive."

She took a long and deep breath and continued.

"As I said; determined not to part with my load, I kept running after the train, and losing the race as the locomotive gathered speed. Just as I thought all was lost, however, the guard in the caboose at the end carriage grabbed be and pulled me on. Mind you," she added smiling, "as you can see, I never dropped the sack of potatoes."

Once Mother settled in, she started taking stock of our belongings. Eventually she worked her way to the two wooden tubs in which she brought her supplies of berries. She knew that one was already empty, but the other still contained a substantial amount of blueberry preserve. She peered inside and to her horror saw that the container was completely empty. Of the preserve there was no sign. "Maybe the children ate it all up when I wasn't there," she thought. Turning to Stasia she enquired, "Have you and the others been eating the berries while I was away?" At that my sister went beetroot red and after a long pause responded. "No Mother. None of us has touched it. We were all too worried and upset to even think of food." Then a look of puzzlement and concern appeared on her transparent face and she enquired. "Why do you ask? Is there something wrong?" Mother, by now quite angry pointed at the tub and said, "Look for yourself. When I left, the thing was a quarter full. Now it's completely empty. How do you think this happened? Tell me honestly; did you keep a eye on our things or not?" Stasia, by now realising she was being accused of neglecting her younger sister and brothers felt hurt. "As I told you before, we were all beside ourselves with worry, thinking we may never see you again. I would have thought you'd show that you were pleased to see us all instead of straight away telling us off again." She moved away into a corner and started weeping silently.

Mother feeling rather awkward, wanted to do something to patch things up but didn't know how. In the end she got on with preparing for us a meal of baked potatoes, hoping that the matter will simply blow over.

I don't know when potatoes tasted better. We all enjoyed the "lavish" meal and having relaxed, soon all fell fast asleep.

New supplies of food proved harder and harder to come by. I'm sure that without Mother's hard-won potatoes none of us would have survived the journey.

We travelled south for many weeks. After some time we realised we were not the only Polish travellers. As time went on we came across more and more trains loaded to the brim with resettled Polish families, desperately trying to make their way South and hopefully out of the "Soviet Heaven".

Here and there people would succumb to one or another disease. A lot of infections were obviously brought along by some of the passengers, and in this close proximity the danger of epidemic was ever present. It was therefore a regular occurrence for the train to stop on occasion in order that a person identified as being struck by an infectious disease was removed from the train. It didn't surprise us therefore when, after a long run, the train stopped, and a group of officials from the station approached the carriage in front of us. It was only when we all heard the commotion that people stepped out to find out what was going on. With our door opened we could all hear and see a woman, being physically restrained, desperately calling, "My boys! What'll become of my boys!" The woman was duly taken away and the train resumed its journey. It was soon after that I recall a conversation between two women sitting next to us.

"You know who that was, don't you" said the woman to her neighbour. "No I don't." she answered. "She created quite a commotion. I wondered what it was all about." The other responded, "Why; I'm surprised you didn't recognise her! That was Anna Wasek. You remember her and her famous foreswearing, don't you? Well, as you know, she lost all her children with the exception of the two boys, and they were in a bad way even when we boarded the train. It seems her husband was left behind about a week ago, and hasn't been seen since. She was left alone with her sick children, and then, herself fell victim to typhus. She was screaming in panic, not for herself, but because she was terrified she might loose the only two remaining children left out of her large family." The other nodded and said. "Yes. I remember. It's the Curse she herself brought about. God moves in mysterious ways." At that they both became silent; deeply lost in thought.

We continued our journey. It was over a week later that our train stopped again to discharge a cargo. This time two small bodies were removed from the carriage in front of us. They were the bodies of the two Wasek boys. Nobody said anything, but most exchanged knowing looks. Anna was surely punished for her false oath. The thing she most feared had come to pass.

In hindsight it's difficult to make a judgement on the episode. It was an undisputed fact that Anna Wasek had falsely sworn an oath on the lives of her children. It was equally a fact that, against odds, she lost them all. Her compatriots, with their simple faith had no doubts. "God had punished Anna by taking her at her word" they would say. I can't help wondering about that, however. Was it one of those self-fulfilling prophecies? Would all the children have died if some of Anna's friends had made more of an effort to help them?

Weeks were passing and we still continued our journey. As I said, my own health wasn't good even before we set off. With the constant opening and closing of the massive wagon doors, the temperature in the place fluctuated from hot to freezing cold. This situation was not conducive to my recovery from the chill. In fact, my condition worsened and I developed very high temperatures associated with Influenza. Mother, as always, did all she could. No medicine was to be had on the train or even at any of the stops. All she could do was to try to keep me wrapped up as best she could, and keep trying to get me to swallow liquids. As time went by, and we continued to travel south, the climate started to become a little milder. The moderate temperature was a little late in coming for me, however. My illness was by now progressing on it's own cycle. I had, by then developed full-blown Pneumonia. I was almost completely unable to accept food. My body, and particularly my scalp, was covered with open wounds and scabs that refused to go away. By he time we arrived at the main junction in the town of Kujbyszew, I was in a bad way. The fact that the air was warm and summery no longer helped. In Kujbyszew, we were transferred to another train and sent onto the main collection centre on Taszkent in Kazakhstan. On arrival we discovered that we were not alone and certainly not the first. The platforms and the surrounding fields were filled with Polish escapees from the Russian work camps. Representatives of the Polish Authorities milled around, doing what they could to provide some food and basic shelter. New trains full of Polish refugees were arriving every hour, making matters even worse.

Next morning an announcement came on the station loud speakers.

"This concerns Polish people awaiting resettlement," the voice announced.

"An empty train is pulling in on platform three. The destination is the railway station of Arysa. The Soviet Authorities have assured us that workers are required in the Communal Farms in that area. Any boarding the train can expect to be allocated accommodation, a food ration and, of course a job. If you are interested, please move onto the platform and board the train as soon as it arrives. Thank you."

Mother didn't hesitate. She immediately picked me up, (by then I was not capable of walking under my own steam), organised the rest of the kids to carry what remained of our belongings and made her way across to the platform in question. By the time we got there, the place was already crowded. Before long, however the train pulled up and pushing and elbowing with the best of them, we managed to scramble on board.

The train pulled out of the station without delay and rapidly developed high speed. As we looked out through the open door, to our dismay we soon realised that we were retracing our steps. We were literally going back where we came from. Some passengers started panicking.

"Is this some fiendish plot?" they enquired, "Are we all going to finish up in Siberia, where we came from?"

Unease and suspicion quickly spread throughout the train along with the other virulent infections.

We travelled for the rest of that day and the whole of the following night.

As the sun rose, we were able to observe the countryside. The land was very different to the Siberian forests we had left behind. It was also nothing like Poland that we had parted from (it seemed) ages ago. The land seemed parched. We could see settlements, surrounded by expanses of cultivated land. In between, the countryside looked like a sandy desert, occasionally adorned by clumps of greenery. Vegetation and trees also looked strangely different. Grass, when there at all, seemed dark and often faded by the scorching sun. Of the trees, tall palms seemed to predominate. Before long the train started slowing down. It appeared we were about to reach our destination. Maybe we weren't being repatriated back to the Northern Forests after all.

Slowly, the train pulled into the station clearly sign-posted Arysa, and stopped. Soon the driver and his assistants started walking down the train, pulling open all doors and shouting for us to disembark.

Before long the train, having discharged its cargo, departed leaving us all standing there, wondering what would happen next. As we stood there, we saw, on the horizon, a dust cloud forming. The shape seemed to travel in our direction and also appeared to be growing rapidly. As we watched, a long row of vehicles appeared, moving quickly ahead of the billowing dirt. In no time at all, the convoy had arrived and came to a halt in front of us.

Puzzled, we went over to inspect the strange apparitions. In front stood a long row of strange and identical vehicles. Each looked like a cart supported by two large wheels, and fitted out with very tall-racked sides. In front harnessed, was a draught animal most of us had never seen before. "What kind of devilish creatures are they?" some people muttered. The animals certainly had a curious appearance and seemed hostile and dangerous.

Someone called out, "Camels. These people are using camels to pull their carts."

Pacified somewhat, but still uneasy, we could only marvel at what we saw.

In short order, we were all loaded onto the carts and the vehicles moved off. We travelled, at a surprisingly high speed, for most of the day. In the late afternoon we reached a large settlement and the animals came to a halt. Around us we saw numerous small mud huts with large round and un-glazed holes for windows. We could see no straw overhanging the tops of side walls, and presumed therefore that roofs were not thatched. It was only later that we discovered that the roofs were in fact flat. In this hot climate and with no snow and very little rain, the protection of sloping roofs was not needed.

My Mother, still carrying me on her back, was directed to one of the nearby structures. We first entered a dark corridor and then as a door on the right hand side was opened, we entered. The room was quite substantial in size, but before we had a chance to spread out our belongings another family was ushered in to join us. So it seemed, at last we are settled for the time being. "At least we won't freeze to death here." Mother said, thinking out loud.

Six and a half weeks had elapsed from the time we had left the Siberian camp of Szamp Oziero. We soon discovered that, as one of the first transports, we were luckier that some. After the announcement of the amnesty, a trickle of Polish travellers started appearing on the road South. This steadily grew until the flood became so large that it strained the resources of the Russian transport system. People poured down from the northern forests, Ural salt mines, towns and State farms. They travelled however they could. The preferred mode of transport was of course the train, however when this form of transport wasn't available they set off by riverboat, by horse and cart and even on foot. Everybody aimed in the direction of Taszkent. The authorities tried to cope with the influx as best they could but the system eventually became hopelessly overloaded and transports into that town had to be halted. The new arrivals were re-routed to Alma Ata, Frunze, Buhara, Aschabad and many other towns and locations in Kazakhstan, Kirgistan and Turkestan. Some people travelled over three months before reaching their destination. Starting points and routes were as varied as were the final destinations. Journeys also differed greatly. Some, like us, managed to make it without stopping, and survived by selling off our warm clothing, supplemented by some begging. Others, having run out of resources, stopped off in towns and farms and took up employment for long enough to build up stocks of food. Many months later small numbers of Polish people still continued to arrive at the Polish Consulate in Taszkent and other locations in the area.

We introduced ourselves to the people we were to share the room with and proceeded to unpack and arrange our belongings to form a habitable space. The head of the group that joined us was a youngish woman by the name of Jadwiga Sliwinska. With her, was her old mother, her son Janusz and, (and this may now seem surprising), a young girl who used to be a servant in the Sliwinski household at the time of deportation. This odd situation can be best explained by trying to appreciate the kind of relationship Polish families often developed with their servants. Often a young girl or boy would be taken into service because the youngster either couldn't be maintained by his or her parents, or, through some misfortune, found him or herself orphaned. In such cases the family concerned would take responsibility for the child and the young person would in turn grow up to think of them as his own family. Such was the case with Sliwinski's young servant girl named Kasia. In fact to the best of her knowledge, both her parents were dead, and she was all alone in this world, except, of course for the Sliwinskis. Janusz Sliwinski was eight years old. He was, everyone agreed, rather tall for his age, and handsome. Needless to say, he was the apple of his mother's eye.

We were all soon introduced to the way of life and normal practices in a State Farm settlement in the Soviet region of Kazakhstan. A standard ration of wheat grain was to be issued weekly, a measure per member of the household. In return, all able-bodied adults were to report daily for work in the fields.

Like the locals, we were issued with hand mills. With these we had to grind the grain into flour, and then make our own bread, if we were to eat. Mother didn't find the process particularly strange and soon got things going. After all, there were times back home when she had to carry out similar labours before freshly baked bread appeared on the table!

My pneumonia was at last subsiding. Mother at long last allowed herself the hope that her youngest child may live after all. As the fever left me, I started to regain some strength. The illness however left some serious side effects. The worst of these were two boils on my eyelids. Soon after we got settled, it was time to celebrate Christmas. Mother did what she could with her meagre resources. She turned the wooden bathtub she dragged with her all the way from Poland, upside down thus forming a kind of tabletop. On it she arranged her food dishes with which she tried to follow the tradition of the Polish Christmas Eve supper, as best she could. On a hotplate she baked some thin unleavened bread, which was to serve as the wafer that is normally shared by all the participants. She managed to barter some beetroots from the local farmers to make beetroot soup, or "barszcz". To complete the feast she made some "pierogi" by cooking some pasta-type pastry stuffed with goat's cheese. She even managed to lay her hands on a couple of small portions of local river fish - a must at the Christmas Eve Supper table.

The table was laid and, after all had gathered, Mother went over and picked me up from the corner where I spent my time. When I stood up, everybody gasped with shock.

"My God! Gienek! You look terrible!" shouted Stasia.

Although they all knew I wasn't well, only Mother was fully aware of the seriousness of my condition. As I stood there, I looked like a skeleton, with nothing but skin hanging loosely from my frame. All my flesh had wasted away. My close-cropped scalp was covered with scabs. My left breastbone seemed to have collapsed making the right one seem to protrude unnaturally. On both my eyelids sat large dark boils, forcing the eyelids into a permanently shut position. I must admit that the above description comes from my siblings and my mother. My own emotions at the time were quite different. I was heartily sick of my earlier semiconscious state and lately bored with just lying around and not being able to do anything. At that moment my main emotion was that of excitement. I couldn't see a thing, of course, but as I heard the description of what was in front, it all came to life in my mind's eye. But I wasn't shocked or upset. In fact I was overjoyed to be sitting down with my family, and delighted to be out of bed if only for a short while.

Early in the New Year, three men were moved into our hut to live in the room on the other side of the passageway. Up until then the place had been standing empty. In those strange times, odd happenings were the norm. In spite of that, however, like the episode with Anna Wasek and her children, what happened with our new neighbours qualifies as extraordinary.

After the newcomers moved in and settled, one of them knocked on our door. Mother answered and saw all three standing there expectantly. The one closest stepped forward and said, "I trust you won't consider it an impertinence. As we appear to be neighbours, we thought it proper to introduce ourselves and make your acquaintance." Seeing no negative response, he then followed, "My name is Mojsze Lewy, my companions are called Itzak Golden and Abram Szmidt. You may be surprised to see grown and able-bodied men joining you here instead of joining the Polish Army. Let me explain," he continued. "I'm sure it didn't escape your notice that we are all Jews. As you may or may not know, not all born Jews take their religion seriously. Unfortunately for us on this occasion, we three have always adhered strictly to The Law. Our teaching tells us that taking up arms against a fellow human being is wrong under any circumstances. When we reached Taszkent, we were directed to the Polish Consulate there. The Assistant immediately started explaining to us how to reach the local Polish Army unit.

"Once you join up," he said, "you'll be safe. The Russians won't be able to touch you."

"It was my unpleasant duty to explain to the helpful young man, that we can't join the Polish Army and to give him our reasons for refusing such a generous offer."

At this point he looked straight at my Mother, a look of deep despondency on his face. "The people in the Consulate had no alternative but to redirect us to the Russian Authorities, who in turn assigned us to your work unit."

Looking even sadder, he continued, "I know that the Polish Army is bound to leave the Soviet Union soon to fight at the side of the Western Allies. I'm also sure that most, if not all of the women and children will follow. That gives you some hope for the future, at least. I'm afraid for us there is nothing to look forward to anymore."

Mother, touched by this sad story, asked them all to come in. Politely, she introduced each one of them to all the inhabitants of our cabin. After a brief exchange of pleasantries, Jadwiga Sliwinska asked,

"Tell me, where do you come from? Clearly, you don't belong to one of the Siberian transports."

It was Abram's turn to provide the explanation. He took a deep breath and started. "All three of us used to live in Lwow. We were fully aware of the deportations of the Polish settlers in 1941. The Russians left us alone then and our lives continued more or less as normal under their occupation. We are all professional and educated people and the lives we led were comfortable and purposeful. I am a qualified dentist, Itzak here is a lawyer, and Mojsze practised as an accountant. Yes. Life was good and we felt reasonably secure. A couple of months ago, however, rumours started circulating to the effect that remaining intellectuals are to be rounded up and deported. It didn't occur to any one of us for a moment that this might include us. Soon after however, came the famous knock-on-the-door in the middle of the night. Before we knew it, we found ourselves on our way to Taszkent."

After some further conversation, our new neighbours withdrew to their chamber, presumably in order to settle in.

They were put to work in the fields alongside other Poles. Mother observed that, as days and weeks passed, the threesome became more and more morose and withdrawn.

One morning, Abram didn't present himself at the collecting point. The Khazak team leader asked his colleagues why their friend was missing. "He's dead. He died last night," matter-of-factly answered Mojsze. The Khazak immediately left the group where they were and marched over to our hut. In the cabin he found Abram's dead body laid out on his bed. "This is most unfortunate," he thought. "I must get the Commandant straight away."

When the chief of the camp arrived, he was immediately shown the body. The Commandant inspected the remains of Abram carefully. It was important to ascertain the cause of death. After all, the man might have been the victim of some deadly and possibly contagious disease. If that were the case, he had to be careful to prevent an epidemic. Cautiously he approached the body. The corpse showed no obvious indications of infection. The next question was; did he die of starvation. If so, awkward questions would be asked. The Commandant could certainly do without an NKVD investigating team descending upon him from Arysa. No. Thankfully, the body definitely didn't look emaciated. The last possibility he had left to consider was murder or suicide. He was certainly unaware of any possible motif for murder. As to suicide, "who can tell?" he thought. Still, those possibilities also had to be looked into. He inspected the body yet again, this time looking for any telltale signs of foul play. There were none. The Chief was baffled. There appeared to be no reason for the man's death. He pondered the problem for a while and eventually turned to the Work Unit Leader. "Bring both the dead man's companions over here at once." he ordered.

When the two men arrived the Commandant looked at the two glum faces.

"Maybe you can help me out here. I've looked your friend over carefully and can't determine the cause of his demise. So," he said turning to Mojsze, "tell me; what did your companion die of."

Mojsze turned his face to the Khazak; eyes showing a total lack of expression, and uttered only one word in reply.

"Despair."

The Chief could see he wasn't likely to get any sense out of these two. He simply waved them away and ordered the body to be removed for burial.

On his return to his office he entered the name of the deceased in his records. Against the cause of death he wrote, "natural causes".

Life returned to normal. Mojsze and Itzak continued to live in the chamber opposite our own. They carried on working in the fields, but their demeanour became even more sombre and they were now completely silent. After work they stayed inside their room, presumably preferring their own company to that of others. Some four or five days thus passed off without a further incident, and everybody was ready to put this curious event behind them.

One evening soon after, however- late - we were all woken by loud hammering on our door. Full of trepidation, Mother approached the passage and called out:

"Who is this, and why are you making such a racket in the middle of the night, waking everybody up."

In reply she heard our neighbour Itzak's trembling voice:

"Mrs Krajewska; please let me in. I swear to you; this is a matter of life and death. Please let me in!"

Mother hesitated. She wasn't happy about allowing into their room a man clearly in a state of agitation. "Should he get out of control or if anything happened, the safety of all of us would be in danger" she thought. "The room is full of defenceless women and children."

She called out to the man: "I'm sorry. I can't allow you to come in. Go back to bed and come and see us in the morning." She thought for a moment and then added, "Where is your friend Mojsze? Why isn't he here with you now?"

Itzak, sounding more desperate than ever replied: "Mrs. Krajewska; Mojsze is dead. Please let me in. I won't come anywhere near any of you. I'll just sit there by the door; you'll see. Let me in please. I'll explain everything."

Still uneasy and full of misgivings, Mother opened the door. Itzak, white as a sheet and shaking like a leaf entered and immediately crouched down on the ground by the door. It took him some time to calm down sufficiently to explain his behaviour. Eventually he steadied a little and began.

"I know that my behaviour seems strange to you, and I'm not surprised. Let me tell you the whole thing from the beginning. As you know, from the time the three of us got here, the future didn't look good to us. With each day that passed, we all got more and more depressed. The thought that we were to spend the rest of our natural life in this living nightmare, being more and more brutalised, was unbearable. Each evening we would sit and depress each other further by saying how hopeless and degrading our situation was. After a time, words were no longer needed. We just sat there. As we looked at each other our spirits sunk lower and lower. One night, over a week ago, Abram sat there for a time and then simply leaned over and fell down on the ground. Even before we bent down to look at him we both knew he was dead."

"After our friend had gone, we tried to shake ourselves out of this morbid state. It worked for a day. Soon, however, depression set in again, as we sat there, looking at each other. Tonight, Mojsze keeled over, just like Abram. I knew he was dead without any need for closer inspection. An enormous fear gripped me. I was convinced that if I stayed there a moment longer, I'd be laying dead on the floor alongside my friend. I had to get out and join the living, or I would be doomed. That's how I came to knock on your door with such desperation."

Mother heard the story out with amazement. She wasn't the only one. With all the commotion, we were all soon wide awake in time to listen to Itzak's amazing tale.

Mother and Jadwiga Sliwinska had a quick conference after which Mother came over to where Itzak sat curled up next to the doorstep. In her hand she carried one of our blankets.

"Mr Golden," she began, "we were all deeply moved by your story. Of course you can stay the night here – you are welcome. Here, wrap yourself up in this blanket. The night air has been getting chilly lately."

She hesitated for a moment and added, "I will only give you one piece of advice. Don't go back to your room tomorrow morning. Go to the Commandant, report the death of your friend and demand to be moved to another place, with other people. Stay with the living. Don't spend time with the dead or ghosts."

The visitor listened intently, and when mother finished, simply nodded.

Soon after, mother blew out the lamp and everybody settled back to sleep.

Early next morning Mojsze Golden got up and left the room. He took Mother's advice and didn't succumb to the siren calls of his dead friends. We saw him from time to time. He seemed to settle down to the life in the "kolchoz" and even seemed cheerful. I know he was alive and well when we came to leave on the next phase of our journey.

We have often pondered on this strange episode over the years, and discussed its significance. It seems that, to destroy a human being it's not necessary to infect him with a deadly disease, starve him or even shoot him. For a person to be destroyed, it's often more deadly to take away his dignity and remove all hope of deliverance.

My health continued to improve, however, the two boils on my eyelids stubbornly refused to either fade away or burst. I continued to live in a world of complete darkness. Mother, inspecting the growths daily became increasingly worried.

"There's no sign of the puss coming to the top," she thought. "If the boils start growing inwards, they might burst onto his eyes, and my baby would be blinded for life."

The prospect of me being thus crippled absolutely terrified her. This was not the place or the time to become disabled. A child in such a condition would become an unbearable burden on the rest of the family, and was doomed in any case to suffer and in the end, die. The spectre of such an outcome haunted her day and night. Without medicine or professional advice, what could she do?

One day, working in the fields, helping in the planting of cotton, she was approached by one of her fellow workers.

The woman, a local, but quite friendly for all that, turned to mother and asked,

"What's the matter? I know that this isn't the sort of life you're used to, and that to you and your friends, this isn't exactly a bed of roses. In spite of all that, I have always admired you for the way you took matters head-on and somehow coped. I must say; I've never seen you so depressed before. Tell me. What's troubling you so badly? Maybe I can help."

Mother stopped her work, looked at her friend and said, "To tell you the truth, there is something to which I can't find an answer."

She then proceeded to tell the woman the whole story about my illness and about the boils on my eyelids.

"I don't know what to do," she concluded. "I'm terrified that, unless I can find a way to bring the boils out, the infection might go in the other way and my son will be blind for ever."

Mother's friend listened to the story intently. When mother finished she sat there for quite a while, absorbed by my mother's dilemma.

"I well understand what you must be going through," she finally responded. "I had a daughter, about the age of your boy, whom I buried just over a year ago. Without any medicine available, it's difficult to know what to do for the best."

She sat there a little longer, pondering the problem, and finally spoke.

"There's not much anyone of us can do. Our destiny is in the hands of The Almighty. I have only one suggestion, and that may not prove to be the solution either. I don't know if you've noticed, but at the far end of our settlement lives an old woman called Anuszka. She has some knowledge of herbs and, on occasion, helps people get over minor ailments. My advice would be to see her and ask her to help you."

Mother, feeling a little better for sharing her burden with a sympathetic friend, thanked her and determined to follow her advice at the earliest opportunity.

That same evening mother approached the little hut on the edge of the settlement. The hut was set a little apart from the rest, as though the villagers were uneasy about the occupant and preferred to maintain a little distance.

She knocked on the door and entered. Inside she saw a little old woman crouched over a large cooking pot. As mother entered, the woman straightened up and looked up at her expectantly. Even standing straight, the occupant of the mud-hut was very small. She wore a black skirt reaching down to the floor, and a black blouse with large white polka dots. Her dark and deeply lined face was heavily hooded by a rather attractive black headscarf with a pattern of distinctive large red flowers. Despite appearances, mother thought that the woman's eyes indicated an expression of welcome.

Quickly she explained her concerns as well as the reason for her visit. Old Anuszka listened to all the details of my condition, asking

99

questions about my previous illnesses. Having extracted all that was relevant to her from mother, she considered the matter for a while.

"It seems your boy is suffering from the after-effects of pneumonia. He should be in a hospital with proper care and medicines. Without professional help I can't give you any assurances that he'll get better. There is only one remedy I would recommend, and that carries with it no guarantee of success. Try making a poultice by boiling some onions, and mix them with stale bread and some spider's web. Apply the mixture to his lids twice a day, and watch to see if the boils start coming to surface. Remember," she said in parting, "No promises."

Mother returned home feeling very uncertain. What the old hag said didn't make much sense. She couldn't imagine it doing any good.

She decided against following the old woman's advice, hoping that I'd get better on my own. Days passed. Each morning she would inspect my eyelids closely, hoping for some sign of improvement. Unfortunately the boils continued to look inflamed, with a horrible dark blue-to-purple hue, and the colouring getting deeper. Things were looking more and more dangerous. "There's nothing for it," she decided. "I've nothing to lose. I'll just have to take a chance and follow the old hag's advice."

She got the ingredients together, made the mixture as instructed and, with trepidation, applied the poultices to both my eyes.

Days passed and mother saw no change. "At least things don't seem to be getting worse," she thought. After many days of regular treatment she finally saw a little yellow spot appear on top of one of the boils. At the same time the protrusion seemed less inflamed. Mother was delighted. She continued with the treatment conscientiously, delighted at the now obvious signs of progress. In the end the boils burst open, and having been cleaned up, began to heal. Under Mother's constant care the wounds healed so well that there isn't even any sign of a scar on either of my eyelids today.

So it was that even under those primitive conditions my Mother's determination paid off and my eyesight was saved - for which I shall always be profoundly grateful.

Life continued to be hard and the meagre diet combined with hard work kept all our existences on a knife-edge. Mother was particularly concerned about her two youngest offspring - that is the younger of my sisters, Zuzia and I. One day she heard that a Polish Outpost located some five miles away from our settlement had set up a home for Polish orphans and that the children there enjoyed a relatively high level of comfort as well as a regular and nourishing diet. She even heard that some mothers took their small children over there to be "built up". She decided that, come what may, she was going to get us there.

One Sunday morning (the only day in the week free from work) mother made up a small bundle of food for the journey, took both of us by the hand, and set off. After only a short distance she discovered what appeared to be an insurmountable problem. Neither of her children had the strength or the stamina to walk for any reasonable distance. With the food bundle to cope with, she could at best carry one child on her back. To take on the other as well was impossible. It might have worked if at least one of us could walk along unaided. Unfortunately, she soon discovered that this wasn't going to work. She considered her options carefully. No reasonable answer sprang to mind. In the end she settled on a solution not many would have considered. With the food bundle on her back she took me in her arms and walked on for a couple of hundred yards along the road, leaving anxious Zuzia sitting by the roadside. She then set me down, put the bundle on the ground alongside and returned to Zuzia, leaving me alone this time. With my sister on Mother's back they waked on past me for a further couple of hundred yards at which point Zuzia alighted and mother returned for me.

This process was repeated over and over for many hours until, finally, at dusk we reached our destination. Having installed us in the children's home, exhausted, but satisfied, Mother returned home alone.

After a period of emotional upset at being parted from Mother, we both settled-in well enough. The food was to our eyes plentiful, we were issued with new clothes, and we found there were many children of our own ages to play with. Life seemed pretty good to us. Without our noticing, our health quickly improved and we both started to put on weight.

Back in the settlement little had changed. Food in particular continued to be in short supply. The camp Commandant, a rather handsome man in his middle age, with a swarthy complexion and a long and impressive moustache, took a liking to my mother. Every week, as usual he would come to issue the wheat ration. As normal, he would measure out a scoop and tick off one of the occupants, "Konstancja, Stanislawa, Romuald," and then continue as though he noticed no change in our household, "Zuzanna and Eugeniusz." Nobody rushed to correct his "mistake" which he continued to make for many weeks after we'd gone. Mother thought the whole affair amusing but never allowed it to develop any further.

To supplement their diet, people took advantage of every opportunity that presented itself. After harvest mother would send out Stasia and Romek into the fields to gather left over wheat stalks like other children. On some occasions they would come home with a good-sized bundle each. On other occasions, however, they would be spotted by a Khazak farmer and pursued. It was a typical example of the madness of State Economy that, although the stalks were left to rot in the fields, hungry children were prevented from gathering them and taking them away. Typically, when they saw a Khazak in pursuit, Stasia would drop her burden and run, while Romek would follow her, but would return home still carrying his bundle.

I can recall particularly clearly one amusing episode that took place in our settlement. One of the local Khazaks living in the settlement owned a Billy goat. The goat poked it's nose everywhere, as goats do. People's clothes would disappear from clotheslines; the goat would carry off precious vegetables and generally make a nuisance of itself. Many a person looked at the animal wistfully. Most hadn't tasted meat for a very long time.

One day the goat "disappeared".

The Khazaks went about in groups and searched the settlement from top to bottom. Everybody had a good idea what must have happened to the poor creature. There was no doubt that, as soon as some proof was found, the culprits would be severely punished. The Khazak officials searched on for days, however not the slightest trace of the goat was ever discovered. None of us begrudged the clever and brave people who dispatched the animal for their reward. What we all wandered was; how did they manage to dispose the inedible bits so efficiently, and leave not the slightest trace?

Time went by. While Zuzia and I settled into life in the Children's Home, Stasia and Romek attended a newly formed Polish school in their own settlement. All adults, including my mother earned their living by working in the fields. In summer, during school vacations the school children were also required to help. A lot of them, and my brother particularly, resented this instruction, particularly as the order to work was received from the Polish schoolteacher. They felt betrayed. Surely, it wasn't right for them to be forced by their own authorities to help in ensuring the success of the hated Soviet Communist system they thought?

One muggy morning Mother, together with her usual contingent, marched off to work in the fields as usual. The group was somewhat depleted that day. Four of the workers didn't turn up. Their neighbours reported them ill to the team leader. As she walked on, mother reflected that Stasia and Romek seemed unwilling to get up for school this morning. "It must be this muggy weather," she thought. "If even grown-ups don't feel like making the effort, it's not surprising kids want to stay in bed."

Next morning only six women turned up. Something was very wrong. Worried, the charge hand set them to work and went off to see the commandant. He soon discovered that matters were even more serious than he thought. A third of the whole population was ill. The doctor decided that the settlement had been struck with an epidemic of typhus. All work was halted that day. Under the doctor's direction, a group of huts at one end of the hamlet were cleared and designated an isolation centre for those affected. After a couple of days it became clear that Mother's two elder children - the only two she had with her - were down with the dreaded plague, and were duly transported away and placed in the isolation centre. Mother fought her own symptoms as long as she could. In the end she too collapsed and was carried off. The doctor, having examined her said that my mother was suffering with typhus as well as 'spotted fever', another variant of the same disease. The doctor and his helpers were helpless. All they could do was to isolate those affected and care for them. There were no medicines available. A lot of people died of course, but some pulled through. Stasia and Romek made it. Mother lay in her bed, very ill and unaware of her surroundings for many days. Nobody thought she had

103

any chance of survival. One morning, however she opened her eyes and asked about her children. The doctor was called immediately. It seemed that mother's fever broke. She was on the mend at last.

It took many weeks for the settlement to re establish some level of normality. Yet again our family had miraculously survived.

In March 1942 rumours started circulating that the Polish armies were on the move. A few weeks later the vague gossip was confirmed. Polish officials arrived in the settlement and called on each family in turn. They eventually entered our chamber and were greeted by my mother and her friend and fellow occupant, Jadwiga Sliwinska. The man in charge of the delegation started by explaining that units of the Polish Armies, with the approval of Russian authorities, had already started to move towards the Caspian seaport of Krasnowodsk. From there transports were being arranged by boat to neighbouring Persia. He then proceeded to explain that relations with Russian Authorities continued to be delicate and that at that time, no permission had been received to remove Polish civilians. This matter was proving difficult because the Russians found Polish labour on their collective farms particularly useful.

Seeing the despondent expressions on the women's faces he quickly went on, "The situation is by no means hopeless. We are convinced the Russians will let all of you go eventually. It is probably a matter of timing."

He paused to allow the notion to sink in and continued, "As you know, the Children's Home in the next settlement is run entirely for the benefit of small children, most of whom are orphans. As they represent no labour force and only a drain on resources, the Russians readily agreed that we can take them away with the army to Persia." He stopped again, took a deep breath and delivered his final statement, and the point of the whole conversation.

"We cannot take you along with us. I have a proposition for you however. Your youngest children, Mrs Krajewska, and your son Mrs Sliwinska, are at present living in the Children's Home. I would like you to give me your permission to take those children along with us to Persia. I'm sure it won't be long before you and the rest of your families will follow and re-join your kids outside the Soviet borders."

He stopped, looked at both women and added, "Well - what do you say?"

The two women were dumbfounded. They couldn't believe their ears. In the end my mother responded.

"You don't seriously believe that I would let my children go, to be treated by strangers like orphans? No - much as I'd like to leave this place, I'd rather take my chances here, with all my children with me, than let some of them go away. After all, who knows how they'll be treated when there's no one about to defend their corner? My mind is made up. When you leave you must leave my children behind. I'll go over as soon as I can and collect them."

Jadwiga Sliwinska then added her comments.

"I'm in full agreement with my friend Koscia. There is no way I'd consider letting my little Janusz be taken away from me. I must also add that I find your suggestion deeply offensive. I can't help wondering how hard you've tried to secure our freedom. Our husbands lost their lives fighting for our Country. To abandon their widows in this fashion seems to me callous on your part to say the least." Unable to contain her fury further, she left the room into the night.

Zuzia and I were, of course, completely ignorant of the above events. One afternoon our housemistress called both of us over and said, "Tonight we're leaving this place. All the children are setting out on a long journey, across the sea to another country. I'm sorry to tell you, however that you two won't be coming with us. Your mother decided that you must stay behind."

We watched the others gathering their belongings. In all the frantic activities both of us were completely ignored. Frightened, bewildered and feeling abandoned, we crouched in a corner and started crying.

Late at night a string of the same curious carts that brought us to the settlement arrived. Children and carers started loading the vehicles with their meagre belongings. All of a sudden, when almost all had left the building, the head teacher ran up to us and called out. "Quickly children! Get your things together. Your mother's here! You and your whole family are coming with us after all!" Seeing our bewildered expressions she added, "Hurry up, there's no time to lose! The transport is about to set off."

What we discovered later was that; on the day of the transport, late in the afternoon a visitor arrived at my family's hut. The unexpected caller was none other than the Polish Outpost official who only recently called in order to persuade my mother and her friend to give up their children to be taken away to Persia. To their surprise he came this time with a different message.

Having entered and caught his breath, for he was clearly in haste, he said, "Mrs Krajewska and Mrs Sliwinska; as you may already know, the transport with the occupants of the Children's Home is departing for the port of Krasnowodsk tonight. Once there, the children will be shipped across the Caspian Sea to a port in Persia."

Seeing hostile expressions on the women's faces he quickly added,

"No, I haven't come to persuade you to change your minds about your children. I have good news. It seems that a few vacant places have been uncovered on the transport list. If you hurry up you can come along and get across to Persia together with your children and the rest of your families. Time is short, however and if you decide to go, you must leave for the Outpost immediately."

Mother didn't hesitate. She called to Stasia and Romek to gather what belongings they could carry and started herself to make ready and go. With Jadwiga Sliwinska, it was a different matter.

"I don't like his attitude," she said. "He hasn't even attempted to apologise to us for his rudeness during his previous visit. I don't like any of it," she continued. "Sneaking out like thieves in the night at such short notice. Surely, there will be other transports when we can travel with some dignity."

She sat for a moment silently and then announced, "No. I'm not going."

Mother, with a much more practical approach to life, tried her best to get her to change her mind but to no avail.

Time was getting short, so having bundled their belonging together mother, Stasia and Romek set off on foot through the night towards the children's home where Zuzia and I, unaware of these developments, sat in a corner crying our eyes out.

We were delighted to discover that we were joining our Mother, brother and sister and the rest of the people, and all previous despair forgotten, clambered together onto one of the carts.

Chapter 8

At long last we were off. At first, as we started to move away from the shore, everybody stood still as if stunned into silence. After a while however, emotion took over. The joy of leaving the "Soviet Garden of Eden" could not be bottled up. Someone started a religious song about deliverance. Within seconds the whole ship was vibrating with the voices of all on board that had enough strength to sing. The song was followed by another and then another. Later, emboldened, the travellers started singing old Polish patriotic songs that again talked of freedom and victory. Nobody was there to stop them. The Russian crew, being massively outnumbered, didn't dare to interfere.

Once the euphoria was over we soon discovered that the journey ahead of us wasn't going to be a bed of roses. In fact it looked as though we were in for another trial. In reality, as time went on, our time on board the ship "Kaganov" proved to be much more horrendous than we could have possibly anticipated. The little ship was packed tight with passengers. Most travellers were women and children. Most able-bodied men, having joined the Polish Army, made their way across on separate transports. All passengers were weak, malnourished and generally ill equipped for a sea journey. Much less so to travel on this small bouncy and overcrowded vessel. In addition, many people were already ill as they came on board, some very seriously. After all nobody was going to 'miss the boat' so to speak, and particularly not this one. We all thought (probably quite correctly), that this represented our one and only chance of escaping to freedom.

With this kind of cargo, consider the effects of seasickness and you can immediately imagine the long queues forming to the only toilet on board. Add to that the fact that many of those travelling suffered with galloping diarrhoea on arrival and you'll start to suspect the horror that was about to develop. The queues became never-ending. Most, on leaving the toilet, would immediately join the line to go again. Many couldn't wait and relieved themselves overboard or "almost" overboard. The resulting stench right across the ship was unbearable.

The combination of seasickness, diarrhoea and oppressive sunshine caused a heavy demand on meagre supplies of drinking water on board with the result that the vessel soon ran dry. So it was, all of us, thirsty

107

and packed like sardines, travelled for thirty-six hours before finally arriving at a Persian port of Pahlevi. Many didn't survive this latest ordeal and didn't live to see the Free World again. Many others, badly weakened by the journey, lay on the deck, close to death.

We stopped some distance from shore. Apparently the harbour wasn't deep enough to accept even a relatively small craft like our ship. A large number of small boats could soon be seen making their way towards us. As the rowing boats came along side one by one, orders were given for us to disembark and climb into these tiny and rickety items of maritime transport. Most women and almost all the children refused to board them to start with for fear of drowning. It took a lot of persuasion and coaxing to get them to finally take advantage of the facilities, and be transported onto the beckoning sandy beach.

At last we were all on dry land. As we waited to be processed we had to witness another appalling spectacle. Having delivered all the live passengers, the boats continued their shuttles but this time their cargo was that of the corpses of those that didn't survive the journey. The dead, and there were very many of them, were laid out on the beach not far from the living standing in a queue. We were told that the number of corpses being taken off the boats was so great that the burial details were unable to cope. The people we saw lying there would stay on the beach with just a sheet to cover them for anything up to a day, while the teams tried to catch up with the backlog. Some people, discovering that one of their relatives was missing, would walk down the row of corpses, trying to discover their own. The crying and wailing as they recognised the deceased was heartrending. It may seem callous, but I must admit that I, for one, couldn't wait to get inside the reception tent and out of sight and earshot of this open-air cemetery.

The long queue moved on. Eventually we found ourselves far enough away from the dead to be distracted by the sights and sounds of this new and strange land.

Our first taste of freedom.

The beach we were standing on was quite wide and extended in both directions as far as the eye could see. The fine white sand was clean and pleasant to my bare feet. The day was warm and sunny and as we stood there, we could hear the strange sounding calls of Persian

108

traders, like: "kus-kus, hurma, jajca varonie, papieros" etc. Some people brought Russian money with them, which the traders were quite happy to accept. Unaccustomed to the quantities and richness of food available to them, some went on an orgy of eating, often with disastrous results. Many became very ill, and some died in terrible agony before they could be helped. For good or for ill, we didn't take advantage of the traders' offers. The reason was simple. My mother brought no money along. As it happens this fact alone might have helped us to survive, although watching other people eating all that delicious food and fresh fruit, it didn't feel like that at the time.

Eventually we reached the entrance of the Reception tent and went in. Facing us, seated behind a table was a Polish official. The man asked my mother all sorts of questions, intended to establish our identities. Next we were told to separate: women and girls to the left passage, men and boys to the right. I went through as directed. There I was told I was to be "disinfected". This word sounded strange to me and I didn't know what to expect next. Certainly not what actually followed.

First, I was stripped naked and all my clothes taken away to be burned. Next, my hair was cut and my head shaved close to the scalp. As if all that wasn't enough, I was then put under a hot shower and thoroughly scrubbed with some kind of strong-smelling soap. I came out the other end exhausted and bewildered, and in spite of it all, feeling somehow "better" to face yet another ordeal. This time a man in a white coat told me to lie down on a bench and proceeded to prod me around my chest and stomach, asking the rather stupid question, "does that hurt?" every once in a while. Obviously it did hurt, and I said so. He then told me to sit up and took a long time tapping my chest, and looking into my throat.

"You have a bad case of whooping cough," he said. "We'll have to get you into a hospital." Then looking at my worried face added, "Don't worry. You'll be all right. The nice nurses there will take good care of you."

I was given some new clothes and came outside into the fresh air again. There, I saw a large group of people of all ages huddled together. Shortly afterwards a lorry arrived and a nurse came out of the front cab. The nurse asked all those waiting to make themselves comfortable in the back of the lorry. Seeing my forlorn little figure standing near the tent she turned and said,

"Don't look so worried. You'll be going with me to a nice hospital in Tehran. If you like you can ride with me in the front."

"Where's my mother?" I asked, crying.

"Your mum has already been told where you're going. She and your brother and sisters have to stay in this camp for another two weeks. They all seem quite well but the quarantine is there just to make sure. Soon your mother will also be going to a camp in Tehran and I'm sure she'll come and visit you in hospital as soon as she can." She looked at me again and seeing that I still seemed unconvinced added, "Don't worry. Everything'll be all right."

Soon we departed. The views that passed in front of my eyes as we travelled soon diverted my attention. Almost as soon as we left the camp we entered the narrow and busy streets of Pahlevi.

What a sight - streets full of people milling around, standing, talking and laughing. Stalls along the streets brimming over with all kinds of goods and with no queues in front of them. The strangest thing of all was the general impression that the town's inhabitants were relaxed, unafraid and were clearly enjoying life. There was an atmosphere on the streets, which I for one, forgot existed at all.

We soon left the little town and suddenly found an entirely different panorama spreading before us. The sand was left behind. All around us we could see greenery. The road was lined with tall palm trees. Ahead could be seen fields lying fallow and covered with exotic and colourful wild flowers. Yet further we could see the deep green of rice paddies and later, as the hills started appearing, vineyards. The whole view was a feast to the eyes.

Very slowly the picture started changing. The surroundings started looking more and more arid. The air felt cooler.

"We are beginning to climb the mountains of Elburs." The nurse said. "Now, watch the fun start."

Sure enough, the journey soon became very exciting, if not in the way one would have wished. The lorries started climbing along steep, narrow and winding roads. To one side we could only see an enormous wall hewn out of sheer rock. On the other, a precipice so deep that the bottom disappeared in a mist below. This hazardous journey, with

110

stops for rest and refreshments, continued for two days. In the end, at last we saw the white and gleaming walls of the city of Tehran in the distance. I could hear the passengers in the back loudly giving thanks to the Almighty for getting them through the journey safely and "in one piece". We had finally arrived.

`The hospital stood on a small hill just outside the City centre. It was an imposing, fairly modern structure; walls all painted brilliant white. We all alighted and after attending to basic formalities, the hospital staff placed us in various wards, depending on the diagnosed illnesses. My ward was on the ground floor. It was clearly intended for the not-too-seriously ill. My bed was next to the corridor and faced the permanently open door to the garden outside. The view of the flowers and the delicious scents made us all feel happy in spite of our illnesses.

With the excitement and the tensions out of the way I discovered that I really was ill. The doctor wasn't joking. Every once in a while an uncontrollable cough would shake my small frame. It took some time for me to recover after every bout. It was only when I discovered however, that I had started spitting blood that I started to get concerned about my condition. Who knows what depths of despair my imagination would have driven me into if it weren't for our favourite nurse? With her ever-smiling round and pretty face, she really was like a ray of sunshine to us all. Was it only my impression or was she especially nice to me personally? I must admit that with her around all my worries seemed to fly right out of the window. Could it be that at this tender age and in spite of my poor state of health I had suddenly started to appreciate the finer points of the opposite sex? Sometimes I wonder.

By the time my mother came to visit about three weeks later, I was on the way to recovery. She asked me how I was getting on and I told her that things were pretty good in my ward and that I was beginning to feel better. As we were talking, a couple of warders went by, carrying somebody out of the hospital. I remarked on this strange event to my mother and said that this sort of thing seemed to be happening regularly. Maybe four or five times per day. "Do you think they are being moved to another hospital?" I inquired. Mother went silent for some time and eventually replied. "Unfortunately, not everybody was as lucky as you, my son. Some people were too ill to

111

survive, even with the best care and medicine this hospital had to offer. No. What you saw weren't people being moved for further treatment. These were the bodies of those who didn't make it, being removed to the cemetery to be buried." Seeing me saddened by what she told me she started on another tack, trying to divert my attention.

"We've only just arrived in Tehran," she said. "We were given very comfortable accommodation in Camp number 1". Then with some excitement (and that itself was uncharacteristic of my mother) she said, "There was great ceremony when we arrived in the city. The Shah of Persia himself greeted our transport. It seems we were the first lot of Polish refugees to arrive here."

I later discovered more stories connected with this reception. Apparently the young "King of Kings", having discovered that the Polish refugees from the Soviet Union were on their way to his capital, had insisted on greeting them personally At the court of the Peacock Throne a number of visiting dignitaries were present, and the young king invited them all to join him. Most attended in order to comply with protocol. Among tem was Jam Saheb, the Maharaja of Navangar in India. On seeing the pitiful and emaciated lot scrambling out of the vehicles, the Maharaja was shocked. He was especially impressed by a group of children who were, he was informed, orphaned.

Immediately after this event the Maharaja approached the British authorities with an offer to create a home for the orphans within the grounds of his palace in Jamnagar. He offered too a parcel of land near Kolhapur on which could be built a large camp for Polish refugees. This offer was accepted. Recently, in order to express the Polish nation's gratitude for this kindness, a secondary school in Warsaw was named after the Maharaja.

At last I was pronounced well and allowed to join my family. I soon discovered that all members of my family, with the possible exception of my younger sister Zuzia, looked much fitter, healthier and generally "fattened up" since I saw them last. Zuzia, although she seemed well enough, continued to look pale, thin and anaemic. We were housed in a large brick-built house, subdivided to accommodate six families. We all agreed that the accommodation was comfortable and food, after the earlier depravations, was delicious. Many faces from our sea journey appeared to be missing. When I inquired where these people might be, my elder sister Stasia replied, "Most of them are dead. You didn't stay long in Pahlevi so you wouldn't know. We saw literally thousands being taken away and buried. You should see the new cemetery there, near the beach. It's enormous. On top of that, a lot of people died here in Tehran. Some, after being taken away to hospital like you, others fell ill here in the camp. There is another enormous Polish cemetery, this time outside Tehran. If you like, I'll take you over one day and show you."

A little later she did indeed take me over to see the place where so many of the Refugees found their final resting place. Straight ahead, as far as the eye could see, a forest of little white wooden crosses stretched out in front of me. The same applied if I looked to the left or to the right. The number of lives claimed by our Invader was beyond my comprehension.

In spite or maybe because of the above, we enjoyed our stay in the Refugee camp in Tehran a great deal. We realised of course that this was to be no more than a transit stopover. The British (for it was they that were in control of the whole operation), went about in their usual systematic way to arrange permanent placements for us all, at least "for the duration of the war," as they were fond of saying. The implication was of course, that the concept of the Allies winning the conflict was beyond question. It was only a matter of time.

The plight of the refugees was heavily publicised on the International stage and individual States were invited to make their offers as to the numbers they could take in. South American countries like Mexico and Argentina as well as Dominions like Australia and New Zealand gave quotas. On the whole though the response was poor, and the British found themselves having to fall back on their own resources. They took up the Maharaja's offer and constructed a camp near Kolhapur which was subsequently named Valivade. To accommodate the rest, settlements were constructed in various parts of the African colonies.

Having made all the necessary preparations, the next stage was to determine the individual preferences and try to marry them up with the places available. A list of families was prepared and the head of each family (generally the mother, as the adult males were either dead or had joined the newly formed Polish Second Corp. of Monty's Eight Army) was asked to call at the camp's office. As we were one of the first to arrive at the camp, Mother discovered that the organisers employed the "first come, first served" system and listed her as one of the first to be called.

The Polish official was very helpful. She patiently described the options and gave mother as much background information as she was able. It seemed that choices like South America, Australia or New Zealand implied resettlement for life. This, my mother wasn't prepared to contemplate at that stage. "Surely," she thought, "The war'll be over soon, we'll go home, I'll probably find Leon waiting there for us and we'll start again. I've even got our land deeds with me. Once we're back, we'll reclaim our farm from whoever occupied it and life will begin again." After all, it wasn't the first time her family had faced disasters and setbacks, only to stubbornly restart as soon as the situation permitted. So, South America and the Antipodes were out. The other choices were a series of small camps out in the depths of Africa, or a substantial camp that was being erected in India. Mother gave it some thought and in the end opted for India. She figured that the Indian settlement was the more viable option - the fact that it was to be quite large gave her the feeling that it would be more secure than a little camp out in the depths of Africa. In addition, with the camp population being so large, decent schooling for her children should also be possible.

Once the matter of placement was settled we were on the move yet again. This time the familiar Army lorries took us across the mountains to the Persian port of Ahvaz.

On arrival we were told to move into what looked like old Army stables. The single storey building we were led into was long and rather narrow. Although the walls were brick-built, the floor was simply bare clay. The space allocation was not generous and, in fact we found ourselves very badly congested. The responses to complaints were, invariably,

"Sorry, it's the best we could do in the time available. As you know, this is only a stopover. You'll soon be on the way to your destination. Bear with us."

114

In spite of the cramped sleeping accommodation our rather short stay in Ahvaz was quite enjoyable. The weather was pleasant (some even complained that it was too hot), and the surroundings interesting. Many adults made excursions to the nearby town to buy clothes and other useful articles, while others simply went sightseeing. Most, and that included all the children, stayed inside the camp. In the confined space, it was inevitable that whole families, individual adults and individual children started to get to know each other and make friends. It was all the more likely if you discovered that the other person was signed on for the same destination as yourself. We in fact discovered that even in the first transport there was quite a wide range of expected final destinations. Apart from India, we found many waiting to go to various parts of Africa. Apparently this was the most convenient port for large trans-oceanic liners, which would take some of our acquaintances on the very long journey to Africa. However, as I said, many friendships were started. Some were to develop and in many cases, last for years to come. One of these was my mother's friendship with a woman by the name of Strojkowska. Mrs. Strojkowska had a number of children and we soon got to know them all very well. Amongst them was a girl of my own age. Zosia Strojkowska. I will always remember her.

What we were told about the length of our stay at the beginning proved to be right. Indeed, our stay in Ahvaz wasn't very long. After only a few weeks, one day the word came - we were to get ready to move. Our transport ship had arrived.

The following morning we got our belongings together and boarded. The ship wasn't very big, but the accommodation and level of comfort very different from our last experience of sea travel. We were all allocated sleeping bed bunks, regular meals of a good standard were provided and there was plenty of space to move around above and below deck. The journey was slow and ponderous. We seemed to travel all the time within sight of the shore. This gave us a pleasant view of the greenery and the palm trees. Possibly because the vessel never ventured far into open waters, the decks were steady at all times and there were no problems with seasickness and the like. The journey took ten days. Until our little ship had finally pulled into a port in the Indian city of Karachi.

115

On arrival we were taken to a location outside the town, in the middle of a sandy dessert plain, where accommodation was waiting for us. We were to stay in massive army tents. The camp comprised a forest of tents surrounded by a tall wire fence. We were quickly told that the fence wasn't there to keep us in, and that apparently, it was to prevent the various wild creatures that roamed the dessert at night from entering the camp uninvited.

Half a dozen families were housed per tent. The Strojkowski family shared our enclosure together with some others. I must say that I for one, found the sight of the horrible looking vultures, hyenas and other creatures frightening. How glad I was of the tall fence. Sometimes I couldn't help wondering, "Is the fence really strong enough and tall enough to keep some of the more ferocious of the creatures away from us?" The thought that they may come and get us filled me with horror.

In spite of the strange surroundings, we soon started to settle in. Life in the camp started to establish a level of "normality". Rapidly, various social organisations started springing up, a public library was opened and even amateur dramatic circles and a choir were formed. To the dismay of all of us kids, it was discovered that there was a surprisingly high number of professional teachers amongst us. Teachers being teachers, they of course couldn't wait to get their hands on us poor children and save us from idleness and generally enjoying ourselves. As one might expect, soon a school was established on the camp. By then I was seven years old and so, found myself roped in as well. The camp was very short of books and other materials required in a school, and writing paper was in particularly short supply. To overcome the problem the teachers reverted to the ancient system of slates and chalk. Each of us was issued with a small, framed piece of black slate, about 300mm by 200mm, as well as a small piece of hard chalk. The teacher would write on his blackboard and we had to copy the letters onto our slates. Thus begun my first steps into literacy.

We stayed in the camp for about eight months. In that time many transports departed from our settlement, heading for a variety of far away destinations. Most were transported by Allied transport ships. Some of them were major British and American liners. The Polish liner "Batory" (the only liner which Poles managed to keep out of the clutches of the Germans at the outbreak of war) carried one of the transports out. The ship and its crew had in fact taken part in all kinds of war activities as part of the Allied Fleet and had carried out their duties with distinction. Vacant places left by those departing were soon filled again by the continued and constant trickle of further arrivals from the Tehran camp. Some of these were late arrivals from the Soviet Union, but most were delayed through various family illnesses, and in some cases resulting in fatalities. It's not easy to estimate the percentage of survivors, however it may serve as an indication if I say that, of the five thousand travelling with us across the Caspian Sea, much less than four thousand reached their "final" destination. By "final" I mean the place where they hoped to sit out the war.

We discovered later that while families, after registration and selection of their "permanent" homes, travelled on to Ahvaz, unattended children were gathered into an Orphanage Unit and transferred to a camp in Isfahan, also in Persia. There they stayed for a time recovering their health and strength. Another reason for keeping the orphanage "stayed-put" for a time was the suspicion that not all of them were true orphans. In the chaos and turmoil of trying to get out from Russia, many parents found themselves separated from one or more of their children. On reaching the other side they would, of course immediately inquire about their whereabouts. Some were unlucky and had to accept that their children had either died or got left behind. The lucky ones discovered that their little darling daughter or their favourite boy were alive and well and being cared-for in the orphanage in Isfahan. Once all the "non-orphaned" orphans were accounted for and re-united with their families, the remainder could proceed to their next destination. The Maharaja had kept his word. The Authorities were soon informed that the children's new home in India was ready for occupation. The Orphanage departed and formed the very first transport of Polish refugees to be settled in the sub-continent.

Back in our camp in Karachi, we continued to wait our turn.

In February 1943 the word finally came that our new homes in India were ready for occupation. One morning shortly after, a long line

117

of by now famous lorries arrived and parked just outside the camp main gate. We were off yet again. As Mother was one of the earliest to register, I with the rest of my family soon found ourselves sitting in the back of one of the vehicles waiting for the "off". We didn't have to wait long. The caravan set off single file and speeded off down the dusty road toward the nearby mountains to the west of the camp. We travelled through mountain ranges, along precipices and across open deserts for about two weeks, stopping only for meals and to sleep. In the end, exhausted by the tiring, hot, dusty and somewhat frightening journey we arrived in the famous Indian port of Bombay.

What a sight. The whole city seemed to glisten in the bright sunshine like a jewel. All the houses were painted white and appeared to be spotlessly clean. My impression of Bombay may have been exaggerated. It may indeed have been affected by the dusty journey we had just completed.

We stopped outside the town's railway station. A long train was already there and waiting for us. We transferred to the new mode of transport and set off once more. The train sped on, stopping only once to pick up water and fuel. The next morning our train went through the station of Poona at full speed. Some hours later we could see signs indicating that we were about to enter of Kolhapur. Quite soon after passing the Kolhapur station the engine pulled up. We appeared to have stopped in the middle of nowhere. Transport warders started walking down the train, calling us to alight. We had arrived.

Chapter 9

Bewildered, we stood by the side of the empty train and looked around. All around, to our left and right, looking alongside the train, we could only see an open plain stretching out, punctuated by groups of rather strange looking trees. Some distance directly ahead the arid ground was replaced by a something new and out of place. A large square patch of the landscape appeared to be painted a bright and shiny red colour. On closer inspection we saw many rows of long houses, all erected in almost regimental order. The colour of red came from the roofing tiles with which all the buildings were covered.

We were soon brought back to reality by calls from the Official in charge of the transport. Holding a hailer to his mouth he called out: "Ladies and Gentlemen, or shall I say Ladies and Children, we have arrived at our destination. What you can see in front of you are to be your new homes. Before we go any further, I want you to form into groups so that we can allocate to you your accommodation. My assistants are lined up over there as you can see. You will see that each is holding a large card above his or her head with a number. I will call each family name in turn and allocate a number. When your name is called, please move across and join the warden with you allocated number. Thank you and welcome to Valivade."

What followed was a lot of noise, argument and confusion. Polish people don't take instruction and organisation readily, I'm afraid. In spite of that, when the leader started calling out the names some semblance of order started to appear. Eventually all transport was broken up into groups as intended.

We, having found ourselves in the first group, marched down the hill towards the settlement ahead of the rest. We walked past rows and rows of barracks, until we reached the far edge of what appeared to be a section of buildings. The group leader stopped. He invited us all to come around in turn and inspect the first accommodation unit in Block number One. He also suggested that we follow on and also look at the next two or three to get a better feel of the places.

The building we found ourselves in was built on a gentle slope and comprised four levels with steps, as it stretched down the hill. Each of the level sections housed four family units, all being identical in

119

design. The concept was quite simple. Looking from left to right, there was a smallish room, obviously intended as a bedroom. Next to that was a much larger room, which was to be the living room, and further on to the right was a small kitchen. The living quarters adjacent were a mirror image with the kitchens interlocking. As I mentioned earlier, the sloping roof was covered with red clay tiles. You could tell this easily because the tiles had no lining whatsoever - you could see all the battens and tile fixings when you looked up. The floor inside all the rooms was bare earth, compacted to give a firm and level surface. Walls were a low brick wall and double skinned bamboo matting. Windows had shutters but no glazing. On either side was a veranda overhung by the sloping roof. Wooden posts supported the roof along the edge of the veranda.

Our guide settled individual families in the allotted places and passed on his advice and instructions before moving on. We finished up in District One, Block No. Two, Accommodation No. Eight. Before he left us to our own devices, the Official repeated the instructions for our benefit:

"You will see that each bed has a lattice support woven out of hemp rope. This should give you good support. If, however, the string stretches in time and the bed starts to sag, simply undo the knot, pull the netting up tight and re-secure it. You'll find it's quite a simple operation. Each bed, as you can see, has a mattress and a pillow. Both are stuffed with coconut hair. I'm afraid it won't exactly feel like goose feathers, but that's all that's available around here."

We all started inspecting the item. Mother, unaccustomed to this type of bed looked doubtfully and asked:

"It may be all right for small children, but are you sure it'll support a fully grown person?"

The guide assured mother that the furniture was fully capable of long and satisfactory use by adults, larger than her and continued:

"You will see that there is a bamboo frame over the bed with a piece of fine netting wrapped over it. When you go to bed at night you must pull the netting all around the bed and tuck it in. This is to protect you from mosquito bites. Unfortunately they are prevalent around here. Mosquitoes are not just a nuisance. One bite and you may find yourself infected with the malaria bug."

We were all horrified at this terrible prospect and assured him vigorously that we'd make full use of the mosquito net protection. At that, he moved on to the main living room, and carried on:

"As you can see there's a large table and four chairs. If you need more chairs, let the office know. I'm sure an extra chair or two could be found if necessary. On the table you can see a storm lamp. Take good care of it. This paraffin lamp is your only source of light. The camp facilities don't run to electric lighting in each room. There is electric supply, of course on the Camp, but that's confined to main centres only, like Camp Offices, Social Centre etc."

Moving on he continued, " The kitchen is built for use with solid fuel, like wood or charcoal. You'll find that dried cow-dung makes a good substitute." Looking at mother's expression of incredulity he added: "Believe me. It really does work. The locals use it in this and other ways all the time" he said, smiling. As a parting shot he said: "You'll all be issued with tropical kits. One of the items is a pith helmet. Do make sure you wear it every time you venture out. The sun here is very strong and going about with no headgear can have serious consequences. Another thing to mention is shoes. You'll get the type of open sandals used by Indians. Covered shoes are not a good idea in this climate. Do, however wear the sandals all the time. You never know what might be crawling around under your feet."

He left us, and moved on to the next "apartment," taking the entourage of the remaining group with him. We were all stunned by this introduction to our new home. I for my part remember being terrified. After a while my elder sister Stasia said,

"This place seems horrible, what with all this business with mosquitoes, the sun and various frightening creepy-crawlies. Maybe we should have gone somewhere else."

"Where else could we go that would have been any better?" Mother responded. Places like Australia and South America were really for those that wanted to emigrate and make their permanent homes there. Our only alternative was a settlement in the middle of the African jungle. Do you think you'd be any safer there?" she asked, and then not waiting for an answer added, "No I don't think I've made a mistake. You'll all see. It won't be as bad as it looks once we get ourselves settled in."

We unpacked our belongings and, while mother started struggling with her stove to make us something to eat, we went out to explore our new surroundings. As I said earlier, we were located in building number two. This placed us near the front edge of our district. As we came out to our right stretched row upon row of long barracks identical to our own. In-between lay unmade ground, the yellow clay showing through the recently disturbed soil. Ahead was obviously the camp's Social and Welfare Area. The buildings on the left formed our new hospital. Dead ahead was a curious construction with a lot of concrete posts and inter-connecting steel piping. This, we discovered was to be our source of water supply. There was no general water distribution system in place. To the right we saw a couple of buildings, apparently intended to house shops, a Community Hall and a cinema.

Beyond stretched further expanses of housing blocks. Presumably further districts. Coming back we explored the open space along the other edge of our corner. On the left we saw another odd construction. An open concrete water reservoir of about five meters square sat right in the middle of the open ground. The concrete surround projected only half a meter above ground. The tank was filled with water to the brim. It looked like a disaster waiting to happen. (This was to be confirmed by my own experience a short time later.) Much further ahead we saw a group of smaller buildings. Upon investigation we discovered these to be communal toilets and washrooms. Like water distribution, drainage was also confined to one area.

Hungry, we all returned home to find that Mother had managed to work the stove and cooked some soup, which we all ate with relish. This was mother's first go at serious cooking, (not counting any odd bit of work she might have done in Siberia, with the meagre supplies she occasionally managed to secure) and she certainly enjoyed it. In a small way it reminded her of her glory days in Piaski when her regular diners queued up to complement her on her culinary creations that day. She served out the food and as we all sat down to eat, Mother hovered around expectantly. In the end, seeing no response from any of us she asked,

"Well - what do you all think?"

Stasia, remembering what it was like back home in Poland finally got the message and called out;

"It's great Mum. Haven't tasted food like that for years!"   The rest of us, having taken our cue from our eldest sibling, called out in chorus that the food was excellent. At that, mother wandered off, a satisfied smile on her face. This became a ritual in our family that lasted for many years. In fact, right until Mother's death. Even in those days, when she was quite infirm, she would make soup to her own recipe every time we visited her, and we would see the joy in her face when we told her (as we invariably did), how delicious it was. Our praise of Mother's cooking wasn't false - I really did think her creations were delicious.

Mother's words about the place proved to be prophetic. Soon the whole place was teeming with life. Following our arrival, one trainload came after another in quick succession. Before long the camp was almost filled to capacity.

Among the many following transports came many kids of my age group. Soon we started making friends and established relationships. One of the new arrivals was a girl I had known from our camp in Karachi - Zosia Strojkowska. I had also made new friends with boys and girls that moved in nearby. One of them was Piotrus (Peter) that lived opposite and another's name was Bogdan, although everyone called him Buba (no reasonable translation available), who lived on the other side. Needless to say before long we formed a group and tended to spend most of our spare time together.

The camp as I said earlier, by now close to full capacity, housed about five thousand people. These were almost entirely women and children. I say "almost" because there were in fact some men amongst us. These were generally individuals, invalided from the Army due to either some permanent damage received at the Front or some other long-term health problem.

Accustomed to changes, the organisers as well as the camp inhabitants rapidly started to form social structures and generally injecting life and normality into the settlement. As I said, we were located in District number one. There were in fact to be a further four such Districts. Soon Primary schools were formed and children were allocated places in their nearest schools and assessed for classes. There were to be four such schools in the camp. I found myself assigned to the first class in school number one. I was eight by then, and would

123

normally expect to be in my second school year, however, the only bit of schooling I'd received until then was the temporary set-up in Karachi and that, the teachers reckoned, wasn't worth much in educational terms. My younger sister Zuzia and my brother Romek got also signed up to the same school but, of course to classes appropriate to their ages and abilities. My eldest sister was accepted to Grammar Secondary School. Apart from the Grammar School, other facilities for Secondary Level education were also formed. These were: a Higher Secondary School for General Education, a Teacher's College, and a Commercial College. All of the latter were intended for young people that successfully completed the Grammar School. If all this sounds a little unfamiliar, let me say that the whole educational structure in the camp closely mimicked the pre-war system left behind in Poland. Part of the system, unlike the English structure with which I'm a little familiar, was a rule that you would only cross over to the next class if, at the end of the school year you had no "unsatisfactory" or "failed" marks. If you were unfortunate enough to find one of those on your report, you were forced to repeat the school year.

Other Institutions also developed rapidly. One of them was a General Lending Library, another was the Church complete with three priests, yet another a Community Hall, a Cinema and many Social and Youth organisations.

We arrived in Valivade in May 1943. By the time some sort of organisation and normality was established in the camp it was June and therefore the start of school summer holidays. We played in groups, investigated our surroundings and made a nuisance of ourselves to our parents. Slowly, I found myself spending more and more time with my new female friend Zosia. Zosia Strojkowska was about the same age as myself. She was a pretty girl with dark blonde hair, green eyes, a round pale face and rosy cheeks. After a time we seemed to be always together. Somehow eventually we became inseparable. I would run errands for her, carry her coat or her carrier bag, if she had to get some supplies for her mother and generally behaved "like a gentleman". Grown-ups used to laugh at us and called us "love birds" but I wasn't bothered. I WAS IN LOVE and I didn't care who knew it. The relationship was, obviously purely spiritual and emotional. We both had many years ahead of us before we were to reach puberty. It's very difficult to describe my feelings towards Zosia in those days. A good indication as to their intensity however may be my reaction to what I considered her act of treachery and perfidy.

Although we were past the age when kids normally start their schooling and learn to read and write, we were all almost completely illiterate. This wasn't surprising, as up to that time there were no decent opportunities for us to receive any worthwhile formal education. As a consequence the kind of literature we all favoured was the sort that had a lot of pictures. One sort of magazine in great demand was the Comic. There was, (and still is) in existence a book, written by a famous Polish writer under a title of "Mary and the dwarfs". In fact the similarity to the English fairy story of "Snow-white and the Seven Dwarfs" is superficial. The story, told in the form of a children's fable, was in fact intended as a satire on the social order in pre-war Poland. All that was, of course completely over our heads. All we knew was, that there was this great book with a fairy story and fantastic illustrations. It was obviously, and immediately in great demand. As soon as I heard of it's existence I went to the newly opened Public Library and to my joy discovered that a copy was available. Very proudly I carried the book home. At the first opportunity I shared my joy with my girlfriend Zosia, who said she was also trying to get hold of a copy.

One day, having shinned up one of our school veranda posts, as one does, I saw Zosia below having an agitated exchange with our new school Head Master. I overheard her saying,

"I've been waiting for it for weeks. Surely it must've been returned by now."

The teacher seemed embarrassed and apologetic. "I know it's been out of our library for some time. To be honest I'm not sure who borrowed it. As soon as I get it back I'll bring it over to you personally. Until then, as we don't know where the book is, we can only wait."

I decided to come down and find out what was happening. It seemed to me that my favourite girl was getting fobbed off. As I approached, however, Zosia pointed at me and shouted at the teacher,

"Here he is. He's the culprit. I know he's had the book of "Mary and the Dwarfs" for ages and he still has it. Tell him to return it so I can borrow it. "

I was stunned. Here I was running over to her aid, only to be accused of secretly hoarding the book she wanted. Calmly I went over to the School Head and said,

"Yes. Zosia is right that I have a copy of this book at home. The one I have however belongs to the Central Library and not the School Library. You must search for your culprit elsewhere."

Having delivered my speech I walked off home. I was in a shock. I was disappointed in Zosia. I felt betrayed.

On arrival home I went into my room and pretended to read something. The fact was that I wanted to be alone with my thoughts and didn't want any company for a while. Some minutes later I heard Zosia's voice at the front of the house.

"Gienek! Zosia's here to see you," I heard my mother calling.

"Tell her to go away," I said, and added, "Tell her I never want to see her again. Ever." I shouted.

After a while, the muttering outside ceased. The girl has obviously gone. Stasia came over to me and asked mockingly, "What's the matter. Have the love birds fallen out?"

My only reply was, "I don't want to talk about it."

I felt so upset and wounded by the girl's action that, day after day and week after week I kept my vow. Whenever Zosia, apparently sent over to my mother with some errand, approached our place, I would either go out or, if that wasn't possible, turn away so as not even to look in her direction. Years went by as we continued to live in our camp in India. In all that time I can honestly say that I have never seen my ex-girlfriend again. In fact, many years later, whilst in England I was told that Zosia Strojkowska met up with an American GI from a nearby American Base, got married and went away to live in the United States. I knew then that, even if I wanted to call off my pledge, I wasn't going to see her ever again.

So ended my first attempt at a relationship with a member of the opposite sex. After this episode I wanted to have nothing to do with girls who were all clearly deceitful, selfish, scheming and generally not to be trusted. I must add that I was still very young, however, and

126

some years were yet to pass before hormonal activity changed my attitude towards them.

As I said, life soon arrived at a level of normality and stability normally associated with long established societies and settlements. It now seems very strange to me. Valivade quickly became a self sufficient little island of "Polishness" in the midst of the Indian continent. A veritable Polish Brigadoon. The camp seemed to have and needed little or no contact with the outside world. To keep us up to date with the progress of the War, "somewhere far away," a weekly bulletin flier was printed by the Administration and distributed throughout the camp. It was by this medium that we all first heard of the death of our beloved General Sikorski. The shock was deeply felt by all and the consequent mourning was highly vocal, long and very genuine. Everybody knew that he personally delivered us from the clutches of N.K.V.D. and almost certain slow death in Siberia. Masses were said in church for the repose of his soul, and many funeral songs and laments were performed in his memory. Apart from the fact, however that we were all grieving for a person we all genuinely loved there was another question at the back of all our minds. Without our Protector, what would become of us? Would the Allies and the Polish Authorities, now without their illustrious leader continue to care for us or, as has happened too often in the past, might we be sold down the river in some secret deal?

The mood of mourning and dark suspicion lasted for a long time. Eventually as usually happens, daily concerns took precedence and the loss of our General, although certainly not forgotten, moved to a position of lesser priority.

School had started and I, along with the others had to get used to the classroom discipline and harsh treatment dealt out by our teachers. I tried to complain to mother, but soon discovered that in Polish pre-war society, questioning teacher's actions was not customary. I just had to accept that that's how things were and with it the occasional wallop from the teacher, deserved or not.

Soon after the start of the first school year a new transport arrived. It was in fact the Orphanage we left behind in Persia in Isfahan. The children were settled in their own separate section across from us on the other side of the Community Centre. Their existence seemed to be covered in the mist of mystery. They apparently had their own school within their compound. This probably contributed to the fact that little mixing took place between them and us "normal" kids. The Orphanage was always viewed with curiosity, but only from afar.

There was one encounter I recall with a member of the Orphanage that didn't leave me with a pleasant memory. Here I must admit that I was then and still am a devout coward when it comes to physical violence. I've always managed to avoid these sorts of challenges. One day some lads saw me in the playing field and came over. One of them turned to me and said,

"You see that little lad over there. He must be no more than half your size. He reckons he can lick you."

I shrugged my shoulders and moved to go away.

"Come on," the little boy shouted. "You're not scared of me are you? Come on; let's see who's stronger. Put up your fists."

Feeling that I had no choice I reluctantly raised my hands, not knowing what to expect next. What immediately followed was that the little boy jumped forward and landed me a fierce punch on the nose. My face exploded with a sharp pain. Tears started pouring from my eyes. Realising that this was no game, or no game I wanted any part of, I ran off home leaving the victor on the field of battle. After that episode I tended to stay clear of the Orphanage kids. My compassion for them had waned somewhat.

Bit by bit everybody adapted to our new, and seemingly permanent, way of life. One day for instance, my mother saw our neighbour crouched down, spreading some wet substance evenly throughout her living room floor. That seemed like a very good idea, as after some use, the clay floor dried up and became very dusty.

"What's that stuff you're spreading on the floor?" Mother inquired. " I must say looking at the dried up bits it seems to be doing the trick."

Our neighbour, known for her sense of humour got up, looked at her own handiwork and admitted, "Yes, it should do the job. And to think that I've put up with all that dust for so long." Smiling, she added, "and on top of that all it costs is a little labour!"

Mother, puzzled asked her, "Where do you get the stuff? I must get some myself and go over all my floors. What is it anyway?"

Our neighbour, with an innocent expression on her face replied, "Don't you know? Its cows dried up dung. All you need to do is to collect some out in the fields where the cows have left them, bring them home, mix them with water to a nice thin consistency and there you are. A nice new floor surface. And in case you're wondering, " she added, " no, there is no smell."

Mother, still having some doubts, sent us kids out for "supplies" and proceeded to experiment. The result was even better than she could have hoped for. Once the surface had dried, the floor was hard, even and not at all dusty. As well as all that, as our neighbour had said the dung produced no smell, either during the time of application or afterwards.

Another example of learning the ways of the locals was the matter of washing. Washing of dirty clothes was proving to be difficult. What with having to cart all this water for washing and rinsing over from the central mains distribution point, the lack of proper washing implements, washday was certainly not a time to look forward to. It wasn't surprising then, that some of the better off women, paid Indian girls to carry out the chore for them. It was then that Mother and others discovered how the locals did their own washing. They would take all their laundry to the riverbank and wash it there. Instead of scrubbing, as our women would do normally, they'd apply soap to the garment and bash it against a selected smooth stone along the bank. This procedure was followed by rinsing in the river water and repeated as necessary until the item was clean. The process had the advantage of needing no special implements and no backbreaking carting of bucket after bucket of water. Needless to say, the system was quickly adopted by all Polish women and was soon in universal use in our Camp.

Life in the Camp had indeed arrived at a natural rhythm. The shops in the middle of the Camp provided a lot of the necessities. Typical of the resourceful Indians, an open-air market soon developed on the edge of our settlement. There, one could get all the items on sale in the "official" shops and many that you couldn't get in the shops at all. In addition, local villagers soon discovered that the Camp dwellers had a need for fresh supplies like meat, milk, butter etc. Soon a man or a woman could be seen walking down the alleys between the barracks, calling out the one or two recently learned words in Polish like, "mieso!"(meat) and "mleko!" (milk) etc. The accent and the pronunciation were usually atrocious, but the desired effect was achieved. The hawkers were regularly approached and trade soon flourished. The Indians' enterprise didn't end there. Some of them inevitably tried to discover just how much profit could be squeezed out of the Enterprise. One way, something the housewives soon cottoned-on to, was to water down milk and so get more money for the increased volume. They soon learned, however, that these kinds of tricks didn't pay. A Polish woman would first inspect the offered produce. If she discovered the telltale blue line on the margin, the milk would be rejected and neighbours would be warned not to do business with this particular vendor.

The temptation to maximise their (probably) meagre income sometimes took them beyond the margin of pardonable excesses. One day my mother became the victim of just such action. It may now sound silly and naïve, but, like so many other women, mother kept her money in a wallet "secreted" under the mattress of her own bed. It would seem that she wasn't too careful in keeping the place of concealment from Indian vendors. One day, mother reached for her bag in the usual place, only to discover that it wasn't there. Thinking that she might have put her money elsewhere by mistake she searched the house from top to bottom. There was no sign of her purse or the money. In desperation, for the wallet contained almost all the moth's allowance for the whole family, she asked each of us if we knew anything about the affair. We all denied it, of course. Zuzia then mentioned that she saw the chap that usually sells us milk nearby quite recently. Like a bolt from the sky mother suddenly saw what must have happened. Earlier that day she did indeed buy milk from him. That being the case there was no reason for him to be hanging around our place later on.

"It must have been the milk vendor!" she said out loud. "He must have seen where I hid the money and sneaked in when nobody was looking." She then looked around and said to my brother, "Romek. Run over to the Police Station straight away and tell them what has happened. Maybe they can help us." My brother run immediately to the Station and, breathless, reported the theft. The Polish policeman heard him out and started asking, what seemed a series of odd questions, like;

"Is your mother sure that it was an Indian that took the money?"

"Could she have mislaid or lost her wallet?"

"Have any of your neighbours been to visit you today?" etc.

Romek, puzzled and indignant, answered all the questions, emphatically in the negative and anxious, demanded immediate action. Reluctantly, the keeper of law and order got out of his office and asked my brother to come with him. They walked along a few hundred yards and arrived at an Indian Police Post on the Camp outskirts. As they walked, the man explained. "We are only here to keep order inside the Camp. Our unit has no authority over the local population and can't take any action outside the Camp boundaries. In such circumstances, we have to hand matters over to the Indian Authorities. The Indian policeman listened patiently as the story was repeated and disappeared into the back room. A few minutes later the man re-emerged and said,

"I've just had a word with the Sergeant. We're pretty sure we know who the vendor is and where he lives. Leave it to us. A detail will be dispatched to the village straight away. If he's the man we'll soon get to the bottom of the thing. Tell your Mother we'll be in touch."

With trepidation Romek returned home and relayed the events to Mother. She wasn't at all impressed with the way the matter was being dealt with. In despair she wailed, "This is all a waste of time. While these stupid men argue with us and among themselves, the culprit will get as far away as he wants! No use hoping. The money is lost for good."

Needless to say the event represented a major disaster for our family. The monthly allowance paid out to Mother, was calculated on the basis of the age of family members. For some reason the Authorities believed that younger kids like Zuzia and me cost less to feed that adults. The total amount Mother received each month wasn't enough to keep us reasonably fed. To put some aside was out of the question. There was nothing for it. We would have to borrow some money to survive, and then repay it out of our meagre allowances in the future.

To our delight and amazement, an Indian policeman came the next day carrying mother's purse. Almost no money had been spent. The officer reported that it was indeed the milk vendor that took the money. Just as Mother suspected. The man apparently went home to his village with his booty. Having discovered that his family wanted to have nothing to do with his action, he decided to "make a run for it". It took the efficient Indian Police no time at all to track him down and get the truth and the money out of the culprit.

Mother thanked the policeman profusely and promised not to put temptation in the way of any callers in the future. The whole household was relieved and delighted at the turn of events. We all also walked away with a highly elevated opinion of Indian Police efficiency and honesty.

As I said, our allowance was low, and Mother had great difficulties in making ends meet. This didn't apply to everybody. Some were better off because all or most of their children were over sixteen and so eligible for the adult's allowance. Others got a job, for which they received a good salary. Schoolteachers were a good example. Others started one form of enterprise or another. One old man, a cobbler by trade, opened up a shoe (or rather sandal) repair business, a woman discovered she could get a plentiful supply of offal and started preparing tripe on a commercial scale, yet another group of men got together and set up a slaughter-house and a sausage -making shop, also of course for profit.

Mother had to do something. But what?"

In the end she found her solution. One morning, as I was playing on the edge of our Camp I saw the silhouette of my mother appear on the horizon, walking towards me. Puzzled, I stood and waited for her to get closer. I couldn't imagine what she might have been doing out there, far away from the protection of our camp. To my surprise, in her train I saw two Indians carrying something heavy. They came closer and passed me without a glance. It would seem that mother was leading the men towards our apartment. My curiosity got the better of me and I left my friends behind and followed. When I arrived I saw mother proudly displaying her new acquisition. It was a Singer sewing machine.

"Now I'll be able to earn some money," she said. "Back home I used to do all my dress-making. I know there are plenty of well-off women that would be interested in my services."

Mother's assessment proved to be right. Women soon discovered that my mother had a talent and flair when it came to making dresses. It only took a look at a picture, for her to be able to cut the cloth and make a dress just like it. No figure, either thin or ample presented a problem. The income didn't exactly transform us into the camp's millionaires, but it helped. Later, other types of work came along, that also made good use of the machine. A lot of torn and damaged soldiers' uniforms arrived. The camp warden offered a reasonable "piecework" rate for anyone with a sewing machine. I recall mother spending many days and weeks, working through masses of uniforms. The sewing machine certainly proved it's own worth, and more than paid for itself.

I mentioned earlier that the Camp women developed a custom of doing their washing by the riverbank. I should have also mentioned that not far from our camp flowed the mighty river Vishnu. During the dry spells the river wasn't that impressive. After all, the hills where it originated weren't that far away. A little further down-stream was a dam. This was a pretty crude structure. The river span was filled with tall concrete columns, each about one and a half metre square. The distance between the posts was also one and a half meters. During the times of water scarcity wooden planks would be slid into slots to block up the dam and raise the water level. When the wet seasons came, the situation was reversed. At normal times the river didn't seem particularly formidable. Both Indians and Poles made full use of it. For one thing, fish seemed plentiful. I could often see Indian fishermen standing, waist-high in water, usually on the down-stream side of the dam, swinging their curious round nets. On the whole they seemed to walk away with reasonable hauls. My brother Romek developed an entirely different method. He would prepare a long and stout line and to it he'd fasten fishing hooks at regular intervals. In the evening he would take one end of the line and swim with it across the river. Having fastened the string securely and concealed it from view, he'd swim back and do the same on our side of the water. Next morning, early, he would return and retrieve the line. It always surprised me how many stupid fish would manage to get themselves caught on hooks without bait. The rest of the morning would be taken up by all of us cleaning and preparing the catch, followed by a feast of delicious freshly fried fish.

After a Monsoon storm, the river took an entirely different aspect. It broke its banks and grew so large that you couldn't see the other side. The water was fierce and yellowy-brown from the clay it picked up on its way. At those times, the waters seemed positively threatening and only a fool would come anywhere near them.

In spite of the fact that the river seemed gentle through most of the year, it had its deceptive currents and sudden drops. Many an experienced bather found this to be the case, sometimes to his cost. We reckoned that at least one person from our Camp drowned in the Vishnu each and every year of our stay in India.

I made frequent forays to the riverbank with my friends. I wouldn't venture into deeper water, as I couldn't swim. Some would cross the dam by jumping from one post to another. Again, I would refuse to follow. Standing on the top of the first column it wasn't hard to work out the options. If I jumped and made it I would have had to repeat the exercise a couple of dozen times to get to the other side. Even if I succeeded, there were another twenty-four jumps to be made to get back. If I failed and fell on the left hand side I'd surely drown, as I couldn't swim and the river was very deep at that point. If I fell off on the right hand side, I would crash onto bare rocks far below and also die. No. There was no favourable percentage in these kinds of stunts and I wasn't going to be goaded into them.

In spite of my assurances Mother was convinced that my visits to the river were dangerous and insisted that I was not to go there unless accompanied by an adult. It was never my intention to disobey Mother's orders but, on a nice sunny day, when all your friends are on their way, it's sometimes difficult to remember them. In the end, Mother became so exasperated that she took a rope and tied me to the dining room table, for all to see. If it was her intention to humiliate me, she certainly succeeded. I remember the feeling of being there, "on show," as if it were yesterday. Later she allowed me to go bathing in the river, provided that I went with my other friend Buba and his mother's friend. We both thought it was quite funny. Buba's "protector" was in fact invalided from the army. He had had a throat operation that had left his voice box inoperative. To speak he had to cover a hole in his throat with his finger. The opening was otherwise left uncovered and served as an airway to allow him to breathe. As I said, one day he took the two of us to the river for a paddle. Everything was fine until the man decided to join us in the water. As he waded over to us he suddenly fell into a dip and took in water through his unprotected tracheotomy hole. What followed, to our amusement, was a massive amount of noise and spluttering. It is amazing how cruel kids can be.

It's very strange. I always thought that there was little risk of me drowning in the river, as I was too cautious, or too cowardly if you prefer. Mother's actions were, in my view excessive and un-necessary. On the other hand it wasn't necessary to go all the way to the river to face such a hazard. One evening, one of my friends managed to wangle his father's bicycle for a little ride. A group of us gathered around. Each hoped that he might get lucky and this friend would let him have a go. I stood on the dwarf wall surrounding a local fire reservoir, absorbed in my friend's antics on the bike. Suddenly I lost my balance and fell in. In an instant I was drowning. The water was a good two meters deep, and my feet were nowhere near bottom. I started trying to shout and began thrashing about. The other boys saw what was happening. The proud owner of the bicycle dropped the machine, ran into his place and dragged out his father to help me. The man grabbed me as I was about to go under for the third time and pulled me out. Bewildered and shivering with cold and fright, I ran off home. When she saw me, Mother asked me what had happened.

"I nearly drowned in the reservoir up the top there!" I told her. I don't recollect Mother responding to that in any particular way.

I had always been afraid of water before then, and even more so since. It just goes to show. Sometimes you can try your hardest to avoid something, and it still manages to catch you unawares.

Another of my little adventures concerned cats. I have always been fond of all kinds of animals. I pleaded with Mother on many occasions to be allowed to keep one or another cuddly puppy, but on each occasion to no avail. I suspect she thought a dog would be too expensive to keep and perform no useful service in return. With cats it was a different matter. We seemed never to be without one or more cats in the house. Our first tomcat was a good mouser, but soon proved to be a severe embarrassment. We started getting complaints that the cat was stealing people's food. When one day we caught him with a large slab of meat belonging to our next-door neighbours Mother decided that this couldn't go on.

"The cat must go," she said. Then turning to my brother she continued, "Take him on a bus somewhere far away and lose him. I don't want him anywhere near this place a moment longer. "

Romek put the cat in a bag, tied it with a piece of string and set off. He travelled many miles by local bus, passing a number of villages. In the end, thinking he'd gone far enough, he alighted, let the animal out and took the next bus the other way.

"I've done it," he told Mother on his return. "He'll never find his way back here."

Mother was relieved and soon the whole incident (and the cat) was forgotten. Weeks went by. Until one day, lo and behold, the cat reappeared.

"That hasn't worked too well," Mother said. "There's nothing for it. You'll have to drown the rascal in the reservoir," (yes, the very same one that was nearly my undoing).

My brother wasn't very pleased with his task, particularly as all of us, and me most of all, started to loudly plead with mother for the cat's life.

"No," was her answer. "The cat must go. Get on with it," she added, turning to Romek.

The whole household went very quiet, as my brother took a stout rope, tied it around the animal's neck and attached a large stone at the other end.

"That should do it," he said. "I know cats can swim, but I'd like to see him try with this stone pulling him down to the bottom."

Off he went, cat under his armpit. Five minutes later he returned empty handed. Nobody wanted to hear any details of the foul deed he'd just carried out. We were all in mourning for the hapless creature. Later that evening we heard some movement in the bedroom. I went to have a look and, to my astonishment discovered the cat huddled under my bed, the rope still trailing behind. After that, Mother no longer had the heart to devise a new way of disposing of the cat and allowed him to stay.

The cat lived out his natural life with us. That is to say, until some natural disaster befell him and he never returned home. After this one, we kept other cats with varying success. At one time for instance, we had two young cats that had the habit of sleeping with me in my bed. One morning, to my horror, I found both the animals lying next to me - dead. I ran to Mother with the bad news and asked what could have caused this tragedy.

"I think you must have rolled over in your sleep and suffocated them," she said. "That's the only cause I can imagine. They certainly don't look as though they died of any disease or any other mishap."

That gave me double the reason to be upset. Not only did I lose my pets, but also on top of that I now felt like a murderer.

After that, other cats followed. We later had a she-cat, which eventually presented us with a litter. This was a source of pleasure for all of us until some unexplained plague befell our camp. Suddenly all cats throughout the settlement started showing signs of sickness and soon after keeling over and dying where they stood. To my distress our she-cat and her kittens suffered the same fate as other camp felines. This last loss hit me enormously. I buried them all in our garden, fashioned a cross for each, and planted flowers over their remains. It took me a long time to get over it.

Social life continued to develop in our community. My eldest sister was able to take part in pastimes not available to small kids like myself, joining various organisations like scouting etc. The rest of us managed to find our own amusements. For example, there was the camp cinema. The prices were nominal and most of us took full advantage of the facility. This was the time when I became aquatinted with "Popeye," "Zorro," "Cisco Kid" and other stars of the silver screen.

Mother favoured the Indian films. It wasn't that she understood the language. No. It was the fact that, as she put it, the love scenes were very romantic. By that, she meant that the lovers only sang to each other from afar. Seeing any touching, kissing or "worse" was out of the question.

Another matter that absorbed a lot of our time was church activity. It is well known that Poles are a Roman Catholic nation, and most of them practising Catholics and churchgoers. It was therefore fully in character that the church and activities connected with that Institution held an important place in our lives. Every Sunday we all went to mass, of course. In fact that was when I discovered my interest in music in general and my enjoyment of singing in particular. As I got on and started participating in church ceremonies, it was noticed that I had an outstanding boy's soprano voice. This was not a problem, except on occasions, at home when this or that woman would come and ask me to perform for her. I would be stood on the dining room table and asked to sing some well-known ditty. I usually did as I was told, but I certainly did not enjoy it. What I found fascinating was the notion of harmonising. In church I heard the Head teacher harmonise to various hymns. This I thought was beautiful and enchanting. I became determined to mimic her and learn this art for myself. With time, I in fact taught myself to harmonise to a moderate level without anybody's assistance.

Another aspect of religious practice was Confession and Holy Communion. Soon after arriving in Valivade, I joined other youngsters in Catechism instructions. Some time later, when the priest decided that we were ready, we made our first confessions and then, with great ceremony, our First Holy Communion. For me it was an interesting and an elevating spiritual experience. The trouble was that, having made the first step; regular visits to the confessional became obligatory. I have yet to meet a person, however devout who can honestly say that he or she doesn't dread the thought of their next confession. In that respect I was no different from anybody else. Luckily, we had a number of priests, and it was up to you which one you chose to go to. Opinions about each of them were soon established in the community. The story was that; the Parson, nicknamed "the elderly," was such a saintly person that he'd never tell you off in the confessional or give you a heavy penance to perform. A good choice. Another was nicknamed "the young". The story about him was that he was deaf in his right ear. He was another good choice, providing you approached him from his deaf side. He would prove to be no trouble, as he wouldn't even hear your sins. The last of our priests was called Nowak. He had no nickname. Nowak was the priest you went to only as a last resort. It was interesting to observe the situation in church during days of general confession. The largest queue was aimed at "the elderly". The next largest (but from one side only), was to "the young". To Nowak there was no queue.

Life for me on the whole was what everybody's childhood should, in my view, be. In the morning, not on school days of course, I would just slip on my denim shorts and off I'd go. The idea of wearing pith helmets, sandals and the like had been long forgotten. Every day was warm and sunny and fun with adventures around every corner. There were, of course, no fancy factory-made toys or games to be had. We had to make our entertainment and toys out of whatever came to hand. The usual material was clay. This was certainly plentiful. At some stage somebody hit upon the idea of making spinning tops. You simply took a solid piece of wood and, with the aid of a pocket-knife, fashioned it into a cone. The next process was to take a large nail, cut off the head and drive it into the cone's apex. That was all there was to it. You were now the proud owner of a spinning top. The real trick was to make it spin. To do that you had to take a string and, very carefully, wind it onto the top, making sure that, while on one hand the string is kept taut, the whole coil does not to fall off before you had a chance on the other to make use of it on the other. Other ways of entertaining ourselves included climbing liana trees; messing about with the many stray dogs roaming the camp...the list of possible amusements was endless.

Most of the year the weather was hot and sunny. The clay soil baked hard, and the sun burnt what little grass there was. The only time the weather changed was during the monsoon season. The hurricanes were something we all dreaded, young and old. First, a great stillness would descend. It was the kind of thing you could almost touch. Then the rain would start. Very large and widely spaced drops to start with. It would slowly grow in intensity until it became a deluge. Next was the wind, and this was the thing of which we were all most afraid. More and more ferocious hurricanes would develop. As soon as the tell tale signs would start, we would hurriedly prepare for the approaching onslaught. All window shutters would be shut tight and fastened, doors secured and fires in the kitchen put out. As the rain poured and the ferocious wind howled outside, we would all huddle, terrified, in the only place we thought safe. An onlooker would probably find it amusing to see the whole family huddled under the dining room table, looking very worried. What we were mainly afraid of was the roof tiles being blown off and coming down upon our heads.

We were lucky. Unfortunately not everybody escaped scot-free. After the attack was finally over we would come out and survey the damage. The rain would no longer be coming down, but all the isles between the barracks became torrents of fierce brown muddy water. We had to wait for the flood to subside before venturing out any further.

Eventually we could walk out and see the havoc caused by the storm. Telegraph poles would be lying, strewn about, clearly blown around by the wind like matchsticks; massive trees torn out of the ground roots and all. The power of the thing was incredible. Here and there damage could be seen also to human habitation; walls blown in, roofs collapsed or verandas destroyed. We all hoped that the occupants had escaped unhurt. This was usually so, but sometimes we would find out that one or more members of this or that family had been killed or seriously hurt.

The monsoon hurricanes, terrible as they were, were soon accepted as part of life. It was amazing how quickly life would go back to normal after each storm, all fear and damage forgotten - until the next time.

Years went by. My eldest sister finished her "Gimnazium" ('O' level equivalent), and went onto Liceum ('A' level equivalent). My brother later followed suit and, having finished his primary education took an entrance exam for the Grammar school, which he passed easily. To Mother's dismay however, just at that time a new school opened in the camp. The Authorities decided to offer a facility in technical education. Academically it was clearly intended to be below the level of the Grammar school. Having heard of the newly formed centre, he couldn't wait to apply. No amount of persuasion from all members of the family would make him budge. He was definitely going to the technical school. In fact, on reflection, it was the right choice for him. Although academic knowledge was easy for him to absorb, his heart was not in it. The type of thing offered by the new school was much more to his liking. He would come home, excited, and tell us about the technique of working wood or metal he'd just learned or, would actually bring the result of his labour home for us to see.

I too moved on. I was beginning to grow up, absorbing more and more at school. I readily took in as much information as I could to do with what it meant to be a Pole, even if temporarily deprived of the homeland I could only just about remember. Lessons in school, historical novels, stories and reminiscences being told by adults - indeed the whole society that surrounded me spoke to me of our homeland. After all, the camp really was a miniature Poland.

With all this to help me, I had no difficulty with my identity or imagining what it would be like when (and not if), we returned home. What I could not easily picture in my mind was what it *felt* like to be there. I was confident that I knew enough about the people, but what was the place itself like? It had to be very different from this parched land that surrounded me. I was, after all only four years old when we were "invited" to leave. Much too young to have absorbed any significant knowledge of my surroundings.

Almost by chance I got my wish. One day the librarian, having noticed that I had become an avid reader of all things Polish suggested that I take a novel by Boleslaw Prus entitled "Chlopy" (The Peasants). The work was in four very fat volumes, and many an older person might have considered the task of taking it on, onerous. I on the contrary, having been given an idea of its contents looked forward to immersing myself in its pages. The storyline involved life in a particular village in Poland and as such was not of particular interest. The parts in the book I found invaluable were the detailed descriptions of Nature. Each of the four volumes was named after a year's season; i.e. the first was called Spring, the second Summer, the third Autumn and the last, of course Winter. At the beginning of each volume Prus devoted many pages to detailed descriptions of the changes in the fields and forests brought about by the arrival of the new season. This was just what I was looking for. I lapped it all up. In my mind's eye I could see the buds breaking out in the Spring; riots of colour in the meadows during Summer; the peace and quiet of a forest under a thick blanket of freshly fallen snow. I read the whole four volumes avidly.

141

The contents left an impression on me, which was to stay with me forever.

Although our life was completely divorced from that of the locals, this fact didn't stop us from observing Indian customs with interest. One event I recall was a particular day each year when our hosts would chase each other with bottles of coloured water and sprinkle the victim in a variety of greens, reds and yellows. To us it was particularly noteworthy, as it was similar to our own custom called "Smingus Dingus". In Poland, this is an old pre-Christian custom and is probably still practised in some families. It entails pouring water (but not a coloured variety as is the case in India), over each other on the morning of Easter Monday. Another annual occasion was the "drowning of the Gods". A great procession would proceed towards the sacred river Vishnu. A great many images of various Indian Deities would be carried on biers. Among them, the largest figure belonged to "Ganesh" - a God with a man's body and the head of an elephant. The procession, flutes blaring and drums beating, would come to the riverbank and there, again with great ceremony the people would "drown" the figures representing their Gods. This was to bring them fortune and prosperity in the coming year.

Although we were unaffected by the war being conducted so far away, it's progress was followed by all with great interest. We heard of the Allied victory over the German Reich with great joy. It seemed that the time when we would return home couldn't be far away. Next we heard of moves in the now liberated Poland to form a new and democratic government. Although Communists, supported by the victorious Red Army were in ascendancy, Poles in exile were invited to return and participate in forming the new government. A representative of Polish Government in Exile, Mikolajczyk in fact took our Russian "liberators" and their henchmen at their word and returned. Many people in our camp followed his example and also asked to be repatriated. Alas, we soon discovered this to be another of Stalin's Machiavellian tricks. The communists took full control and Mikolajczyk had to flee for his life. I'm sure the people that chose to go back had good reason to regret their decision. My Mother was of course much too wily to be taken in. We stayed and waited.

In 1947 another momentous event took place. India was formally granted its independence by Great Britain. Needless to say, we again observed massive ceremonies and celebrations by our hosts.

The war was over. The news trickling across to us talked of Allied Armies returning home to England and other countries of origin like Australia and New Zealand. Polish divisions, forming part of the British forces, found themselves transported to England. Next, followed the process of demobilisation, and the reunification of families. Transports to the British Isles started to be organised. Those with husbands and sons in the forces were first. Many people left and the camp started to look deserted. We were still there. It looked as though we were never going to leave. Eventually Mother managed to track down a distant cousin in the Second Corps, now withdrawn to England, and on the strength of that, got us on to the next transport to England.

After weeks and months of uncertainty and anxiety, we were all delighted when Mother told us the news. Then, preparation started for yet another journey. This time the situation was different from our previous moves. Unlike earlier stopovers, we did live here in Valivade for many years. In that time, people can be expected to acquire and accumulate various articles of property, some too valuable to leave behind. Our main such article was Mother's sewing machine. Here my brother Romek came to the rescue. Since he still attended his technical school with all their workshops, he asked the instructors to be allowed to make a large wooden trunk. Appreciating the situation, the school authorities readily agreed and soon Romek proudly presented Mother with a magnificent and massive travelling casket.

The sewing machine was dismantled and packed in the coffer together with the rest of our belongings. On the 29th of January 1948 we boarded the train yet again, this time on the way back to Bombay. We travelled for many hours. During the night the transport briefly stopped in Poona. After we started moving on again somebody told us the terrible news. That night Mahatma Gandhi had been assassinated.

This act of violence shocked us all. Reprisals were expected. We only hoped that we wouldn't get caught up in any disorder as a consequence. Luckily the train reached Bombay without mishap and we were promptly transferred to the waiting ship.

The vessel was very large and impressive. *The Empress of Scotland* was a three-funnelled liner with a displacement weight of thirty six thousand tons. Having boarded, we could all enjoy our last view of the city of Bombay while waiting for the tide. As we waited, we watched the Indian boys diving by the ship. This wasn't done for sport alone. Passengers would throw coins into the water and the boys would dive to retrieve them.

Another matter also caught my attention. In parting, many people came to see us off. I noticed young Indian men involved in highly emotional farewell embraces with some of our women passengers. In some instances the women would be holding a bundle - a baby, obviously the result of a liaison between the woman and the Indian.

"She's taking her little Indian bastard to her husband in England, you know," I overheard some woman saying to her neighbour.

It seems not everybody kept their distance from the locals. "And yet how could she so brazenly take the proof of her infidelity to her husband? I was only twelve and still very naive. I had not yet learned that life is not just black and white, but many different shades of grey in between.

At last, on 1st February 1948 we were off on the morning tide.

Chapter 10

Imperceptibly, the enormous vessel started to drift away from the dock. Slowly, very slowly it edged away till in the end all the people lined up at the water's edge looked like dots on a distant horizon.

Once out onto the open sea, the Empress's engines came to life, all three enormous funnels smoking profusely. It didn't take long for the ship to attain the speed of knots that could be expected of a liner of her class.

Before long first the port and later all signs of land disappeared from the horizon. The day was bright and sunny and the sea was calm. We were cruising steadily. Conditions were ideal for us kids to set about investigating our new surroundings.

As could be expected we, the refugees travelled "steerage". The communal spaces with sleeping bunks way down in the bowls of the vessel. Up top we discovered a spacious open deck – a perfect space for all kinds of games. Ahead and towering above us we could see a further structure with another deck above it. Access to this section was barred. These were the first class cabins of members of the British Raj - British administrators and their families, now redundant, returning to "old Blighty" as India had become independent.

Journeys through the ship were to us one long series of discoveries. Everything seemed fascinating, complex and at the same time incredibly orderly. One of the novel gadgets we couldn't leave alone was the water closet. Not only did it contain this incredible flushing mechanism, but each cubicle also had a pocket full of beautifully clean white sheets of paper. Perfect for writing, and you could have any amount you wanted "for free"! As could be expected, toilets became rapidly denuded of paper, and the crew had quite a task refilling the paper holders as we emptied them. The novelty eventually wore off as we found other matters to occupy us.

As I said earlier, most of us kids spent a lot of our time on and around the deck, playing "hide and seek" and various other games. We found some of the crewmembers to be rather helpful and friendly. Some even joined in with us. It seemed a little surprising to us that "grown-ups" should want to spend so much time with us. This was certainly not our usual experience. It didn't take us long, however to discover that the crewmen had an ulterior motive. Whilst our transport carried no men to speak of, it did include a large number of pretty young women of "marriageable" age. I don't think marriage was foremost in the minds of the sailors however, as they tried every way they could think of to make their acquaintance with some of our girls. This was apparently where we kids came in. In an effort to improve their chances, they would ask us to teach them some terms of endearment in our language. We soon realised what was happening and agreed amongst ourselves to have some fun. The unsuspecting victim would be taught some rude phrase or a swearword and sent on his way to a potential conquest. The results, to our delight, were invariably disastrous. The approached girl, instead of rewarding the man with an inviting smile, would look dismayed, blush and run away. Sometimes the aspirant would also walk off with a smack across his face as a reward for his trouble. Eventually the sailors cottoned on to our games and gave up trying to enlist our aid in their romantic approaches.

The journey continued with good weather and steady seas. The word came that we were nearing the African continent and that soon we'd arrive at the port of Aden. Stories started circulating about Arabs trading with ship's passengers and the bargains that could be struck. We became very excited at the prospect of this new adventure and impatiently awaited the forthcoming new experience. For me however, Fate decreed otherwise.

One typically hot and sunny day, as we played our usual games on deck, I started feeling a headache coming on. Quite rapidly the pain increased to the point where I could no longer bear being exposed to the naked sun. I left my friends and made my way down to our temporary home. Mother was sitting on her bunk chatting with newfound friends. Not wanting to interrupt, I sat quietly by.

After a while one woman turned to Mother and said, "Your son looks very pale, sitting there. Is he all right, do you think?"

Mother turned and looked at me closely. "Is anything the matter?"

By that time my headache increased to such a point that it felt as though my head was about to explode. I was in such pain that I was hardly able to utter a word. Finally I managed to get out, "My head hurts," and burst into uncontrollable tears.

146

Worried now, Mother ran off to get the duty nurse. The woman came within a matter of minutes.

"The boy doesn't look right," she said. "I think I'd better get him examined by the ship's doctor."

The English doctor didn't take long to make his diagnosis. "The child has sun stroke," he said, "and a very severe case at that. He will need immediate treatment. Leave the boy with me. I'll find him a bed on one of my wards."

Before I knew it, I was stripped of my clothes, dressed in hospital pyjamas and placed in a hospital bed. A nurse gave me some kind of pill to swallow which, after a while eased my pain. What followed a little later wasn't quite so pleasant. The doctor returned, but this time in his hands he held an enormous syringe.

I must have looked a little anxious because the doctor turned to me and said, "Don't be scared. It won't hurt much. I'm afraid we'll have to give you an injection like this one every three hours day and night for a while." With that he proceeded to turn me over and stick the enormous needle into my left cheek.

I must say that I was too weakened by the illness to care. Day or night, a nurse would simply turn me over and stick the injection alternately into one or the other of my cheeks. After a few days I felt a little better. Mother on her visit was visibly relieved.

"You gave us quite a fright," she said. "The doctor said you have a bad case of sunstroke. To get you better, they're injecting you with penicillin. Still, you certainly look better now."

I was amazed: five years in tropical India, mostly running around without any headgear and I get sunstroke.

I was kept in hospital for over a week. Eventually the doctor pronounced me fit and allowed me to return to my family.

As I started walking down the corridor and onto the deck, a strange scene started to unravel in front of me. People were queuing to get into toilets, on deck, rows upon rows of people were being sick overboard. The whole place was in a mess. Eventually I reached my Mother and the rest of my family. All looked pale. Nearby stood a bucket into which someone would occasionally vomit. The fittest person at that moment seemed to be my sister Stasia so I asked her what this epidemic was that had clearly been spreading through the ship.

147

"It is simply sea sickness. In case you haven't noticed, the sea is quite rough. We're apparently crossing the Bay of Biscay. The sea is always rough here, they say."

I was spared the discomfort of "sea sickness" but, as I later discovered, lying in hospital I had missed many fascinating events when the ship stopped over in Aden, and later in Port Said, while passing through the Suez Canal.

Soon we left the notorious Bay of Biscay and the sea returned to its normal calm state. Passengers also returned to their previous routines, the discomforts of the rough seas forgotten.

After a few more days, on the early morning of the 14th February the *Empress of Scotland* slipped into Liverpool harbour. We had finally arrived in England. Together with others I came up on deck to look at our new surroundings. The sky above was leaden gray, vision limited by mist showed no more than the shadowy outlines of cranes and warehouses. The air felt damp and very cold.

"What miserable place have we come to?" I heard my elder sister exclaim behind me. "Maybe we should've stayed in India after all."

Later we disembarked and climbed into waiting lorries, which were to take us to our destination. After a couple of hours' travelling we reached the transit camp, which was to be our temporary home. Again I must admit the place was uninspiring. This is the first time I had seen the English Nissen Huts or as we named them, "Barrels of Fun". For the uninitiated, these simple and quick to erect structures were used throughout Britain in setting up military camps during the time of war. The barracks had the appearance of an enormous barrel cut in half and placed on its side.

On arrival we were allocated sleeping accommodation and taken over to the Stores to be "kitted out". The new clothes seemed to me very strange. The shorts in particular were not at all what I was used to. The material was thick and heavy, the garment had an internal lining and most of all, the leggings looked as though somebody had taken a pair of slacks and chopped them off just above the knees. On reflection, the clothes were obviously more suited to the English climate than the tropical gear we arrived in. It's just that I for one was by then, completely unaccustomed to temperate climate clothing.

As we started to settle in we discovered that the camp was largely deserted. Most buildings were empty and even the ones we occupied had many unused beds. The place was unbearably cold. The small cast iron stove in the middle of the hall seemed to give little heat. I and other kids took to running around and performing all kinds of exercises, simply to stop ourselves from freezing to death. Bedding consisted of a thin mattress laid on top of a wire-sprung frame, a thin pillow and two blankets. The first night I shivered under my covers, unable to fall asleep. The next day Mother came up with a good idea. She discovered that there were some loose bricks lying about outside and brought a few in. Before the night came she put a brick on top of the stove and allowed it to get really hot. Then she wrapped it in a piece of cloth and placed it in one of our beds to act as a "warming pan" or a "hot water bottle". She repeated the process until each of us was suitably fitted out. Thanks to Mother's inventiveness, that night and the following nights were not very comfortable, but bearable.

We didn't stay in Dalingworth (for that was the name of the place), very long. Soon we were off yet again. This time we were brought to a smaller camp further down South. The camp was called Howberry Park and was located by the river Thames, just a mile or so away from an old historic town of Wallingford in Berkshire.

Howberry Park made a very different and much more favourable impression on us from the first moment. The place was already partly occupied by Polish arrivals from other parts of the World. The camp was smaller, separate accommodation was provided for each family, and on top of that there was no sign of snow. Time had passed since our cheerless arrival in Dalingworth. Now the air was much warmer and there were definite signs of Spring in the air. The small camp huts were arranged alongside a driveway from the main road to a deserted Stately House situated by the river. Clearly, like so many English aristocrats, the owner had handed his property over to the Government as part of "the war effort". I must say that, in my view the contribution of the British Aristocracy in the Second World War was substantial, and on the whole largely unappreciated.

I should add that although ours was a strictly civilian camp, we soon discovered that there were at least two military camps nearby occupied by Polish units. Before long a stream of Polish soldiers started visiting our camp. The reasons weren't hard to work out. The fact that a lot of young unmarried Polish soldiers, about to be demobbed, would make contact with newly arrived polish girls made obvious sense. I would also add that our young ladies were no less interested than the soldiers were.

In our household the only "marriageable" female was Stasia, my eldest sister. Soon I began to see one suitor after another appear on our doorstep. After a few false starts, my sister finally made her choice and later married one of them.

We all settled in what appeared to be our new permanent homes. The British Authorities "processed" each one of us, issued us with Registration Documents and Identity Cards and proceeded to integrate us into their system. All people of working age were interviewed by Labour Exchange officials and offered employment. Both my sisters ended up working for Huntley and Palmers, sorting and packing biscuits in their Reading factory. In fact the number they took on was so many that a special coach was laid on to transport the workforce back and forth. My brother was placed in a local repair garage as a "gofer" on minimal wages. Later Romek looked around and found a job that paid a little better. Mother was also interviewed, but as her health wasn't good, she was crossed off the list of workers. After the War the country was rapidly rebuilding it's industries and required masses of labour. With this enormous choice, many unattractive manual jobs tended to be left unfilled. The new Polish labour force was therefore in many ways a Godsend for the much put upon Labour Exchange officials. At last they were able to provide a young strong and able-bodied workforce for all those low paid and unattractive vacancies. After all the Poles didn't speak English and didn't know the System. They didn't even know that there were better paid jobs out there or that that they had the right to refuse the employment offered by the officials. I suppose this happens everywhere with immigrants. They're bound to end up with the jobs nobody else wants.

I found that there was a substantial group of children in the camp. The age-range varied from pre-school to those who would soon be invited by the Government officials to join the country's labour force. In the beginning we wandered about getting to know our new surroundings and each other. The tireless authorities soon put a stop to all that. An instruction was issued to all Camp parents that went something like this.

"It is noted that within your household you have a number of school age children, specifically your son John aged nine, your daughter Anna aged twelve and your son David aged thirteen. Please note that it is illegal to prevent school age children from attending school and receiving education. Your children have been allocated places in the Primary School in Wallingford. Please ensure that they attend without delay to register and to regularly attend classes thereafter.

Your servant etc."

The letters were of course written in English. Not knowing what this was all about; parents queued up in the Administrator's office to get their letters translated. After they had discovered its contents they invariably became annoyed and more than a little worried. The correspondence certainly sounded to them like an unwarranted threat and not like a message from a "servant" as it was apparently signed.

The following Monday morning a whole group of boys and girls marched out of the camp and up the road to the Wallingford Primary School. On arrival we were registered and allocated classes.

As instructed, we all started attending daily. There was about six or seven of us boys in total. Girls attended a different establishment. The group was broken up into three different classes. The experiment was soon discovered to be a complete disaster. One must bear in mind that none of us except for one boy, who arrived at the camp much earlier, spoke any English whatsoever. We sat there in the classroom, saying nothing and absorbing nothing. The discourse around us was all gibberish as far as we were concerned. At break-times we all gathered together for comfort. The school and the teachers seemed uninviting, cold, uncaring and even hostile. We needed each other's company for reassurance and to hear our native Polish tongue. After a while the Headmaster realised that, although we'd been forced to obey the law by joining his school, now it was he himself who was not fulfilling his legal obligation by not providing us with any form of education whatsoever.

He tried another experiment. All of us were taken from the individual classes and put into one special group. A teacher was appointed to take charge of this newly formed "special unit". One must give the poor chap credit for trying. He used pictures and illustrations to try and communicate with us. Unfortunately the language gulf was too great. As I said, we spoke no English and needless to say, the teacher spoke no Polish either. The experiment continued for some time although it was becoming more and more clear that this attempt was also doomed to failure.

As time went on, children started reporting the goings on to their parents. The picture being painted began to look more and more worrying. Mothers started getting together and comparing notes. The situation appeared very serious. In the end a deputation went to the Camp Administration Office and demanded that something be done.

"My son finished five classes in India. He's short of only one year to complete his primary education," said my Mother who made sure she was on the Team. She continued, "The last teacher told me I've got a bright boy. I don't think its right that he should be pushed around in that English school and treated like a Dunce."

Other mothers and fathers made similar comments. In the end one of the fathers expressing general consensus unannounced;

"That's it. We've had enough. We're not sending our children to that school any more. They can put us in prison if they want. Our children's future is more important than their silly rules."

The Polish Camp Administrator worried by the turn of events, responded:

"I must apologise to all of you for what's happened. I fully understand and appreciate your concern. It probably doesn't help much but I can assure you that all that happened was done with the best intentions. I really don't know the answer to this problem. Before anybody does anything rash however, I must remind you that the British law requires all children under the age of fourteen to attend a recognised school and receive proper educational instruction."

Not knowing what to do next, they all fell silent. Suddenly somebody from the middle of group called out:

"Surely, we've got one or two teachers in the Camp. I know that my neighbour used to be a professional teacher back home before the war. Why don't we organise our own school here and allow our children to complete their education that they started in India?"

The Official's face brightened.

"That's a very good idea," he said. "To the standard educational curriculum we must also add a new element. We must provide them all with an intensive course in the English language. They'll all need it badly in the future whatever they do or wherever they go."

There were no dissenting voices and the meeting broke-up after the Camp Administrator promised to put a plan together as a matter of urgency and put his proposals formally to the Educational Authorities.

The Civil Servant responsible for this area at the Ministry of Education was delighted to receive the Proposals. He had already had numerous complaints from the Wallingford Primary. Until now he had considered the problem insoluble. In short order he replied, not only agreeing to the Plan, but also offering to allocate the necessary funds for school equipment, materials and, of course for the teachers' salaries. Soon afterwards the Camp school was formally launched and all children duly registered.

There were no more than a dozen of us altogether counting girls and boys of all ages. Not enough to form separate classes. The new teachers solved the problem by placing us all in one room and grading us and our lessons according to stage achieved in "normal" circumstances in India. I, together with three more boys and one girl were to do the last year of Polish primary education.

Rapidly, yet again, the camp organised itself into a self-contained Polish community. A tiny microcosm of pre-war Poland. A Roman Catholic priest was found to cater to the community's spiritual needs, various organisations were formed and various facilities like a library set up. I suppose the speed and efficiency with which the new community developed shouldn't be a surprise. After all by then, we were all used to "starting again".

Musical talents were soon discovered amongst the resident young men and a dance band formed. Dances proved to be very popular and well attended. As I said earlier, our community was an important "fishing spot" for the many Polish soldiers in the near-by camps waiting to be demobbed. After all, what better opportunity to meet a

153

nice Polish girl and prospective future wife than a dance in Howberry Park?

I, "for my sins," found myself conscripted by the priest to be his Altar Boy. In addition, I joined a newly formed Boys Scout Unit and also found myself dragged into a Folk Dance Team. Although I didn't exactly volunteer to serve at the Altar, I must admit that I rather enjoyed the prestige associated with my position as the Priest's only assistant. To encourage me in my duties, the Parson dug up from somewhere some impressive looking vestments and had my mother adjust them to fit me. Mother was, of course delighted to help. She had a secret hope that this might just be my first stage towards a spiritual calling. Little did she know. If anybody had suggested such a thing to me at that time, I'd have run a mile.

Scouting, on the other hand, I was eager to take on. The whole business of being a Scout lived up to my expectations. On reflection, I must give credit for that to our young Scoutmaster. In the evenings he would organise Campfire meetings where we sang various Scouting songs and received instruction on orienteering and other Scouting activities. Once, I remember, he took us on a trek. To all of us it was a great adventure. We seemed to be walking on for miles into some strange countryside. Eventually, when we became tired out and a little anxious, we saw our camp ahead of us and realised that we were in fact never far away from home. He simply made us walk around in circles. Still, we enjoyed the experience and I for one, never held this small deception against our Leader.

With the dancing team it was an entirely different story. Here I must admit that I found my youthful appearance a distinct disadvantage, and cause for bitter regret. The dance we generally practised (and on Polish national holidays performed), is called Krakowiak. This regional folk dance form originates from the area around the town of Cracow (or Krakow in Polish). It involves wearing strictly formal regional dress and is generally performed as a type of formation dance by four couples. To my dismay I discovered that, whereas all the more attractive girls made eyes at my tall friend Henry, and competed with each other for the privilege of partnering him at the dance, none were interested in exchanging any pleasantries with me. They even had to be forced to be my dancing partners. I suppose to them I looked like some sort of snotty nosed little kid. They certainly didn't want to be seen with me, not to mention any closer involvement.

I was devastated. I may have had the appearance of a small boy however; I was thirteen years old, going on fourteen. Inside I was very much an adolescent, rapidly developing an interest in the opposite sex.

As usual, life continued together with the usual mix of moments of excitement and periods of disappointment.

One day however, something unusual happened. My eldest sister Stasia, having spent some time whispering in a corner with Mother, announced to us all:

"You may all like to know that Edmund and I have decided to get married."

I was vaguely aware of the fact that her latest escort was a soldier named Edmund Gajewski. Of the fact that their relationship had blossomed into a full-scale romance, I had no idea. Still, the rest of the family and I were happy for her and said so.

The next thing to occupy us was the excitement of preparations for the wedding and the following reception. The ceremony was to take place very soon. Apparently Edmund was about to be released from the Service. In preparation for the civilian life, he contacted his sister in Bolton in Lancashire asking her to help him find a job. Unlike us, Edmund's sister, along with many other people of various nationalities, was DP This abbreviation stands for "Displaced Person". Whereas we came to England as "Political Refugees," fleeing the Soviet oppression, D.P.s had no such status. Our situation was justified by our experience in the Soviet Union. D.P.s circumstances were quite different and did not have the "political oppression" element. During the war, Germans would occasionally round up people from the streets and cart them off to their own country. The exercise wasn't intended as a holiday or a sightseeing tour. They were taken there as slave labour. People of all ages and different backgrounds were forced to work in German factories, "helping the war effort," or taking the place of farmers in the fields. With a few exceptions, work was very hard and treatment harsh. When the war ended and Allied forces had finally defeated the Germans, the English and American new occupying Authorities discovered these "displaced" people, often hungry and lacking shelter. Sometimes they were worse off, now that the war was over, than under the German yoke. This very substantial group presented a major problem to the Allied Authorities.

Most of them originated from Russia, Poland and other countries now under Stalin's control, and refused to return. The Officials had a problem. The English and the Americans couldn't be expected to just simply take them on. In spite of their difficult and distressing situation they couldn't be classed as political refugees. None of them could provide sufficient proof that their life would be in danger on their return home. It was decided that all that could be done to help them was to see if any Countries or Undertakings were prepared to offer them jobs.

The people were all interviewed, registered, sorted by age, gender and nationality and placed in camps where they were given food, clothing etc. One question each person was asked at the end of interview was, "If a suitable job could be found for you, which country would you like to live in? Please state three destinations in order of preference."

Needless to say, most put United States as their preferred option with other countries such as England, France, Australia etc as alternatives. Not many managed to find their way to this new country of "milk and honey". The Americans didn't have large demands for labour, and controlled the influx of immigrants very carefully. England on the other hand was in full flow of reconstruction and various Industries and individual businessmen were crying out for more labour. Representatives of British State-controlled Industries as well as Personnel Managers of major companies started coming over, interviewing selected candidates and in some cases, offering jobs in the United Kingdom.

Normally the offer would be to come and live in Great Britain, on condition that the lucky candidate continued to work for the Organisation making the offer. Moving around once in England wasn't allowed. Most jobs were located in the industrial areas like Yorkshire, Lancashire or the Midlands. The type of industries included coal mining, wool and cotton mills and heavy steel industry.

It was no coincidence that Edmund's sister lived and worked in Bolton, a centre of wool production. In fact she had secured a job in one of the Mills. After hearing from her brother, she enquired about vacancies and discovered that her employer was still short of labour and that getting a job for him in the same Establishment would be no problem.

With their immediate future secured, the couple made their final preparations and were soon married in our little Camp chapel. The reception was organised by Mother and took place in our living quarters, cramped that it was. The number of guests was by necessity small. As was our custom, one of the main guests of honour was our priest who had earlier presided over the ceremony. We all had a good time. It was on this occasion that I was first introduced to alcohol. Unaccustomed to these sorts of beverages, I got drunk good and proper. My brother was shocked and said that I was on the way to becoming an alcoholic. Mother surprisingly, seemed much more tolerant of my condition. Perhaps this could be put down to the fact that her experience of life was much more extensive than Romek's.

After the wedding, the couple, having spent their obligatory honeymoon in a London hotel, departed to Lancashire. Our family group was now reduced to four.

I found my last year of Primary School quite interesting; I particularly recall some Polish history lessons. The subject was very different to the kind of stuff we had to memorise in previous years. We had finally arrived to a stage in our history, which was so recent that some older, still living people might have lived through it. This made the events much more real and relevant to me. Similarly, I found myself learning about recent exponents of Polish prose and poetry. This I also found fascinating. Unlike my early years in India I enjoyed school in Howberry Park. Even learning English was engaging. "All those strange new words," I thought. The language seemed to have no rules. The only way to progress was to learn it "parrot fashion". Still I persevered. After some time I started to develop a "feel" for it. I discovered that I could put together sentences in correct order and even spot errors in badly phrased statements. "This business of learning English is fun," I thought. I discovered later that my aptitude for this new language was a distinct asset.

Extra-curricular activities were a different matter. One of our teachers took it into his head to teach us book–binding. He obviously thought this craft represented a useful trade, which would put us in good stead for the future. I must admit that I didn't share the man's opinion. I found the work boring, tedious and dirty. Try as I might, I couldn't develop any enthusiasm for the tasks involved. Judging by my teacher's occasional comments, it showed. I must confess that bookbinding was the last thing I imagined myself doing when I reached adulthood. My mind moved on higher planes in those days. Given a choice I'd have wanted to become a philosopher. The type of matters that absorbed me were more along the lines of whether life had meaning or not, and why we were here. Pedestrian activities like bookbinding in my mind were completely irrelevant in the great scheme of things.

Time passed. In the summer of 1948, the school year ended and I received my Certificate. I passed all the subjects without great difficulty. We were, at last free to simply have fun.

One day Mother called me in and said she wanted to have a "serious" talk with me. I didn't like the sound of that much, and immediately searched my mind to discover the reason for which I might be in trouble. Still, the only thing I could do was to sit still and wait for events to unfold.

"Yesterday all the parents of children from your year had a meeting with the Headteacher," she said. "He told us that he had some good news. Apparently there's a Polish Technical Secondary School not very far away. He asked if we'd like the boys to go there. Of course, there would be an entrance exam, but he didn't think it should be a problem for us." She paused and then asked, "Well? What do you think? I'll be a great opportunity you know. Shall I ask them to put you down on the list?"

I couldn't hide my disappointment. "Mother," I cried out. "You know very well I'm not mechanically minded like Romek. This school would have suited him, I imagine, but I can't see myself getting anywhere in a school like that. Surely there's got to be something else."

Mother, looking concerned explained, "I know what you mean. I asked the Head-teacher to explain what the school is all about. He told me that this is not, definitely not, the kind of set-up Romek attended in India. It's not just a place to train future mechanics. I have been told that this is a high standard establishment. The education you'll get there could help you get on in all sorts of jobs. Who knows, you might even be able to continue with some kind of further education afterwards. And the answer to your question is no; there seems to be no other school available. I must tell you that the teacher was delighted to have secured this chance for you. He's sure this is a golden opportunity for all of you boys."

I remained unconvinced, however it seemed clear that I had no choice but to go along with the arrangements. "Put me forward," I finally said to Mother. "We'll see how I get on. Anyway, I might not even pass the entrance exam and come straight home." All the arrangements were duly made.

On a rainy morning on the twenty second of August 1948, I and three of my school friends set off on our way to Lilford; the new school. Mother packed a suitcase full of clothes and anything else she thought I might need during what would be a long stay away from home. I could hardly lift it. With trepidation we all boarded a bus bound for Reading, accompanied by the teacher responsible for our predicament. He saw us off to the Reading railway station and gave us his final bit of advice,

"This is the train you are to board," he said, pointing at the waiting carriages. "Don't forget. You get off at Thorpe, just after Thrapston station." He then looked at the four of us, all huddled together. "Good luck to all of you. I'm sure you'll all pass with flying colours and do well afterwards. Off you go and have a great time."

Chapter 11

Although full of apprehension, I found the journey quite exciting. To start with there was the view of the ever-changing panorama of the English Midlands countryside to be seen out of the compartment window. Looking out, I suddenly realised how little of England I'd seen up to then.

In fact I found the view fascinating and absorbing. We passed through the pride of English farming country. The land, gently undulating, was neatly divided into fields of varying shapes and sizes. The most favoured method of fencing appeared to be the hedgerow, although occasionally one could see fields separated by stone walls. Here and there clumps of trees would break up the skyline. Some fields displayed golden, ripening wheat while on others I could see grazing cattle and occasionally some horses. It all looked rich, lush and well ordered.

"How different it all seemed from the arid, dry and sun-scorched countryside I left behind in India such a short time ago." I mused.

The train kept trundling on monotonously. Nothing was happening. Locked in our private thoughts, we all sat silently. My friend Henek suddenly interrupted our reveries.

"Listen guys," he shouted as he entered the compartment. "I've just been to the next carriage. A load of boys boarded on the last stop and guess what. They're all Polish!" he continued. "I've just been chatting to them. It seems they and many more are on their way to Lilford to sit the Entrance Exam like us." Seeing little response he added, "The rumour is that the test is going to be tough. Depending on how many applicants turn up, they may reject half of us or maybe even more."

Seeing consternation in his companions' eyes, satisfied, he sat down.

My immediate mental response was, "If the exam is to be so hard, maybe I'll be going straight home afterwards. After all I've never been any good with mechanical things."

The thought of going back cheered me up. "Maybe failing to get into the Technical School will be a good thing." I thought. "Who knows. There may well be opportunities afterwards that suit me better."

The journey continued without further interruptions. We passed station after station. At long last we saw the name "Thrapston" on a platform as the train went past.

"The next stop is ours." I said.

It seemed only minutes after that the train came to a halt. My friends all grabbed their belongings and made for the door. I too started tugging at my heavy suitcase and manoeuvring it the same direction.

We finally alighted. What confronted us was bewildering. Apart from us four and some lads next door that we knew about, almost half the train seemed to have emptied. We had all however, found ourselves literally "in the middle of nowhere". Thorpe wasn't a station. It was really no more than a halt. There wasn't even a platform there, nor was there any Railway Guard or any other Official. We all simply stood there bewildered, watching the train pull away.

We were stranded. Nobody was there to meet us. We all knew that our destination was "The Polish Technical School at Lilford". Unfortunately we could see no signs directing us to the school or even to a place called "Lilford".

A whole bunch of us, probably over a hundred in number stood there not knowing what to do next. Eventually some boy called out,

"There's only one path leading away from here. Our destination is bound to be somewhere along that road. I don't know about the rest of you. I'm walking."

Everybody followed the boy's lead and the trek commenced. Before long the line stretched hundreds of yards along the road. I found myself at the end of the line. Hardly able to lift my case, I couldn't see how I was going to keep up.

To my relief after a period of time, some assistance did arrive. This consisted of no more than two small vans. To provide transport for this number of boys with these two vehicles was clearly out of the question. The only thing our "School Representatives " could offer was to transport out luggage. We ourselves had to make the journey on foot.

We walked for what seemed hours and hours. My stature or physique wasn't suited to such long and arduous exercise. Even without my suitcase I was getting to the end of my energy reserves. At long last we appeared to be reaching our destination. As we turned into the straight road (so typical of approaches to English stately homes), we first saw some small huts of the type we occupied in Howberry Park. The huts were dilapidated and obviously abandoned some time ago. We then crossed a small bridge and at last found ourselves on the grounds of the School.

This time the barracks were of the larger variety; the sort we encountered in our transit camp of Dalingworth. The camp seemed quite large, with the buildings, in groups, separated by generous areas of open space. Everything, by contrast, looked neat and well maintained.

What followed was the usual bureaucratic procedure. We were all marched into an administration building and one by one gave our particulars, which were meticulously recorded by the one clerk processing us all. Eventually exhausted, we were taken to the canteen and given something to eat. Afterwards the applicants were broken up into four groups and allocated temporary sleeping accommodation.

Like the others I was given a bed with a thin mattress, a hard pillow and a blanket. In spite of the obvious discomforts, exhausted, I was soon fast asleep. Next morning, after a sparse breakfast we were marched off to examination rooms. I must admit that I was relieved. I expected the exam to comprise some impossible questions. Instead I found the arithmetical tests quite basic and demands with regard to the Polish language a positive pleasure. Of the English there was no examination.

Some hours passed, during which the authorities left us alone. This gave us an opportunity to look around the Camp and get to know other newcomers.

At three o'clock as instructed, we all reported at the Dining Hall to discover our fate. A list of names of successful applicants was prominently displayed on the Notice Board. Everybody rushed forward to find out if they could see their name. I, not feeling like a fair match to most of the boys, stayed back and waited. Soon I heard shouts of joy, interspersed with groans of disappointment from those who, having not discovered their names, concluded that they had failed to get in. In the end the crowd thinned out and I was able to look up my own name. It was there all right. I went to search out my friends

162

from Howberry Park. It seemed all four of us got through. This either spoke well of our Camp teachers, or meant that some lads' basic education was sadly neglected. Probably a bit of both.

Anyway, I was in. My hopes of going back and trying something else were blown.

Later that day, while the unsuccessful applicants got ready to go back home, the rest of us were allocated what was to be our permanent accommodation. I found myself in one of the large barracks together with twenty-nine other lads. My friends from the Camp were also in the same class as me. The facilities were, to say the least, Spartan. Each one of us was allocated an iron bed, a thin mattress, a hard, Army style pillow, a couple of blankets and two sheets. In addition we were provided with little wardrobes, which were stood next to each bed, and one last piece of furniture; a chair. This last item was to serve a double purpose. Firstly, it allowed the "owner" to sit within his minute space on something other than his bed. The second use for it was to be during lessons. We were expected to take our chairs out of the dormitory every morning and place it behind our deck in the top section of the building, designated as our Classroom.

After we all settled in, our Form Teacher introduced himself and gave a little talk on the rules we were to live by.

"In the first instance," he commenced, "you must understand that I, as your Form Master bear the responsibility for, not only your education, but also all other functions which would be normally controlled by your Parents. I am in effect to be your "In Locum Parentis". This means that, if you need something, or have a problem of some sort, you are to come and talk to me about it."

He allowed us to digest what to most of us and certainly to me, was a profound statement. It never occurred to me that somebody, other than my Mother, could have the kind of power over me this stranger was talking about. It was certainly something to think about.

After a suitable pause he continued. "As you arrived, you will have seen a large bell on a frame in the middle of the Camp. From now on your life here will be ruled completely by this instrument. The bell will ring for Reveille. It will also signal the time to go for breakfast, it will let you know when each lesson period starts, and so on and so forth until the time for Lights Out which, by the way is at eleven o'clock every day without exception."

"One more thing," he added. I appreciate that it may be difficult for you to come to me with some of your concerns. To help you settle in, we've appointed a Senior Boy to be your Prefect for the first year. I will introduce him to you later. You'll find him a very friendly and helpful chap."

With that he went away and left us to our own devices.

A little dazed by the developments, I started to unpack and place my meagre belongings in my little wardrobe. Later that same afternoon our Master returned briefly, bringing with him our Prefect.

"This is Staszek," he said. "He's here to get to know you all. If you have any questions, I'm sure he'll do what he can to help."

The teacher then promptly left, leaving us with the young man he'd just introduced. Within minutes we were all crowding round him. Staszek was by appearance and clearly by Nature a very friendly, amiable and approachable individual. What a contrast from the ascetic, austere, cold and humourless image our Housemaster presented. Staszek looked to us kids like a grown man. He was of medium height and bulging with muscles.

"Let me first tell you something about myself," he started. "I am about to start my last year here. When I first came, this was a Sea Cadet Training Centre. Even then the Authorities realised that there's likely to be little call for trained soldiers of any kind, and switched to Technical Education. I'm sure you're all homesick and want to be with your mothers. I can understand that and I don't blame you for a moment. You're lucky. In only a few weeks, at half term you'll go home. I am an orphan. There is no mother or father waiting for me during School breaks. It may not feel that way to you just now, but I for one think you're all lucky. Lucky to have a family to go to. Not so for me."

Seeing our sad faces he brightened up and added. "Never mind. For now you all will be my family. Any questions whatsoever, don't hesitate to bring them to me. If you get any trouble from other boys, again come straight to me. I don't like violence, but I reckon I can lick any body in this Camp if I have to."

164

We all took to our prefect immediately. Soon we sat around while he told us all sorts of stories about himself and about life in the School.

After his visit, somewhat heartened, I went outside to look around. The Camp was quite large. Barracks, similar to our own were organised in groups of six to eight, with large open spaces in between. The groups were connected by covered passages. It all appeared very clean, orderly and well maintained. Far away on the other side of the main road I could see a large structure. Curious, I decided to investigate. As I came closer, I realised that I was approaching an "English Stately Home". At first I wasn't sure whether or not to continue. "I might be trespassing." I thought. "What if somebody comes out and asks me what I'm doing here?"

I saw no movement or indeed any sign of life emanating from the house so decided to continue. When I finally arrived, I saw that the whole Establishment was empty and deserted. Although it looked undamaged, it was obvious from its general appearance that the place had not been inhabited for some years. The place was certainly imposing, and originally designed in a grandiose style. A typically straight road crossed an open lawn to arrive at a large open driveway in front of an imposing double stairway. At the top I could see enormous entrance doors set within a portico with Ionic columns. The three-story building stretched to either side. The whole facade was constructed in grey limestone, presumably a product of a local quarry. The two wings turned away through ninety degrees to form a large yard at the rear of the Mansion. As I walked further on I saw intricately laid out gardens, now of course in a state of neglect and decay. The whole area might have at one time, been sculpted by the famous "Capability Brown".

Quite fascinated by my discoveries, I walked on.

Soon I came to the bank of a river. This was, I was to discover later, the Dene. The River wasn't very wide. On my side I could see, what was clearly a bathing area. On the other, a footpath running along the bank, and open fields.

Pleased with my investigations, I returned to my barrack. - my "new home".

165

We all chatted and generally tried to get to know each other. The evening came before we knew it. It was eleven o'clock and "time for bed". As the lights went off we all climbed into our beds. After such an eventful and tiring day sleep came almost immediately. Suddenly lights came back on and I heard loud voices at the end of the Dormitory.

A couple of women from Administration were standing near the entrance. One of them called out,

"Don't get alarmed. As you were told, it's unhygienic to go to bed in your underwear. We're here to check that none of you have gone to bed with your pants or vests secreted under your pyjamas." As we all sat up in our beds, dazed, the two marched down each row approaching each boy in turn and sticking her hand down his pyjamas. We weren't overjoyed at this performance but tired, we soon settled back and fell asleep.

When the performance was repeated the next night and the one after, a lot of us started to get concerned.

"I know what the old witches are up to," said my neighbour. "Well they're not getting any more cheap thrills at my expense." We all agreed that to say the least; the women's behaviour was suspicious and decided to put a stop to it. The next night, when the "night patrol" arrived the first boy approached refused to be manhandled. The next was the same. The women, puzzled, stopped and one called out: "What's this? A mutiny?" she asked, laughing. At that one of the lads replied, "We all think there's no more need for your inspections. If you'll recall the last two nights you didn't catch anyone of us "with our pants on" so to speak. We now understand the School Rule about that very well and think your "inspections" are no longer necessary any should be discontinued." Rather boldly he added, "If you don't like what I'm saying, and I speak for the others as well, I suggest you make a complaint to the Headmaster."

The women never reappeared after that. This confirmed our suspicions about the zeal with which they carried out their duties. Still, the matter was over and done with. Soon, apart from the occasional joke, the whole episode was forgotten.

The School routine was the most strictly regimented way of life I'd experienced until then, and, I must confess, also ever since. If anybody equates our "live-in" circumstances with the English Boarding School type of Establishment, then I can assure them that they are sadly and profoundly mistaken. Our life was certainly no easy ride. Our days were regulated by the School Bell. This meant that we were all marched from one place to another all day without a moment to ourselves. The only brief period during which we were left to our own devices was a couple of hours in the afternoon between lunch and afternoon tea. Even in the evening we had to get back to our classrooms and do "supervised homework". This may all sound horrible and reminiscent of a Borstal regime. In fact life was quite cheerful, and teachers not inhuman. I think, having all spent years in the Army, this is the only way they could envisage organised life. I'm sure they'd all be shocked if they were to be told that they run the Establishment like a Penal Colony. Another difference between our Camp and an English Boarding School was the matter of service. The School was clearly run on a shoestring as far as finances were concerned. Apart from teachers and instructors, wage-earning staff were kept to a bare minimum. The pupils themselves carried out most of the labouring tasks. This for example, included kitchen duty, where the boys would peel all potatoes and other vegetables, wash dishes and cooking pots, clean the floors etc. Another task was for a "Duty" team to go around cleaning the whole Camp. If a new football pitch was required, the boys would provide physical labour. Goalmouths would be fabricated, again by pupils, in the School Workshops.

The first year seemed to take forever. I was certainly not the only one that counted the days to the next trip home. During my brief visits to Howberry Park the biggest joy was simply to do nothing. This was an obvious reaction to the regimented and busy life in School. Another pastime, also a reaction to school-life, was sleeping-in. For the first few days after my return I would luxuriate in staying in bed, sometimes right up to noon.

At last the first year was over and we all went away for long summer vacations. On our return we discovered that, unbeknown to us, the School Authorities carried out assessments of our individual performances and rearranged us into Streams based on our abilities. The top two streams were intended for the more theoretically able while the following ones were meant for the boys with a more practical bent. I and the three other boys from my Camp found ourselves in the first stream. Whether this was due to a superior intellect or, again the result of our Camp teachers' labours, I cannot tell.

We were re-housed into a different barrack, named "J". This block and this class name were to be ours for the rest of our stay in Lilford. After a period of settling in again and getting acquainted with boys we hadn't met before, life returned to the usual School routine. I coped with schoolwork well enough, although my place in most subjects was no more than a "good average". One possible explanation for my lack of outstanding accomplishment was the fact that my adolescence was a period of emotional intensity and turbulence. I would also add that I've never made any claims to brilliance in any subject.

One area I was particularly ill equipped for was Workshop Practice. Try as I may I seemed to be unable to fashion anything with my hands to anything like an acceptable standard. I simply wasn't cut out to be a mechanic. My talents, if any, lay in more theoretical fields.

As I have said before, I looked much younger than my age. This, in a youth going through puberty, can lead to terrible frustration. Girls, after all, are not inclined to show any interest in lads that look half their age. Adults, also tend to ignore the opinions of somebody that looks like a child. There were, on the other hand, occasional moments when this "affliction" of mine worked to my advantage. Here I must mention that one of the lads from Howberry Park by the name of Henry Okolotowicz and I developed a close friendship, which lasted throughout my stay in Lilford. Another thing I should mention was the fact that, although Henry was a little younger that me, he was much taller and generally looked my senior. Once, as I recall, we were both returning to school by bus. I, as was my custom I'm ashamed to say, asked the conductress and received without a quibble, a half-fare ticket. She then approached my friend who also asked for the concessionary fare.

The woman looked at him and said, "You're not under fourteen. Who do you think you're kidding! Let's have your money for the full fare, or else get off."

My so-called friend then proceeded to "sell me out". "Of course I'm under fourteen." He shouted. "Anyway, you just gave him a half ticket," he said, pointing in my direction, "and he's a year older than me."

The conductress glanced in my direction and retorted, "Rubbish. The little boy must be half your age. You can stop this nonsense here and now. Either you pay your full fare or out you go." Frustrated and angry, Henry dug deep into his pocket to find the extra money for his full ticket. Throughout all the proceedings, I sat quietly, not uttering a single word.

In spite of all I've said, I settled down to life in School and began to enjoy it. The strict routine ceased to be a burden and became second nature. Although I spent most of my time on the Campus, there were compensations. One of them was a cinema. For a sixpence one could see a main feature film every Saturday evening. In addition, a Polish Touring Theatre would occasionally come to visit us. I must say that everyone always enjoyed the Revues tremendously. On reflection, I think the performers; old wartime lags like Refren for example, did as well. After all, I doubt that grown-up audiences would have received them with equal enthusiasm. To them we responded with youthful joy. Something they in turn revelled in themselves.

Another of my diversions was to be music. Our severe-looking first year form Master turned out to be the Music Teacher. I always associated music with emotion, and so found it incongruous that a man so apparently cold and lacking in any sort of exuberance should have taken up music as his profession. In fact he proved to be a very able teacher of the subject. He not only taught us to sing Polish and English songs, but also introduced us to the art or reading musical notation. It was to him that I must ascribe my later preoccupation with the subject.

As time went by, it became apparent that our class contained an unusually high number of budding musicians. After each trip home one more of my classmates would turn up with some musical instrument. Pretty soon our Dormitory was filled with a cacophony of sound each afternoon "free-time". One chap would sit on his bed and start playing some tune on his accordion, another would work through scales on his cornet and yet another would start making indescribable sounds on a violin. You would think all this would put me off music and cause me to spend as little time inside our hut as possible. In fact, strangely enough, on me these activities had the opposite effect. I started getting more and more interested in what they were up to. Occasionally discussions on the subject of music would ensue. These I also found fascinating. I began thinking, " wouldn't it be great if I could put my hands on some sort of instrument and also learnt to make music like the others". This obsession occupied my mind for some time.

"It's all very well, but what instrument should I take up?" I debated with myself. A piano would be great but this was completely impractical. The few instruments on the Camp were spoken-for. To get the use of one for regular practice was out of the question. Accordion wasn't much to my liking and, in any case, the instrument would be much too heavy for my small and feeble frame. I simply couldn't make up my mind. One day I overheard a conversation amongst the more musically "immersed" classmates. One expounded how the violin was the noblest of musical instruments because it most closely imitated the human voice. "That's it," I decided. "Somehow or other I have to acquire a violin, but how?" I wondered. After some thought I decided to approach my brother and my sister Zuzia who by that time lived in London. In both cases I drew a blank. They either didn't know where one could get such a thing or pleaded poverty. To be fair to them both, their wage level didn't make saving a particularly painless exercise. I shouldn't have been surprised that neither felt themselves in the position to satisfy, what looked like a mere fancy of mine. Although I understood, I couldn't help being disappointed. It was therefore a great and an enormously pleasant surprise when I got a letter from my elder sister Stasia telling me that she'd solved my problem. "I've got some good news for you" she said. "I met a man in the Polish Club in Bolton who had a violin he no longer needed. I bought it for you and this beautiful instrument is now here and waiting for you to collect it. If you come over to visit us here during your summer vacations, you can take it away and start using it."

I was overjoyed. As soon as I could, I went to see the Music Teacher. "I'd like to start taking violin lessons next term," I said. And added with pride, "My sister bought me a violin. I'll bring it with me on my return from vacation."

I couldn't wait to get my hands on the instrument. Eventually I made my way to Bolton. After initial greetings Stasia went upstairs and returned, carrying a long black case. Excited, I opened it immediately. The instrument looked beautiful. Apart from the violin, the case contained a bow and all the necessary accessories. I knew nothing about playing technique, but couldn't resist having a go. Even in my inexperienced hands, the instrument produced a loud, rich and velvety sound. Overjoyed, I put the instrument carefully away. Next day I went out to a music shop and equipped myself with the necessary volume of "Violin for beginners". I was now ready. I only needed to get back to school and commence my instructions and my career as a musician.

As arranged, on my return I started attending individual lessons and being tutored in the use of the instrument by our teacher. During afternoons another screeching sound was added to the cacophony in our living area, as every day I practised my last lesson. As time went by my enthusiasm and dedication to music and the violin in particular kept on growing. I started copying tunes out of other people's books for myself, ordering various additional volumes of exercises and music and even acquired a book on Harmony and Counterpoint. My imagination was completely captivated by the Muses of Music. In my dreams I could see myself performing some impressive composition on a stage like my hero Yehudi Menuhin, or being acclaimed as an outstanding composer. The fact that my stubby little fingers weren't well designed for my chosen instrument didn't discourage me. It only made me practice all the harder.

The Form Master of Class "J" was a rather jovial and easygoing teacher. His subject was Geography. He too was a music "nut". Many a time he'd come into our hall, pick up someone's violin, (usually mine) and pace up and down playing some tune or other. His favourite was the Argentinean tango by the Spanish name of "Arana de la Noce" - a piece of sheet music I bought on one of my many excursions to a music shop.

Schoolwork proceeded at its own pace. As time went on, changes in the Curriculum became noticeable. One obvious change was that, possibly under the pressure of the Ministry of Education, some subjects were dropped. Unfortunately one of them was Geography, which meant that our Form Master became redundant and was forced to leave. Another was the increasing stress in the teaching of the English language. This applied to both academic vocabulary and

171

technical jargon. It was amusing to observe the workshop instructors and classroom lecturers struggle to communicate with us entirely in English. By these moves our futures and future prospects were being formulated. I must admit that nobody especially missed the subject of Geography. What did disturb us however, was the sudden loss of our Form Master. After all we'd been with him for two years and by then had established an easy and relaxed relationship. This is not to say that he was lax on rules or discipline. When the need arose he was able to be as tough as anyone else. In fact the need hardly ever arose. The fact is that we all grew to rather like him and wouldn't have wished to do anything which would cause him problems. We were helpless in the face of such decisions. Unfortunately some of my colleagues took out their frustration on his replacement. Although, as the highest stream and the most "intelligent" class we were not known as troublemakers, the new man was almost reduced to tears on many occasions, and after only a month gave up the post. To put a lid on it, the Head decided to place us in the tender care of Deputy Headmaster, a known disciplinarian. We didn't push our luck any further and the mutiny fizzled out.

Other aspects of Curriculum changes came to the fore much later. As the highest stream we received the highest level of theoretical tuition, most of us reasonably expected to continue onto Higher Education. It was therefore a terrible shock to discover that The Head's application for permission to hold G.C.E. Exams was refused. The only form of external tests made available were the Part-time Educational System of Ordinary National Certificate. As the English Educational Authorities seemed unable to assess our attainments, we were obliged to take Preliminary exams, these to be followed by the first year examination called S1.

Although I did not regard myself to be one of the classroom "geniuses," I passed the first and then the second examination without any difficulty. In fact all the questions seemed too simple. The material we were covering at that time was far in advance of that required for S1.

At last the final moment started to appear on the horizon. Our final year was soon coming to a close. Strangely, by then I grew out of being homesick and counting the days to the next leave. To me at that time Lilford was home, and the place where my Mother lived was just somewhere to visit.

Our Careers Officer started calling us in one by one. The idea was presumably to assist us in our future progress. In fact two boys, considered to be top of our class, were given an opportunity to continue further education. I'm still not sure what form it was to take, as a Degree Entrance required satisfactory GCE results, and we weren't even given the opportunity to sit for them. Another two, the next highest in the eyes of the School Authorities, were lined up with some Polish engineering firms. The deal was that they were to take up apprenticeships as draughtsmen. For the rest there seemed no special favours. When my turn came, the woman seemed off-hand and showed little interest in my future.

"I'm afraid I haven't much for you," she finally pronounced. "The only thing I can offer is work on the floor in an Engineering Factory."

Trying to remain polite I replied, "Thank you for your help. I think I'll find something by myself."

I left the interview unhappy and deflated. After such high-handed treatment from this ignorant woman I became determined to prove them all wrong. I had to show them all, and also convince myself, that their assessment of me was wrong. I decided that I would achieve something worthwhile, and one day, become "somebody".

The week we were to break up a ball was arranged for the school leavers. I suppose the American equivalent would be "the Proms". To make it realistic, last year girls from a Polish School at Stowell Park were to join us. We led a rather sheltered life, isolated as we were, and opportunities for meeting girls were few. Chances of getting acquainted with members of the opposite gender were few and far between, let alone meeting girls of our own ethnic background. It was therefore with great excitement and anticipation that we all awaited "the Angels from Stowell Park".

The night finally arrived. I, along with the others, dressed in my best School Uniform and feeling very nervous made my way to the hall. After such a build up, it turned out that I found the event a complete disappointment. The number of girls was considerably lower than boys. The braver ones, of which I was decidedly not, moved in

173

first and the rest of us didn't get a look in. Still, it was something to mark the ending of our stay in Lilford.

A week later the final moment had arrived. All our belongings packed, we were driven to Thrapston to catch our trains home. I must admit that I was leaving the place with mixed feelings and with some apprehension. I arrived there, a frightened child and was now leaving as a young man, no longer tied to Mother's apron strings and accustomed to making my own decisions without reference to anyone else. On the other hand, I was acutely aware that I was leaving the place ill equipped to face the future. I, just like the rest of the boys, received a "School Leaving Certificate" to mark my period of Secondary Schooling. A "School Leaving Certificate". What sort of document is that? We all knew that to the world outside it would prove to be of no value whatsoever. I was luckier than some, I thought. At least I had a Pass Certificate of the S1 Exam. This would enable me to continue my education further - something I was determined to do.

Yet again I was about to make a leap into the unknown.

Chapter 12

I arrived home on a late Sunday afternoon in July of 1953. "Home" was in fact a first floor flat in a house in South London being rented by my brother Romek and my sister Zuzia, and occupied also by Mother. From now on there was to be an additional occupant and, in due course, another person to share the rent.

Tired and unsettled, I greeted Mother and my siblings. After a while, food appeared on the table. What a pleasure it was to yet again taste Mother's cooking in place of the unexciting camp food I was accustomed to. We chatted for a while and then, overtaken by fatigue I went to bed.

Next day I got up very late. My brother and sister had long gone to work leaving only Mother and me at home.

Over breakfast I said to Mother, "I suppose I'll have to start looking for a job. They weren't much help in that respect in school."

"Don't rush into anything," she replied. "First of all, I think you need a good rest," she continued. "Relax, and get yourself acquainted with your new surroundings. A week or two from now would be soon enough for you to start looking into this job business."

This benevolent approach from my Mother took me a little by surprise. It simply wasn't like her. Still, I couldn't but agree with what I heard. At the back of my mind, I must admit, lay much anxiety and fear of what was ahead. Delaying the moment when the matter had to be tackled therefore suited me well enough.

I spent a couple of weeks kicking my heels and at the end found myself getting bored and anxious to get on with my life. Having made the decision, I went along to my local Labour Exchange to register and see if they could help me with a placement.

The clerk meticulously filled in my particulars. He then looked up at me and asked, "What sort of job are you looking for then?"

"Something in a Drawing Office," I replied.

He pulled out a little box full of yellow cards and started wading through them. After what seemed to me like ages he set three of them aside.

"I'm afraid I can't help you with any Drawing Office jobs," he finally said. "The only thing I've got here is a number of shift-work jobs in engineering factories." Seeing my look of dismay he added, "I think you should follow these openings up. The sort of job you're thinking of isn't easy to find these days."

"Sorry," I replied, trying to contain my frustration. "This is not what I'm after. I'll wait until you get some more openings. I think I'll come back next week and see if you get something more suitable on your books by then."

With that, disgusted, I walked off. I couldn't believe the story I was being fed for one moment. I was getting fed-up with people insisting on treating me as 'factory fodder'.

On my way home I picked up a paper and took it home. In the flat I started carefully going through the 'situations vacant' columns. I couldn't see anything local that would suit me. Eventually however, I came across an advertisement that looked interesting. A firm called Slough Engineering had an opening for a Junior Draughtsman. "Slough isn't that far away," I mused. "From there I should be able to come home every weekend. There seems to be nothing on offer locally. Who knows when a decent vacancy might appear in South London? I can't after all expect my brother and sister to finance me much longer. There's nothing for it," I decided. " I must have a try for this one."

Having decided, I sat down there and then, composed a letter of application and posted it. Almost by return I received an invitation for an interview. The director I saw seemed very friendly and well disposed towards me. I later discovered that the Company already had some Poles working for them. The good impression they established must have worked in my favour. The man offered me the job. The starting wage was a princely five pounds five shillings per week. I accepted, but asked for help in finding local digs. A couple of days later I was informed that lodgings with full board were taken up on my behalf and was given a starting date for my new job as the following Monday.

That Monday soon arrived and I started my first wage earning position as arranged. I found my Landlords friendly and helpful and soon settled into my new and fully independent life. I found the job quite straightforward and not too demanding. In the beginning my English speech was awkward and halting. This however didn't last

176

very long. I soon discovered that my original problem simply stemmed from lack of practice. In fact my new problem was the opposite of the old. My knowledge of English grammar and range of vocabulary was apparently wider than that of my workmates. Frequently, I would use a word, which my colleagues wouldn't know. "Don't show off," my young apprentice fellow worker would say. "Don't keep using those long words." The other side of the coin was that I lacked the knowledge and understanding of colloquial speech and English proverbs and sayings. When some problem came up Ron, the apprentice would say, "It's just one of those things." To me this innocuous comment would sound like some kind of recrimination directed towards me. I would immediately jump up and respond, "one of what things?" The lad would immediately see that his friendly remark was being taken the wrong way and try as best he could to assure me that his comment wasn't intended to offend. I accepted his explanations for the sake of office harmony but remained unconvinced. Exasperated, Ron would sometimes tell me that I had "a chip on my shoulder". To this I also took offence (although on reflection he might have had a point).

Another matter I had to get accustomed to was the English diet. Until then I didn't realise just how Polish the food and drink served to us in Lilford really was. The one thing I found difficult to come to terms with was; English tea. The sort of tea I always drank until then was relatively weak and sometimes served with a slice of lemon. I my work place, as I discovered, one of the benefits was free tea mid-morning and afternoon provided by the Company. The liquid the woman brought around had milk added (something I'd never seen in tea) and tasted unbearably strong. I asked if she could make mine a little weaker. After that she'd come around and say, "here's your weak tea, Eugene". I could swear the stuff was as lethal as before but saw no point in making an issue of it and instead, poured what I couldn't manage to get down, into a sink.

Soon after settling down in my job I enrolled in the local College of Further Education in order to continue my O.N.C. course. I was determined to get the education I needed by whatever means available and qualify as a professional engineer. I discovered that it was normal to combine the course with training as an apprentice like my colleague,

Ron. Unfortunately the sort of money paid to apprentices meant that to survive, one's parents or relatives would have to assist financially, and I had nobody in a position to do that. I discovered that I would simply have to do it "the hard way" and "under my own steam," to use a colloquialism or two. I also considered continuing with my violin. I was sure I could have found a teacher, but the problem was where to practice. My digs were out of the question. I couldn't come up with any solution to that problem and left the business of violin playing for future and more suitable circumstances. I regret to say that conditions never improved and what with one thing and another, I never played my instrument again. In spite of this, I shall always be grateful to my sister Stasia for giving me the opportunity, even if for a short period, to enjoy the process of making music. Although I never played again, the experience left me with a love of music in general and classical music in particular, which has never left me.

I had now reached a ripe old nineteen years of age and was fully-grown to my present height, which I'd describe as "the lower end of average". In spite of my increased height however, I apparently still continued to look young for my age. For instance; if I wanted to go to a cinema where an "A" category film was being shown I always had to produce my Aliens Certificate verifying my claim to being "over eighteen".

Although I made frequent trips to visit my family in London, I always considered the job away from home a temporary arrangement. Eventually I found a suitable position as a draughtsman in Streatham, and moved back to South London. At long last my brother and sister had a third partner to share the rent as well as all sorts of domestic expenses. One of the first items we bought between us was a radiogram. I must confess to making the most use of the instrument. To me, those were the days when English radio comedy was really in its prime. After work, in the evening I would sit by the radio alone and curl up with uncontrollable laughter while listening to *Hancock's Half Hour*, *The Goon Show or Take It From Here*. My mother and siblings would look at me with concern; convinced I'd gone mad. They couldn't see what was so funny. Unfortunately, neither my brother's nor my sister's English was sufficient to understand and appreciate the weird and way-out humour in the programmes. It was my first

178

indication of the large differences in the command of English between myself and others who were three or four years my senior.

As I entered my early twenties, my elder brother (to my delight) had accepted me as an adult. He'd often invite me to go with him to some local English dances "on a hunt for birds". More often than not the venue would be The Streatham Locarno. We soon developed a strict routine; on arrival we'd immediately saunter into the bar, order a pint of draught Guinness and 'Gin-and-It' each. (For the uninformed, the "It" in 'Gin-and-It' stood for Italian Vermouth.) So fortified, we'd split-up and go out to try our luck with the girls. If fortune wasn't on our side that evening, and this unfortunately was usually the case, we'd meet up again half way through the evening and repeat the process of "fortification".

It was on one of my "hunting" forays in the Locarno that I came across a small group of Polish lads of my age. I hadn't met any of them before. This wasn't surprising considering my short stay in the capital. However, we soon became good friends, although my original nickname of "stranger" stayed with me for a long time. Some of the chaps, having finished a Polish Secondary School similar to Lilford took up some unskilled or semiskilled jobs and used their spare time for recreation. A couple of them were completing their University degrees. One in particular, named Bogdan, once told me that like most of us he'd started off by going to a Polish Secondary School.

"Fortunately, soon after I arrived, I was involved in one or two incidents. The Headmaster decided that my behaviour was unacceptable and threw me out." He smiled as he continued. "As you know, attending secondary school is a legal requirement in this country. The Authorities placed me in a local English school where I continued my Education. At the end, all the pupils, including myself, sat G.C.E. exams and passed with flying colours. On the strength of my results I was accepted by the Imperial College and now I'm finishing a Degree in Science in this Famous Institution."

I must admit to a bout of jealousy at this point. "If only I had the good sense to misbehave and get thrown out like Bogdan," I thought. "How different my situation might look now." Still there was no point in crying over spilt milk. Fortune had dealt me my cards and I was determined to play them out to the best of my ability.

I continued with my part-time education and progressed at work to a position of Design Draughtsman. When I passed my Higher National Certificate examination I considered myself qualified as an engineer. I was working for a mechanical handling firm at the time.

I looked around: I couldn't see any engineers anywhere within the organisation. Even the much older and experienced people went under the title of "Design Draughtsman". No. This place was definitely not for a freshly baked and ambitious engineer like myself. "I must change my job and possibly my direction," I thought to myself. "My next position mustn't carry the word draughtsman in its title," I decided.

I moved into the sphere of Building Services and gloried in the initial title of Junior Design Engineer to be followed by some more senior prefixes in due course. By then I realised that my H.N.C. was not a sufficient qualification. To be recognised as a professional engineer in England it was necessary to be accepted as a Member by a relevant Professional Institution. The relevant institution for me by this point was the Institution of Heating and Ventilating Engineers. After taking some further evening courses I applied, and was finally accepted, as a Member of the Institution. Surely, I was now a "proper" engineer in anybody's eyes.

After a few years, a new development appeared in the British Engineering circles. More and more people began to realise that the British Professional Engineer was labouring under a disadvantage. It seemed that; as the British were the ones that first employed the title of Engineer so were they also the first to debase it. If workers in an engineering factory went on strike for instance, the Media would make an announcement that, "The Engineers are striking". Something had to be done to rescue the position of the Professional Engineer. Eventually a solution emerged. Major Engineering Institutions banded together and decided to seek a Royal Charter. Having been granted this distinction, all of their Members would be entitled to add a "C. Eng." Behind their name, thus setting themselves up as the only true Professionals in the Engineering Industry. This was fine. I fully agreed with the sentiment.

There was only one problem: "The Institution of Heating and Ventilating Engineers," of which I was finally a Member did not hold a Royal Charter. This left all members of the I.H.V.E. out in the cold,

180

me included. As we weren't allowed to use the "C.Eng." Title, all the most senior jobs in our industry were going to Chartered Engineers of different disciplines. So here I was, all over again struggling to gain recognition for my skills. This battle would last for many years but I'm glad to say, that at the time of writing I add the letters of "C.Eng." after my name in accordance with my entitlement.

The period of my partnership with my brother wasn't to last very long, although I've always looked back on that episode in my life with particular pleasure. I spent most of my spare time in the company of my newfound friends. The pastimes consisted of just those sorts of things that one might expect of young red-blooded males of course. Pubs, dances - they were all just hunting grounds. What we all continually sought was the "pleasure of female company".

I must admit to some modest successes with the local girls. As far as Polish girls were concerned however, things were very different. There weren't many of them about, and those that there were, were picky. Once my sister told me that a girl of our mutual acquaintance told her she wouldn't consider going out with me because I was far too serious. This came to me as a severe blow to my ego and dented my self-esteem. The thing was that this female was in my view particularly ugly. However desperate I might have become, never would I have considered asking her out! To be told that even a creature as repulsive as that had already decided she didn't fancy me was too much. My strong sense of National Identity and my awareness of differences in culture, customs and temperament convinced me that marriage with an English girl would lead to disaster and a lifetime of misery. "No," I would say to myself. "If I can't find the right sort of Polish girl then I shall probably not marry at all."

Time passed. One after another, my friends started getting paired off and deserting the pack. The few of us that remained continued to frequent the same old haunts. Things were getting stale and boring. Our situation was a lot like an episode I remember from a Walt Disney film *Dumbo*, which paraphrased would go something like this:

A group of vultures are sitting on a branch of a tree.
One says: " So what shall we do tonight?"
Another answers: "I don't know. What do you want to do?"

The first one replies: "What do you say we go to Battersea Gardens and try to chat up some chicks?"

The second one comes back: "There aren't any girls over there these days worth picking up. It's boring."

The first one again: " So what do you want to do."

The second again: "I don't know. What do you want to do."

I'm sure the picture must be familiar to most of you. The situation was getting me down. I felt trapped and needed to get out. I looked around and found a job being advertised in a town called Pontefract in Yorkshire.

"That would suit me," I thought. "Its well away from London, my old crowd and all that goes with the whole scene. What I need is to start again somewhere new, without all this baggage I seem to be inevitably dragging around with me."

I applied and got the job.

The situation was certainly different. Maybe a little more so than I bargained for. I found myself alone, and without friends or even acquaintances. I was getting very lonely and depressed. I located the Polish Community Centres in Leeds and Bradford. The Polish people there had their own structures and pecking orders. Some outsider from the Great City wasn't welcomed with open arms. I continued to visit the places, particularly on Sundays, when I attended Polish Masses. I must admit that my re-discovered religion was more to do with the need for affirmation of my cultural identity than Faith itself. What I really mean is that I particularly needed to hear and participate in Polish Mass rather than its equivalent in English or any other language.

I attended various social functions, but as for girls the situation seemed hopeless. I was by then knocking on thirty. Any female likely to be in my age group was long since married. The only single members of the opposite sex were girls of not more than eighteen. I was certainly no cradle-snatcher and in any case, wouldn't find any common language with those 'kids'.

One day, however, an incident occurred that was to change my life forever. Here I must be very careful what I say, as the first person I expect to read this will most likely be my wife, Halina.

Leeds Polish Community Centre organised dances from time to time. I attended a few and soon concluded that for me they were a waste of time. People tended to stick together in their own little cliques. Outsiders were on the whole not welcome. In addition, any woman likely to be of appropriate age was usually married, with the jealous husband not taking kindly to her dancing with some stranger. After a while I stopped going. One night however, feeling particularly bored I decided to go, if only to break the monotony. I turned up rather late, stopped and looked around.

There was nobody on the floor. The band had a brief interval. As I looked around, a couple of women crossed the floor, walking in my direction. As they passed me by I had a good opportunity to make close inspection. One in particular was stunning. I soon saw them again going back to their seats. Normally I don't approach such women, on the assumption that with their looks, they don't stay single or unattended for long, and anyway they'd be looking for somebody more attractive. "There's no point in even trying when there's not chance," I'd normally say to myself, and leave it at that. On this occasion however, for some reason I felt particularly reckless. I observed her sitting there in with a group of friends and decided to have a go at approaching her when the music started. "What have I got to lose?" I reasoned. "She can only say no, after all."

The band started playing and I immediately proceeded to march right across the whole floor towards her. I asked her to dance and, to my amazement she immediately got up. While dancing I managed to carry on a conversation with her. I found her very easy to talk to. "The first hurdle's over," I thought. But then the fear dawned on me – what would happen when they stopped playing! I knew very well that this was a vulnerable point in proceedings when it came to chatting up girls. The only line I knew was to offer her some refreshment. More often than not, the girl's response would be "no thanks," and before I could think of something else to say, she'd be gone, and my chances blown. On this occasion, my chat up line didn't fail me. When invited she willingly went across with me to the bar. After she had polished off a couple of vodkas, I was beginning to feel more confident. "I may be on to something here," I thought. She later invited me to join her party and we spent the whole evening together. Later I drove her home and made another date.

People often talk of "love at first sight". I'm not sure if that's the right phrase to describe my experience that evening. I would certainly admit to a feeling of "lust at first sight" when I first saw her outstanding figure! I prefer to call it "love at first meeting". I certainly felt serious about her. So much so that, I was determined that there must be no deceit between us. As it happens, I had arranged a date with a girl in London on a previous visit back there. I decided to keep it, but only in order to break the relationship off once and for all. Halina was suspicious at my reasons for going away and wouldn't accept my assurances. Still, we continued to meet and our relationship soon blossomed.

Our courtship was intense, passionate, exhilarating and exhausting. We would talk to each other for hours. We met most evenings and I usually finished up driving home in the not-so-early hours of the morning. In the end I think I said something highly romantic like, "let's get married so I can catch up on my sleep," and believe it or not, to my delight, she said "yes".

Halina and I have now been married for many years, and although to some it may sound trite, our love for each other has never faded. Life has thrown some obstacles, problems and difficulties, none of which I propose to talk about here. I would only say that whereas a lot of couples seem to break up when they come across hard times or other difficulties, in our case the reverse is true. In fact adversities seem to have drawn us even closer together. Her eternally cheerful and sunny disposition has certainly helped me to get through some of life's setbacks. We have two beautiful, intelligent and highly talented daughters, of which we are both very proud. Both Susan and Julia speak Polish although this is inevitably their second language. They are both interested in our family history and, like Halina both gave me a lot of encouragement in writing this book. As for customs and traditions, I can't claim that all are kept faithfully in our household but no one is ever missing at the table on Christmas Eve Supper. This in spite of the fact that many miles may separate us during the year.

The notion of putting pen to paper crept upon me slowly and imperceptibly. The causes were various. These are the ones that finally provoked me into undertaking this work.

The subject of how I got to be where I was seemed to come up regularly. Typically some young Englishman, noticing my foreign accent would shower me with questions like:

"What nationality are you?"

"How long have you been here in Great Britain?"

"Do you like it here?"

My answers would vary. To the first question I would tell them I was Polish and skirt around the technicality that; for many years past I had also been a British Subject. In response to the second I would sometimes reply, "Longer than you," and what 's more, I'd usually be right. The last I wouldn't usually bother with. If pressed I'd say, "I can't say whether I like it here anymore than you can, considering how long I've lived here."

Most of them find the situation fascinating and press me for more information. In the end the Enquirer gets treated to a much-abridged version of what you have read here in these pages. The result is usually amazement bordering on incredulity. The usual response is: "You should write a book."

Another series of events that in the end pointed me in the same direction were related to visiting my mother.

My mother, in her later years moved into sheltered accommodation in South London, built and administered by the local Polish community. I, together with my wife Halina, and on occasion, with one or another daughter, made regular visits. At times we'd meet up there with other members of my family. Inevitably our conversations would turn into reminiscences and talk of old times. Often my mother would trigger these conversations. Like all old people everywhere she'd start complaining at the selfishness and self-centredness of the "younger generation". By the younger generation, by the way, she meant her by now ageing children. She might say something like, "to think how I fought, slaved away and suffered to get you all through Siberia, and now there is no one to even hand me a cup of water when I need it".

What would follow would be a chorus of protests. Of course Mother would be grossly exaggerating. In fact she received much more

185

attention from us all than most other old folks in the Establishment. Her thing about "a cup of water" was almost a ritual gripe that can be heard from most Polish old women everywhere. We all knew she didn't really mean it. Next, a conversation would develop about what it was like in Siberia, Kazakhstan or even India. Sooner or later someone would remark, "We should write some of it down, you know. With us gone, nobody will know or remember what it was really like".

On other occasions we'd actually encourage Mother to talk about those times. When one gets to a certain stage in one's life there seems little to look forward to. The only way to avoid gloom then is literally to look back to one's young and happy days. Mother's countenance would brighten up and she'd start telling us what it was like when her and father met, her times of courting etc. We felt satisfied that we'd achieved our aim in cheering her up, but also found additional details from the past interesting and somehow important. "This should not be lost," one of us would always say.

The whole business of chronicling our family story hit me forcibly with the passing away of my mother. Suddenly I realised that the main source of information about the history of my family was no longer accessible. With my siblings beginning to get on somewhat in years there was a real danger that other sources may in due course follow suit, and hard facts would be less and less easy to discover.

Two events that followed made up my mind. One was international in nature and the other at family level. In 1986 Gorbachev, the new Russian leader announced his "Perestroika". This was to be the start of world events, which were to prove unstoppable. Three years later the Soviet Union was dismantled and various satellite countries gained or regained their independence. One such country was the newly formed state of Belarus. The significance of this event for me was that this new independent country, amongst others, encompassed the places where I was born and spent the first years of my life. Before all that, Belarus was just a region of the Soviet Union and as such completely inaccessible to people like myself. The thought obviously crossed my mind:

"Would it be possible to visit my birthplace?"

The next piece of news further cemented my decision. My brother used to make regular trips to Poland to visit some of our relatives that had moved from the "Soviet Sector" immediately after the War. One day, on his return from one of his trips he announced that he'd been to Belarus and visited the place that used to be our home. He came back with stories and photographs. I must admit that what he had to impart made a huge emotional impact on me. Our conversation turned from places to people and general conditions over there. From what he had to say, the place still seemed a little unstable, but free movement for visitors was no longer a problem and the Authorities seemed prepared to dig into their Archives and impart to us information hitherto inaccessible.

I decided to give it a little more time and then make arrangements to go there and discover what I can about my Father's fate. After that, and having picked up what additional information I could, I would finally start to write our story.

Time passed and I observed International political developments and tried to assess how they might impact on the situation in Belarus. I didn't relish the thought of walking into the place during a time of some political turmoil. After a couple of years of apparent stability in that part of the world Halina and I decided to make our move.

Not wishing to go there "cold," I considered whom I should use as a contact at the other end. Suddenly it hit me:

"I know," I said to my wife. "A long time ago my mother used to correspond with my cousin by the name of Zuzanna. Zuzanna (or Suzan in English) is the only daughter of my uncle Juszkiewicz. My mother probably kept up a contact with her because she was always close to her brother, Zuzia's father. I think I'll start with her."

I set about the task. First I got her address from my brother. Next I wrote a long letter of introduction, describing to her our relationship and telling her something about my family. Supported by evidence in the form of some family photographs, I posted the letter and waited for a reply. Time passed and no response was forthcoming. Puzzled, I tried another tack. I made a parcel with what I guessed would be sought after items and sent it. Again time passed, and I was beginning to think that I'd made a mistake, when one day I received an unexpected phone call.

"Halo, Krajewski speaking," I said in my usual official tone. There was a long pause, after which a woman's voice responded in Polish,

"Am I speaking to Gienek?"

Puzzled, I replied, "Yes. Who's speaking?"

"Zuzia," was the response.

"That's strange," I thought. "What does my sister want this time?" But something seemed strange about her voice. Warily I continued the conversation:

"Is everything all right, and how is Mundek (my sister's husband)?"

There was another pause and my caller said, "This is Zuzia from Belarus. Not your sister from America."

I was so shocked I didn't know what to say. At the end of a rather stilted conversation, my cousin gave me her 'phone number and I promised to ring her back the following day.

That evening I shared my excitement with my wife. Next day, as promised I rang my cousin in Grodno. We had a longer chat this time. She told me why she hadn't responded to my letter. Apparently, although her spoken Polish was very good, she had never learnt to write in her native language. It's a notion that simply never occurred to me. When one thinks about it however, she grew up in the Soviet Union, and not only was all her education in Russian, but no doubt, the use of Polish language actively discouraged.

"But how did you get my telephone number?"

"From the parcel," was the reply.

I had forgotten that in completing postal documents I was required to put on not only the sender's address but also the telephone number. That label was on the parcel when it arrived at its destination. What happened afterwards "is history" as they say.

After again thanking me for the parcel, my cousin went on, "Why don't you come over for a visit?"

That was just what I was waiting for. "Thank you for the invitation. I'd love to." I said quickly. Maybe we could organise something for this summer?" I added.

My cousin agreed and said she'd arrange for Halina and I to receive a "formal invitation". Apparently these were still necessary. Clearly not all of the old Soviet systems had been abandoned yet in the newly independent Belarus.

After the conversation, we started our preparations for a (for me), historic journey.

We first went out and did some major shopping. We bought all sorts of items we thought might be in short supply over there. Having brought our haul home, we made another parcel and sent it on it's way to my cousin. It was our intention to use this as a way of financing our stay over there. Judging by what we knew of Poland, nobody would take any money over there from a guest. A present on the other hand, has to be accepted.

A little later our official invitation arrived in the post. With this document we went off to the Belarusian Embassy in London to get our visas. A young man there dealt with our request efficiently and politely. He also advised us on the matter of air travel. Apparently the only way one could get to Minsk (the capital of Belarus), was to book a seat with the official Belarusian Airline, "Belavia".

On our return home we made the necessary booking and started our final preparations for the journey.

Before long, the time came for us to make our way to the airport. I must admit to being a little anxious.

"After all," Halina would say. "You don't really know these people. The only time you saw Zuzia was on the day she was born."

I wasn't going to admit it, but some of her doubts had rubbed off on me as well. Still, this was not the time for hesitation or second thoughts.

This was it. I was to make another leap in the dark - but this time, I was calling the shots.

Chapter 13

Full of apprehension we set off for Gatwick airport. We had previously heard stories about the quality of Russian-built planes and were therefore not overjoyed to discover that our journey was to take place in a TU 1502. "TU," by the way stood for Tupolev, the name of a well-known Russian aircraft designer.

The start of the journey appeared to confirm our worst fears. The queue for booking–in was slow, confused and chaotic. When at long last we got on, we discovered that; not only were the fittings sparse and basic, but the standard of internal maintenance also left something to be desired. Some warning lights, for example were not working, lighting fittings were parting company with the cabin structure and to top it all, I found my seat anchor broken resulting in the item swinging around in a very disturbing fashion.

Before we set off, Halina, determined to avoid falling foul of any rules, read the Airline's Regulations carefully. Among others there was an item that prohibited passengers from taking on board any gas-filled item, including even cigarette lighters. This was a bit of an inconvenience as Halina was still a smoker in those days but, in compliance with the rules, she left her lighter behind. In view of this sacrifice, she was particularly annoyed to discover that; not only was everyone lighting up their cigarettes with gas lighters on the plane, but they were doing it before the plane took off in complete disregard of instructions and warning signs.

On the plus side, I must admit that the plane seemed to fly smoothly and the journey was concluded without mishap. As the pilot brought the craft to a smooth halt, all the passengers started clapping. I have since discovered that this is a tradition amongst Russian travellers, but at the time I couldn't help but wonder what mortal danger we had escaped!

Our entry into Minsk Airport lived up to the earlier part of the journey. The place looked grey and drab. As we walked along we could see no signs in English or, for that matter, any other language than Russian. Before passing through Customs we had to fill in Declaration Forms. To our horror all questions were in Russian. Neither one of us had enough of that language to make any sense of

190

the forms. We were stuck. We just stood there looking helpless. In the end a fellow passenger took pity on us and helped us with the papers.

Confused, bemused and generally shattered, we proceeded to the Customs gate. There by sign language we responded to the Officers questions, basically indicating that we had no idea what the hell he was saying. Exasperated the man let us by.

At long last we were through, but where was my cousin who was supposed to take care of us?

As we looked around helplessly we suddenly saw a couple in the distance frantically waving, in what seemed to be our direction. As they started getting closer I realised the older woman was my cousin Zuzia. I did not know the tall young man accompanying her then, although I was soon to discover that it was Yuri, Zuzia's son.

To say that we were relieved would be an understatement. The meeting was very emotional. We all hugged and kissed each other and tried to respond to their inquiries about the trip, and whether it was very tiring.

Soon Yuri, having grabbed our suitcases, was getting us settled in his car. My immediate observation was that it appeared to be a pretty good quality vehicle. As I recall, it was a fairly recent Mitsubishi saloon. We set off and on leaving the Airport, found ourselves in open country. I tried to relax a bit and look around at the scenery. I didn't get to see very much because the sun started setting quite soon after, however from what I observed the place seemed to me strangely flat and under-populated.

The car went along smoothly and we were soon deeply involved in all sorts of conversations with our hosts. About an hour and a half passed without us realising it. Suddenly I realised that Yuri was pulling over. "Anything wrong?" I asked. He only smiled and said nothing. Moments later the car was parked in a pull-in on the edge of a forest, just next to a table with a couple of benches.

We all got out to stretch our legs and attend to other bodily needs. The nearby forest was certainly handy. When I returned, to my surprise I discovered the table covered with all sorts of delicious-looking snacks. Zuzia certainly did herself proud. Hungry, we all tucked in. The food proved to be as tasty as it looked. We ate, sat, chatted and generally relaxed. It was then that we suddenly encountered our new tormentors. MOSQUITOES. The place seemed full of them. To cap it, the monsters seemed particularly fond of foreign blood. I don't know if there's something different about our smell, but without a doubt they homed-in on Halina and myself, leaving Zuzia and Yuri very obviously alone. The creatures seemed enormous, unafraid, thirsty for our blood and produced a terrifying buzz. The after-effects of their feasting on our vulnerable bodies were certainly painful enough to warrant our fear of the creatures. After a while, we decided that enough was enough and left the field of battle to the victorious mosquitoes.

We travelled in the dark for maybe two or more hours, but with all the conversations going on, the time flew by quickly. Before we realised it we were driving through the wide and well-lit streets of Grodno. We turned off towards one of the many multi-storey monoliths and the car came to a halt outside a main entrance doorway.

"Our flat is on the third floor," said Yuri. "Don't worry about the cases. You follow Mum upstairs and I'll bring all the stuff up myself."

In the darkness we made our way carefully along the corridor and up the stairs.

"Be careful," said Zuzia as we felt our way along. "I'm afraid it's always like this. As soon as someone puts in a light bulb in the corridor, it gets pinched or broken. We are all used to it by now."

Suddenly a shaft of light shot out towards us. In the open doorway ahead stood the silhouette of a man.

"Come in, come in and welcome!" boomed Joseph, Zuzia's husband. He must have heard the commotion and come out to investigate.

With the landing now lit, we quickly made our way in. From the moment we entered we faced customs and habits that were different and new to us. Firstly, all attempts to greet Joseph across the doorstep were discouraged. "Bad luck," we were told. Secondly, as we went through two sets of doors (one opening outward and the other inwards), we were asked to take off our shoes and put on some slippers.

At last the ceremony of entering was out of the way and the one of greeting began. Again we hugged and kissed everyone present. Apart from Joseph, we met Ania (Ann), Zuzia's daughter together with her two young sons.

As we were led further into the flat we took time to look around. The place was large, well decorated and adequately furnished. What a contrast to the drab, grey and dilapidated exterior of the place!

After some further chats, we were led into the dining room for a "formal" reception dinner. Again, the food was a credit to Zuzia's obvious culinary abilities. After cold snacks, she served a couple of hot dishes such as 'pierogi' (pastry stuffed with meat), and mushrooms in sauce followed by a variety of cold dishes, and of course vodka.

Having eaten our fill we sat down to relax. "Let's give them the presents we brought them," whispered Halina in my ear.

I made some excuse to go to our luggage and brought out the gifts. As we were about to hand them out, another surprise awaited us. The presents were taken without a single word of thanks from any of the recipients. When at last we were left alone in our room Halina expressed her concern.

"This is all very odd," she said. "I thought they were supposed to be poverty stricken around here? Surely, our gifts must be highly valuable to them. I don't expect massive gratitude, but some sort of appreciation wouldn't go amiss," she mused. "And another thing," she added. "The parcels we sent cost even us a pretty packet. I can still see most of the sweets and toiletries stowed away in cupboards and display units. You'd think they'd at least acknowledge the fact that they'd received it!"

"Don't make too much of it," I responded, without any conviction. "Maybe it's just the way they are in this part of the world. After all this is a harsh land. Not at all like Krakow, down South where your family are from. People are probably much less demonstrative here."

"I don't mind that so much," she replied. "What bothers me is that I can't tell if the presents are good enough. Maybe they were expecting something more. It's difficult to tell."

"Don't worry yourself," I replied. "As far as I'm concerned, they've had adequate recompense for putting us up. Don't forget why we're really here. It isn't just to visit our relatives. Our main mission, if you remember, is to see what we can discover about my Father's fate." Mollified somewhat my wife returned to the party with me following.

With our private conversation in mind I started my inquiries.

"I've been told back in England," I started, "that it's possible these days to access all kinds of official documents, which would have been unavailable in the days of the Soviet Union. My main concern is to find out about what really happened to my Father. As I understand, he was arrested in Piaski and later transferred to a prison in Wolkowysk. I can well imagine that records in Piaski might not have been adequately maintained but I can't believe that a Main Centre like Wolkowysk would not account for every prisoner brought to them. It is my impression that, in spite of all the local excesses, the Communist bureaucracy worked at least at District level. I would have thought that if we were to go to, say, the Police station in that town, we might find the documents I'm looking for."

A moment of silence followed, with everybody trying to think of the best way to solve my problem.

Suddenly Ann called out, "I think you're on the wrong track my dear cousin. This kind of information would be kept in the Main Archives for the region, and the place for that is here in Grodno. I think we should start our inquiries in the Archives right here in this town."

"Is there such a place?" interjected Zuzia, "where on earth is it?"

"That's easy," answered her daughter. "The address will be in the telephone directory."

She grabbed the book and started to leaf through it. "There it is," she exclaimed, "on Ozeskowa Road, and here is the 'phone number. Tomorrow morning we can ring them and find out."

Her brother stepped in. "No need to ring," he said. "After breakfast Uncle Gienek and I will jump in the car and go there. That's much more likely to produce the desired effect than any 'phone calls." After a little pause he added, "Another thing. Before we go, we'll need to do a little shopping. Its best on such occasions to bring the Official a little present you know."

I was delighted. Events were developing well. We carried on chatting about the day when they took father away, about our own deportation and so on. Suddenly I remembered the Document I had brought with me.

"Let me show you something," I said and rushed over to where our luggage was stowed. Moments later I returned with the Title Deeds to Father's farm in my hands.

"Have a look at that," I said. "Maybe we can find out if we can use this to re-claim our land."

They all inspected the document thoroughly. "Amazing. Where on earth did you get it?" Joseph chipped in. "Well," I told him, "When they were about to take us away, they let Mother gather some belongings together. This was one of the items she considered important enough to take with her. After Mother passed away, the original stayed with my sister Stasia. Before coming over I made this copy to bring over here and show you."

"So this is just a copy," said Zuzia with admiration. "I must admit, it looks like a proper document to me."

We sat and talked well into the small hours of the morning. In the end, exhausted by the journey and the whole experience of arriving there, we were allowed to go to bed.

The next morning, straight after breakfast, young Yuri, Halina and I set off into town in search of the Central Archives. Before going in, Yuri suggested that we stop at a shop and buy some "presents" for the officials.

"This is to oil the wheels," he said grinning. "You'd be surprised how much help and co-operation can be gained by the odd box of chocolates or a bottle of wine," he added.

On arrival we were shown into the Head Archivist's office. The woman was polite and quite helpful, although I couldn't help but detect a certain undercurrent of hostility towards us "foreign interlopers". She listened politely to our requests as set out by Yuri. Her first reaction was that we were in the wrong place if we wished to discover my Father's fate. "Your best bet is to enquire at the Police Archives," she said. "It's only down the road and on the first street to the right." Disappointed a little we ploughed on. "What about our land?" I said, producing my father's Deeds. The woman took the document and inspected it very carefully. I suspect she hadn't seen many of it's kind before. In the end, clearly not noticing that this was only a copy she pronounced, "Yes I can see that this is a genuine document. Unfortunately the issuing Authority, i.e. Poland, has no jurisdiction here. This is The Republic of Belarus; not Poland," she said with pride in her voice. Seeing dismay on our faces though, she quickly added, "Of course I can place your document in the Deeds File and attach our own certificate to make the original valid." We readily agreed and Yuri arranged to come back the next day for the official document. We then asked about Birth Certificates. "That's yet another Archive here in Grodno," she said, and gave Yuri instructions on how to get there. Not too happy, but feeling we'd achieved at least something, we departed.

Next morning I went with Yuri to pursue the new addresses. The Police Archive was quite an experience. I was already getting accustomed to seeing figures of Lenin in public places, but to discover a bust of Stalin in a place of pride inside the Archive Building was definitely a surprise. In spite of appearances, a major change in attitude by the occupants must have taken place. The young policewoman was helpful, polite and even pleasant. I can't believe even locals could have gained access to the documents held in that place. For people like me this would have been out of the question.

Yuri introduced me and explained what information I was after.

"Take a seat," she said to me. "I'll go through to the Filing Hall and see what I can discover."

After what seemed like an eternity she reappeared. "I'm afraid I can't help you," she said. "I've looked everywhere. There is definitely no record of your father ever having been arrested."

Disappointed I asked, "Would it help if I went to the Police Offices in Wolkowysk or even Piaski?"

The woman, her face now sombre, shook her head. "I'm sorry," she said. "This is the Main Store of all the papers from those days. If it's not here then it simply doesn't exist." Then, as though she though it might help to convince me she added, "As I said, all documents from those days are here. We have, for example a fully documented record of you own deportation together with the rest of your family."

Somewhat discouraged, I thanked the young lady and made to leave. It was then, possibly because she felt she was of little help, the policewoman added,

"I don't know whether or not you realise, but you could apply for a Rehabilitation Document. This can only be done here and by individuals presenting a written application to this office in person. Postal applications are not accepted. As you can imagine," she added smiling, "this cuts down the number of applicants drastically."

I wasn't sure what benefit, if any, such a document would bring me, but as I was there already, I promised to prepare such an application and hand it to her the next day. I must admit that the notion of somebody like me, having been uprooted at the age of four, being now required, like some criminal, to apply for rehabilitation seemed amusing. "Still," I thought, "It'll be something to show around when I get back."

Our next port of call was the Archive Building holding all the Church Records.

I must admit that for a change, the Official seemed surly and not inclined to help. In the end, after a long wait we were called into her office. "What exactly is it you want then?" she said, her manner clearly off-hand.

With Yuri interpreting, I replied, "I and my family were deported at the outbreak of the last war. Mother didn't take our Birth or Christening Certificates with her at the time. This meant that we have all had to spend our lives without vital documents proving our Identities. It would mean a lot to see the actual Registration Document. As it is, sometimes I wonder if I really exist."

My long speech got through to the woman. "Wait here," she said. "I'll see what I can find out," and having taken a piece of paper she asked, "What's your date of birth, and your parents' Christian names?"

I told here and she marched off.

After what again seemed like an unbearably long time she popped her head in and asked, "Was your mother's maiden name Juszkiewicz?"

The emotion at hearing the question was overwhelming.

"She's found it," I thought. Unable to summon any words I just nodded violently. She disappeared again and came back a few minutes later.

"Your papers aren't here," she said. I was on the phone just now to our Centre in Mosty. That's where your records are kept." Then, as though the matter was resolved she added, "Is that all?"

"No, far from it," I retorted. "I want to see the document with my own eyes. Can you please ring again and ask if we can drive over immediately and view the book in question?"

The woman clearly thought my notion fanciful but telephoned Mosty and got their agreement for us to come over and view the papers.

The journey to Mosty wasn't very long. Soon we arrived at the town Centre and parked. The square and the surrounding buildings were interesting. The architecture was certainly different from what I was used to in England. The roads were very wide. On either side, the buildings were fairly tall, of heavy construction and of monumental and somewhat pretentious design. In the centre of the market square was a large statue of Lenin. After a few false starts we finally found the Archives, only to discover the department closed. I was just about to start panicking when the ever resourceful Yuri, disappeared into one of the nearby offices. He soon emerged and asked us to wait.

"The chief archivist simply went over to another Building along here to have a chat with a friend," he said, "and of course left the Office locked in her absence."

Obviously, to him there was nothing particularly remarkable about the woman's behaviour. He then added, "I'll go and get her and we'll all then go to the Repository."

Sure enough, moments later my young cousin could be seen walking towards us, with an elderly woman alongside. I was a little uneasy. "Surely the woman will be annoyed at being dragged over in such an unceremonious manner." I thought. "Will she be inclined to be helpful in these circumstances?" I wondered.

To my amazement, the lady was pleasant and very friendly. She invited us all to take our seats and waded through some old books. She opened one of them, and placing it in front of me, pointed at an entry. "Is that what you're looking for?" she asked.

I looked down, and all blood seemed to drain out of me. In front of me was an entry written by hand in, now slightly faded ink. My name. Next to it was my date of Christening and my date of Birth. Reading on, I saw the names of my Godfather and Godmother. I was so overwhelmed to see the record, hand written by my parish priest all these years ago that initially I missed an important detail. The date of my birth was recorded as 25th of March. All these years I thought the actual date was one day later - the 26th. My curiosity awakened by this error, I started looking for the entries of my siblings. With the exception of Romek, each of us had spent a lifetime with the wrong date of birth. Obviously, Mother didn't remember them all and when asked later, had made her best guess. This may seem strange, but one must bear in mind the fact that in Polish culture Birthdays are not celebrated and so there is no particular reason why people should be aware of each other's exact dates of birth. In fact instead of Birthdays it is a custom to commemorate the day of the Saint after which the person is named.

Painfully aware of the lack of proper and genuine documentation all these years, I asked if I could photograph the relevant pages, but the answer was a polite but firm No. I explained why the record was so important to me, to which the Archivist's response was:

"If you need an official copy of your Birth Certificate, this can be arranged."

Delighted, I gave her my home address and asked for my Certificate together with ones for Stasia and Romek, to be sent over to me when ready. As for my sister who now lives in America, Zuzia, I asked if that document could be sent to her direct, and also gave her address.

That day we drove back to Grodno well satisfied. The viewing of the original records was a major emotional experience for me. On top of that, my siblings had a surprise waiting for them. That the surprise was to turn out unexpectedly, I was to learn much later.

That night, over some glasses of Belarusian vodka we sat down to prepare our plan of campaign. The only means of transportation available to us when it came to trips out of town was Yuri's car with, of course, Yuri driving it. We have already taken up a lot of his time, and it became obvious to us that his availability was not unlimited. After all, the lad had a living to make and commitments to discharge. This is where my professional management experience came to my aid.

"I can see that we won't be able to do everything we might like and go everywhere we'd wish," I said. "When faced with such a situation in my job, I prioritise. So; first," I continued, "we must decide which visits are the most important and which we can make only if time permits."

What followed was a long discussion with everybody throwing in his or her suggestions. We all agreed in the end that the priorities were: a visit to Rogoznica, my place of birth, a call on each of my two remaining aunts, and a stop-over at the town of Piaski – the place of my childhood memories. Other, further removed relatives and places would have to take potluck as far as time was concerned.

As Yuri was not available the next day, we decided to go out without him and explore the town of Grodno. This, again I found quite interesting. The City Centre represented the original medieval town. The buildings in this area were old and somewhat dilapidated. The streets were dark and narrow. Clearly Grodno was an ancient City. Immediately adjacent to the Old Town was a very large square, with a Theatre Building facing onto it. Alongside were other post-war government buildings of typically Russian "monumental" design. The square was dominated by a massive sculpture of "post modern" style. In the middle was an actual Second World War Russian tank placed on a podium. We walked on to investigate the inside of some shops nearby. I was a little surprised at what I saw. Judging by the stories I heard before coming, I expected to see a lot of empty shelves and certainly no Western products on sale. In fact most items of Western technology were on sale all round me. Another myth was that Russian gold was a bargain. What we saw was, if anything more expensive than back home in England. Having decided that there were no bargains to be had, we picked up some souvenirs and made our way home. As we travelled, we could see that the City Centre was surrounded by row upon row of monotonous Russian style blocks of flats. One could imagine that Stalin had ordered a design to be produced and that this was used thereafter in every town and on every project throughout the (now defunct) Soviet Union.

Next day, early, we set off for Rogoznica. As we travelled across the flat and open countryside I was overcome by a whole host of emotions.

"So this was the land of my fathers," I thought, looking out at the table-like dry and brown earth around me. It was this view that I had waited to see all these years. Tears began to well up uncontrollably in my eyes.

In the middle of one freshly ploughed field, I saw real, genuine Polish white storks. A sight you never see where I live. I asked Yuri to stop the car so I could get closer to the birds but they flew off at my approach. Eventually, on the horizon we saw the tall spire of the parish church of Rogoznica. We parked and immediately went over to the cemetery across the road from the church. There, in a far corner, we saw the Gravestone erected by my father. As I said earlier, the Parish church was erected in 1925. With the advent of the formal consecration, a patch of land was established as the future Parish Roman Catholic Cemetery. Soon after disaster struck at my family. My parents' first-born daughter died in infancy, to be followed by yet another baby girl. My father, his grief inconsolable had the unenviable distinction of erecting the very first monument in the new cemetery. This had to be my first port of call.

The grave was located on the far side of the cemetery. We walked up and inspected the monument closely. The structure was still in a surprisingly good condition, considering the time that had elapsed and lack of care. The monument was cast out of concrete as one piece. The inscriptions were formed as part of the casting; at the bottom, however, father placed a beautiful poem by insetting letters made out of iron into fresh cement. By the time he came to bury his daughters, father had developed a lot of skill in the art of concrete forming and casting. The monument I was looking at was excellent proof that, not only was he a remarkable man of letters and a talented inventor, but also a very able craftsman.

Once I had spent a while at the grave, and had paid my respects, I looked around the rest of the cemetery. Being used to seeing all sorts of tombstones and monuments in England, some more elaborate than others, I was taken aback at what I saw. Some graves nearby were only marked by badly deteriorated and toppling wooden crosses. Others bore simple metal crosses with no inscriptions whatever. A likely explanation for this apparent lack of respect for deceased relatives could be the fear of the family members still living, at being identified by the Communist Authorities. Practising any faith, but particularly that of the Roman Catholic Religion was, after all actively discouraged by the Godless State. By contrast, and as if to confirm my theory, the most recent headstones were invariably of impressive construction and all had clearly identifiable inscriptions. It would appear that religious persecution was no longer an issue.

Next we crossed the road in order to visit the Parish Church. It was the place where I was christened all those years ago. As the building was locked-up, we decided to seek assistance at the Parsonage adjacent. An elderly Polish priest opened the door. The man was friendly and hospitable. We were immediately invited in and offered drinks and snacks. As we sat drinking coffee, the priest explained that he wasn't in charge of that Parish. The parish priest, it seemed, was away on leave and our host acted as temporary replacement. In response to my request the priest took us over to the church and showed us around. The place was in full flow of renovation. Some pieces of old furniture, probably dating back from the days of my childhood, were still around although most of the original pews were already dismantled. I found the Main Altar of particular interest. It appeared to comprise a number of sections of remarkably fine and well-finished segments cast in cement. I couldn't help but wonder: "Could my father have had a hand in its construction?"

I found the church impressive. It seemed surprising that such a large and magnificent structure should have been erected in, what was after all a rather poor village.

Unfortunately time was not on our side. Regretfully we cut our visit short, thanked the priest profusely for his assistance and hospitality and drove off to our next port of call.

We drove out of the village and stopped outside an isolated hut.

"The man that lives here knew your father," said Zuzia. "Lets go in and see if he can help us locate your land."

Knocking on the door produced no response. We wandered around the back to find an elderly couple threshing a pile of wheat in the age old manner, that is by first beating it with sticks and then shovelling the product into the air to allow wheat and chaff to separate. Clearly, my father's invention didn't withstand the test of time.

Once the introductions were out of the way, both declared their pleasure at meeting us and their readiness to help in whichever way they could.

"You look exactly like your father," was the very first thing the man said to me, looking at me closely. "I knew him well you know," he continued. "As a young lad I used to work for him from time–to–time. I used to help out with the hollow blocks he used to make." He paused and added, "Did you know they were his invention?"

Taken aback by the man's first comment, I replied that I knew about the hollow blocks and thanked him for saying that I resembled my father. At that moment, I felt closer to my father than ever. Slightly overwhelmed, I asked if he could show us the precise location of where Father's farm used to be.

"Follow me," he said. "I can show you the precise spot."

We marched up into a vast open field. Eventually the farmer stopped and pointed to an area in front.

"This is it," he said. "Just there was your house. Over there were the out-buildings, and behind the house was a garden and an orchard." As we looked around he continued, "Your father's place was bang in the middle of the Settlement. Just along here, there used to be a road leading to the village of Rogoznica. As I'm sure you know, once the Russians came, on that infamous night, not only you, but all of the settlers were taken away and deported to Siberia, leaving the settlement completely empty. Over time, villagers grabbed whatever they found useful. After the War was over and the Germans driven back, our New Masters began to introduce the New Order. One of the first things they did was to remove whatever remained of the Ex-army Settlement they so hated, leaving not a trace of Marszalkowa Wola. They even levelled the road that used to pass along here" he said, pointing. "All that is now part of the communal farm."

I looked around. Sure enough, all around I could only see one open flat field of new light-green grass sprouting in place of the now gathered grain. Ahead, not far away, the huts of Rogoznica could be seen, with the Church spire dominating the horizon. Over to the right, far away I could see another sign of human habitation.

"What's that place?" I asked the man, pointing in the direction of the distant buildings.

"Oh that," he said. That's Lawry. I think your mother's family used to live there."

Turning my sights back to the nearby surroundings I suddenly spotted something odd. Immediately in front of me was a patch of earth much lighter in colour to the rest.

"What's that?" I asked.

"That is where your father's gravel pit used to be," our guide replied. "Even after the War, the Authorities used it for a time. Eventually though, they decided to close it own. The pit was then filled in and the ground levelled."

I found the explanation fascinating. If nothing else, it confirmed the man's assertion that we were indeed standing on my father's land. I looked around again. Amongst the surrounding greenery I spotted a patch of blue. I went over to investigate. In front of me I saw flowers in bloom. I picked one and showed it to Zuzia.

"This must've been your mother's flower garden," she said. "They are definitely not wild flowers. These must have been growing here ever since the time your mother first planted them in her new garden."

"However hard you try, you can't erase the past," I thought. "The Communists tried so hard to remove all the evidence of our fine settlement, yet all the signs are still here if one only knows what to look for."

"These must've been great times," I said.

"Yes," the farmer replied. "That's very true. After the devastation of the First World War and the neglect even before by the Tsarist Authorities, it was refreshing and exciting to see what was happening here. The settlers made all the difference. It wasn't just a question of money. They brought with them life, vitality and progress. 'We're building Poland', they used to say, and I think that was really so. To my mind, everybody in the area benefited from their activities. I must say, I for one used to enjoy going to work for your father."

He hesitated, weighing thoughts in his mind. In the end he added, "As you can see, the whole place has gone back to seed under the control of our new Masters."

These were brave words for, even though the Communist system was supposedly gone, not all the vestiges of the Old Order were removed yet.

I looked around one last time and was completely overcome by emotion. "To think that this was the very place where my young parents, full of hope and faith in the future, started their new life together, planted gardens and ploughed fields and started a family," I contemplated. To be able to stand on the very spot, after all these years and after all that's happened was, to my mind a privilege and a rare opportunity.

Time was pressing on. I had to tear myself away from my thoughts and continue on. We got back into the car and drove on to the next village called Podbolocie. There, we pulled up outside a tiny hut by the roadside.

"This is where your Aunt Elizabeth lives." said Zuzia. "Let's go and see if she's in."

The door was opened by a tiny old lady. "Come in, come in," she said. "Sit down over there, and I'll go and make some tea."

We all stepped in and, in the semi-darkness of the interior I looked around. We were standing in a very small and crude wooden hut. The place comprised two rooms only, with no sanitary facilities. In one corner stood a tiled wood-fire stove. It would serve both for cooking and for heating in the wintertime. At the far end stood a bed and a couple of chairs. The floor was simply beaten earth, with no covering at all. The whole place was illuminated by one bare electric bulb - the only indication that we were living in the twentieth century.

In spite of the primitive living conditions, Aunt Elizabeth seemed remarkably fit. It would appear that this harsh country life agreed with her. As Halina and I looked at her and listened to her talk, the same thought struck us both. How incredibly similar she was to my now deceased mother. The way in which she walked, the sound of her voice, the phrases she used - it was almost as if my mother had come back to life again. It was all the more remarkable, considering that the two of them hadn't seen each other for more than fifty years. Even the figurine of Our Lady standing in the corner was exactly the same as the one my Mother used to have.

On being introduced, my aunt, like the man we met earlier, immediately remarked at my close resemblance to my late father. "I always knew I looked like him" I thought, but the way everybody that knew him was behaving, it would seem that I resembled him even more closely than even I had imagined.

We chatted for a while about the old times. Aunt Elizabeth still had a very sharp mind in spite of her advancing years. I don't think she remembered much about me personally, but she'd recall the early days, when "young Koscia and Leon" would go out gallivanting, leaving young Elizabeth to look after the smaller kids. In the end, as it was already getting dark, both Halina and I kissed and hugged her and said our good-byes. I was glad to have met my mother's only remaining sister. After all, if I was to have delayed my visit another year or two, who knows if she'd still have been around.

As we drove back to Grodno, we saw many cars travelling in our direction loaded with all kinds of fruit and vegetables. "Most of these young people are returning home after visiting their parents or other old relatives in the country," remarked Zuzia. "Food is plentiful in the villages, and the old folk are invariably generous. The young take what they can, however they can, and drag it back to their homes in town. Food may be no problem "out in the sticks," but life is primitive out there. The young prefer to make their homes in big towns like Grodno."

The next day being Sunday, we all set off to attend Mass in the nearest Polish church in Grodno. (The city boasts three Roman Catholic churches and one Cathedral.) This experience, I found in some ways was quite strange. The small place was overflowing with the faithful; although observing their behaviour it was obvious to me that practising religion was, to most of them, a new experience. I was pretty sure that my relatives had come along purely for our benefit. I suspected that otherwise, they didn't see the inside of a church from one year to the next. In spite of the zeal of those attending, I was dismayed at the quality of their singing. Poles have heartrending and beautiful church music and songs that they normally deliver in a soulful and tuneful manner. The people in this church, however didn't seem to know the words very well and, what was worse, a lot of them seemed to be out of tune. I was horrified. During the service I looked around in order to gain as much knowledge of the church as I could while I had the opportunity. The thing I found strangest was that the faces of the cherubim all around appeared to be those of grown men and not small children. I could only surmise that, in the old days, work was funded by well-off citizens who insisted on being recompensed by having their images worked into the decorations. Unfortunately not all of them looked like angels. An inscription on the wall next to me caught my eye. It commemorated the foundation of a new Monastery on that site in the year of 1341. The inscription was in Old Polish. "There's proof, if proof were needed that Grodno was indeed an ancient Polish City," I thought.

We spent the next few days getting to know the town. Mosquitoes, by the way although still a nuisance, were not the problem they were to us on our arrival. Either we were getting acclimatised or they were getting used to our scent.

Although getting to know Grodno was interesting, I would have preferred to be spending time visiting relatives or places related to my youth, and Grodno wasn't one of them. Beggars can't be choosers however. Yuri was the only one there with a car and, to be fair, we had to accept that he had to devote at least some of his time to his work. We made one or two trips into the town centre. The old buildings, although crumbling with neglect, were interesting and spoke of the importance the town must have boasted in centuries past. The shops, we found disappointing. Although the range and variety of goods was nowhere near like that of shops in England, I couldn't detect any particular lack of supplies. The famous Russian gold was greatly over-priced, as were most of the other luxury items. We bought little apart from a few small souvenirs.

One evening Yuri announced that, as his affairs were now under control, he was available for another sortie.

The next morning we set off again in the direction of my birthplace. This time however, we bypassed Rogoznica and continued onto the town of Wolkowysk. As this was where my father spent his young days, I wanted to at least get the flavour of the place. In response to my request my young cousin parked the car and allowed us to do a bit of sightseeing. I would describe Wolkowysk as a fairly small if significant provincial town. Few traces of old buildings survived. In their place could be seen the low quality buildings of the Communist era, with village-type huts encroaching at the perimeter.

One of the few items that I thought impressive was the Railway Station. It looked as though it might have been of pre-war design.

We continued on to visit the Gonakowski household nearby. We were greeted by an old man and a little old woman. On being introduced I discovered that the man, still looking pretty good, was my ninety-seven year old uncle, or to be more accurate, the husband of my late aunt Jadzia. Looking at him I must admit at being sorry that I couldn't claim him as my bloodline relative. The shriven little old woman turned out to be his daughter Stasia. Stasia was my elder sister's namesake. She was in fact named after my sister, as was the custom in our family. To look at her, it was difficult to believe that she was actually younger than my sister in London. On being introduced, my uncle immediately, like others before him, pronounced that I was the spitting image of my father. He then proceeded to show me around his little farm. With advancing years he had to curtail his farming activities but, he could still show us some pigs he was fattening up, a patch of ground where he grew some wheat and an apple orchard. Our hostess proved to be quite sprightly, despite her aged appearance. In no time she produced a mouth-watering meal and invited us to sample her fare. All the food was wonderful. I particularly recall fried eggs on cured pork fat as a memorable treat. During our conversation she told us something surprising. Apparently she possessed "the Gift," as she put it. She assured us she was able to heal certain illnesses by the laying-on of hands. She told us that her mother on her deathbed had handed the secret of her powers to her. She reminisced how she spent time in the old days playing with my sister and her namesake and asked me to implore Stasia to come one day for a visit herself.

Having admitted that we had other visits to make, with again thanked our hosts for their hospitality and departed.

On the other side of Wolkowysk we pulled up yet again.

"You see the house up on that hill? " said Zuzia. 'That's Marina's house. I know you wanted to see her. She lives there with her mother Jania Wysocka, your other aunt - your father's sister."

We caught Marina unprepared, and a little embarrassed for it. Marina was a very attractive woman. She looked much younger than her actual age, and I suspect, was well aware of it. She tidied herself up after the initial greetings and took us in to meet her mother.

Unfortunately Jania Wysocka, my father's beloved and only sister was in an advanced state of senile dementia. All my attempts at conversation proved fruitless. Each of her responses amounted to meaningless gibberish. I was very disappointed at not being able to make even the slightest contact with her. One thing though still jogged her memory. Marina showed her an old family photograph with herself as a little girl and my father as a young man.

Marina pointed to my father and asked Jania, "Who's that Mother?"

"That's Leonek," she replied.

As we sat out in the garden, the old woman came up to the doorstep and kept looking at me curiously. "I expect she thinks you're her brother Leon," said Halina. "Poor thing; she must find it all quite confusing."

On the way back we stopped off at the marketplace of the little town of Piaski as we used to call it, or Pieski as it is called nowadays.

I got out of the car into the now roasting heat of this summer day, and stood on the pavement with my back to where my parents' restaurant used to be. Suddenly all the years melted away and I imagined myself, a little four year old, standing there and looking out onto the market square ahead. Strangely, the place looked very much like I'd remembered it. They say places of your childhood tend to shrink when viewed later on. Oddly enough, in my case this didn't happen. As I stood there I recalled clearly all the bustle of town life all these years ago.

"Over to the right, there used to be a Jewish Temple," I said. "Across and to the left I remember a Russian Orthodox Church and just along the main road to the left as well used to be our Roman Catholic Church." Full of excitement I called, "Let's see if I'm right!"

We all started walking in the direction I indicated. As we came to the end of the square, on our right we saw a Russian Orthodox Church. "See," I called out. "It's just where I said it would be!"

We walked on. A little further along, a footpath went off to the left. Looking up I saw a magnificent church building at the bottom. Again I was right. We walked over, hoping to go inside and inspect the place more closely. Unfortunately, we found the doors locked.

"It's not safe to leave churches unattended," remarked Zuzia. There are still people around that hate the Church and all that it stands for. Given half a chance they could do a lot of damage."

Undaunted, I proceeded to carry out a close inspection of the exterior. The church was strangely reminiscent of the one in Rogoznica. The walls were clad with the very same stone and the spire was similar in design. "Could it have been," I contemplated, "that both churches were built around the same time?" I wandered around the churchyard looking for anything that might give me some clue as to its history. There wasn't much to see, however I did find a couple of gravestones with interesting inscriptions. From what I read, it seemed that a church certainly existed in the town in the old days. For whatever reason, it must have fallen into disrepair and was abandoned. The building in front of me, erected on a new site was a fairly recent replacement. "I bet the two churches were built in the early twenties. That would explain the similarity in architecture as well as the use of similar materials," I thought.

We wondered back towards the Square. Inevitably, I came up to the fence that separated the parcel of land where our home used to be from the street, and looked up. In my mind's eye I could still see the tall steps leading onto the pavement. Behind a wooden facade, painted white, with large doors in the middle and a window on either side. Further up the hill I could picture the roof of a house. That was, I knew, our living quarters.

Reluctantly I broke away from my reverie. What I was really seeing was an abandoned patch of ground, with only wild flowers to adorn it. A wave of disappointment overwhelmed me.

"So this place has also been razed to the ground," I thought. "Stalin's henchmen certainly did a thorough job of erasing all traces of the Polish Renaissance of the twenties." The whole place seemed thoroughly Russified. Although I suspected that a very large proportion of the inhabitants of Grodno were of purely Polish extraction, my native tongue was no longer heard on the streets of that city. On top of all that, I had to admit to myself, that I had failed in my mission. I had not discovered the circumstances of my father's demise and still don't know where his bones lie. The reality was that I'd picked up hearsay, some allusions, cautiously spoken scraps of information relating to his fate - nothing but straws in the wind.

Although I realised that I will now never discover the full truth of the matter, from the bits of information I'd managed to glean, and records that were conspicuously missing, I decided I could reconstruct the most likely scenario. In my opinion, Father went out to do some quick shopping, just as I was told. In town he may have seen a man he knew being assaulted by a couple of thugs with red bands on their sleeves. It would have been typical of him that, not thinking of the consequences, he would have rushed to his friend's aid. Unfortunately he would soon discover that the fight was not even. Father would have waded in with his bare fists, but the attackers may well have had truncheons, and perhaps knives. He would have been beaten up alongside his friend. I can imagine these "Communist Guardians of Law and Order" becoming so enraged that they couldn't control their actions. By the time they finally stopped beating and wounding their victims, both my father and the man he went to defend would be dead.

What followed was a cover up resulting in my whole family being duped. The probably series of events following the murder of my father and his colleague might have been as follows. Having calmed down, the thugs realised their impulsive actions might get them into trouble. The sergeant was a strict disciplinarian and did not take kindly to unauthorised excesses. In particular, the killing of my father, a man recently released by the Russians, would be hard to justify. So they finally hit on an idea. Go to the Krajewski's house, inform the wife her husband had been arrested, and pretend to search for incriminating documents. After all, the whole family was soon to be deported and the man's wife would not be able to ask awkward questions. The plan was successfully executed and we were left with their falsehoods.

Epilogue

Having returned, I had to admit that I was not likely to gather any more first hand information about the life and times of my family. Moreover; I was by then convinced that my father's fate was to remain a mystery forever.

While all the information was fresh in my mind, I told myself that I ought to start writing. It was time to put pen to paper (or rather finger to computer keyboard).

I found the visit to the place of my birth and childhood, very useful in filling some of the many gaps in the knowledge of my family history. One thing however continued to gnaw at me. I discovered no resting place or any record of Father's demise. Incredibly, I couldn't even discover any record of his birth. (I'm ashamed to admit that his date of birth is still a mystery to me. My mother unfortunately wasn't very strong on that kind of information.) It was as though he had never existed. Almost as if he were a figment of my own imagination. It didn't seem right that such a remarkable man should disappear into the fast-flowing river of time without even a ripple. I felt it was up to me to do something about it.

One day, we were entertaining a Polish priest from Lithuania who was on a visit to England, when an idea struck me.

"I'd like to erect a monument on a cemetery in Belarus to commemorate my father's life," I said. "Can you advise me how I should go about it?" I asked my guest.

"It's quite straightforward," he replied. "You write to the Bishop of Grodno and ask for permission. After that you make your arrangements with the Parish Priest. Wait a minute," he added. "I think I have the Bishop's address on me." With that he produced his notebook and allowed me to take down the relevant details.

"One day, when the time is right, I'll do something about it," I thought, putting the information away.

By a strange twist of fate, soon after this meeting, I was offered a post in Moscow in my professional capacity as Senior Engineer. It was there in fact, that most of this book was written. It may also be regarded as ironic that I, of all people, should be making a living in

Russia's capital. "At least the Russians are paying back some of their debt to me," I used to think, with some sense of satisfaction.

While in Russia, I made my arrangements regarding Father's Gravestone. Today a modest but appropriate monument stands alongside the one my father himself built in the old graveyard in Rogoznica. The stone modestly, but clearly and openly commemorates the lives of my parents and acts as a marker for the Family of Krajewskis that used to live there once upon a time.

My visit to Father Christopher Karolewski, the Parish Priest of Rogoznica was both illuminating and encouraging.

I found Father Christopher to be a remarkable man. I discovered that, as a young and enthusiastic priest he took over the control of that parish. As priests were thin on the ground, he was also made responsible for the neighbouring parishes in Strubnica and Piaski. He certainly found the places dilapidated and in terrible state of repair. One must remember that the Communist Authorities did their best over the previous fifty years to close down churches and stop religious worship. It was typical of the man that, pouring all his energies into the task, he set about raising funds around the globe, for repairing and renovating these buildings. The condition I found all of them in on my arrival was in itself a tribute to his efforts.

The buildings were not the only part of the Polish heritage he found neglected. The Russians and their Belarusian henchmen were equally stamping out Polish language, culture and traditions. I thought his energetic "re-Polonisation" as he called it, boded well for the future. One can only hope that other Polish priests are as effective as Father Karolewski. During my visit I had the privilege of being shown around the local Collective Farm, or 'Kolchoz' as the Soviets would have called it. The Enterprise was actually named after Adam Mickiewicz, the famous Polish author of 'Pan Tadeusz'. I couldn't help wondering what this Polish patriot and celebrated poet would think today if he saw his name written in Cyrillic at the approaches to the site. I'm pretty sure that most of the employees on the Farm bearing his name had never read any of his poetry and probably didn't even know who he really was.

The Head Office of the Collective was located in what used to be the Muysztowicz Country Seat. The Utilitarian System of the

Communists had obviously degraded the place over the years. As one approached the building however, it was clear by looking at what remained of the facade that this was once the imposing home of an aristocratic family. The Squire was known to be a committed Polish patriot. It followed that the members of the underground Communist Fifth Column hated him. So much so that, as soon the Russians came and the Local Communists took control, one of their first Acts was to drag the man out of his Mansion and publicly execute him.

One of the workers in the Headquarters proudly showed me a flag commemorating the Eightieth Anniversary of the founding of the Belarusian Republic. The red flag displayed two dates: 1919 and 1999. I must confess that my initial thoughts at seeing the item were that our priest's task was even more onerous than I first thought. In the first instance, for the local people to consider that an independent Belarusian Republic was formed in 1919 illustrated their naivety. This name represented typical Communist double-talk. For the word "Republic" one should read: "a Region of the Russian Empire, with its Economy, Politics and Administration controlled from Moscow in every detail." My second point was, and this I found somewhat of an affront, that by implication, my birthplace was included in the mythical date of 1919. A state of Belarus never existed in the Past. The place was peopled by Belarusians, Lithuanians, Tartars, Jews and Poles. Initially the area formed part of the Principality of Greater Lithuania - later on, and for many Centuries, part of the United Kingdom of Poland and Lithuania. After the First World War, when Poles had re-established their Independent State, the soil I was standing on, a rightfully formed part of Poland. In the circumstances I couldn't, for the life of me see how the existence of the so-called Belarusian Republic since 1919 could be celebrated in Rogoznica.

The Communist propaganda and mentality were clearly still heavily engrained in the minds of many young and middle-aged inhabitants of the area. The above, unfortunately, was but one example. I've come across, for instance, young people who, despite the fact that both their parents were Polish, insisted on calling themselves Belarusian, and refused to use the language of their parents. What I was witnessing was the after-effects of yet another

214

attempt at Russification of my birthplace. The process was unfortunately not new in my area.

More than most, we've been subject to much repression in the past. My story after all, is that of a family in Poland (a country considered by some to have had the most turbulent history in Europe) and takes place in the Eastern borderlands known as Kresy (the region usually suffering the brunt of the attacks). In addition and by coincidence, my tale spans the entire Twentieth Century, the most turbulent and violent in our continent's history.

It would appear that the struggle to exist and retain our identity was always to be our fate. I'm reminded of a speech made by Marshal Pilsudski, my father's life-long hero, during the opening of a new University in Wilno. The remarkable thing about this speech was that it was made in the year of 1919. It was earlier that very year that the Martial and his Armies had re-established the newly Independent Polish State, and he therefore had every reason to anticipate and foretell a bright future for our Region. In the circumstances, his speech was strangely prophetic.

This is how it went:

"All Countries have their Limits and their Borderlands. Unhappy and miserable is the lot of towns and settlements in those areas. When a hurricane comes, it shakes the foundations of their homes above all. When clouds come, fierce winds first lay low the Borderland wheat-fields. When thunder comes, it's here that lightning strikes at towers and houses. There, far away, in the Centre of our Culture the sun may still be rising, while here dark night already reigns. When at last it is decreed that the whole Nation is to be covered by a wintry blanket of snow, here the frosts are most severe; here they take the people's breath away and freeze the blood in their veins. Unhappy are the Borderlands. And yet deep is the happiness born out of great suffering and great sacrifice; and not like that born out of pleasure controlling events unaided, but deep and quiet happiness, childishly naive, flowing out of the basic Elements of our own Culture."

As we all know, "the clouds, and the winds" re-visited our lands a mere twenty years later. The Marshal's prophecy of yet another dose of suffering was thus fulfilled. Knowing the people of the area as he did however, he did not leave his audience in despair. Pilsudski, who himself hailed from our part of the country, showed faith in our ability to ride out the storms, and so we did. To those then, who tried so hard and took so much care and effort to eliminate us from the face of this Earth and remove all traces of our past existence I say: "We're here in England, we're here in America, in Canada, Australia and may other places; and we REMEMBER."

To readers with one or more Polish parents or grandparents, I make this appeal; if you have not already done so, try to discover your Polish roots. Learn a little of Polish Culture, Customs, History - and try to learn at least a few words of the language of your predecessors. If circumstances permit, make a visit to the land of your Fathers. Don't be afraid of what others may think or be ashamed of your heritage. Share your discoveries with your friends. You may be pleasantly surprised. You may find that, far from being the target of fun and derision, you will be regarded with increased respect and esteem. Your friends may decide to return the compliment and in turn tell you their own stories. That way you will both benefit by widening your horizons. This advice, by the way, applies equally to young (and not so young), Russians, Ukrainians, Lithuanians and many other people born and living away from their countries of origin.

Finally, to all who read this book: I sincerely hope you found my tale interesting, amusing and even entertaining. If the answer to at least one of the above is "Yes," then I've succeeded in what I set out to do.

THE END

Photograph i   1915 - Leon Krajewski (top right) with his family

Photograph ii   1922 - Leon in World Ward I uniform

Photograph iii   Krajewski family monument and grave of Leonarda and
Regina Krajewska at Rogoznica